CREATIVE CHARACTERS

CREATIVE CHARACTERS

**ELISABETH
YOUNG-BRUEHL**

ROUTLEDGE

NEW YORK

Published in 1991 by

Routledge
An imprint of Routledge, Chapman and Hall, Inc.
29 West 35 Street
New York, NY 10001

Printed in the United States of America

Library of Congress Cataloging-in-Publication Data

Young-Bruehl, Elisabeth.
    Creative characters / Elisabeth Young-Bruehl.
      p. cm.
    Includes bibliographical references and index.
    ISBN 0-415-90369-6
    1. Creative ability. 2. Character. 3. Creative ability—Case
studies. I. Title.
BF408.Y68 1991
153.3′5—dc20   91-173
                                            CIP

For M. T. Beecher,
who provided the etching on
the book's cover, and much more

Le hasard ne favorise que les esprits préparés.
—Pasteur

CONTENTS

Preface

Biographers, I have observed, tend to surface from their long years in other peoples' lives with powerful impulses that are either suprabiographical or autobiographical, or both. Those with the first impulse want to fly into speculation, free at last from the tether of birth dates, daily doings, hard facts, inevitable deaths. They will, they think, make a place for all the generalizations they could not support with documents, the reflections on the human condition that were too large to fit a single life story. The result of this kind of release is either a book focused on biography writing or a book that bends the biography genre toward philosophy. Those with the second impulse demand time and place for themselves, like frazzled parents who would like to be nurtured for a while, even if only at their own hands. They want to lavish on themselves at least some of the energy and intelligence they have been providing for years to The Subject. This is a matter of restitution, self-reconstruction, even therapy for all ambivalences drawn out by The Subject. From this impulse comes either another book about biography writing, this one featuring the biographer, or a more direct memoir to satisfy the great "me too!" Biography is a genre that requires a certain humility, but, I have observed, those who do it well are not naturals at humility. They discipline themselves. And then they have a fling.

Creative Characters contains ideas about creativity that came to me while I wrote *Hannah Arendt: For Love of the World* and *Anna Freud: A Biography*. It is suprabiographically speculative, but there is also a chapter on biography writing and several how-to demonstrations, even though this is less a handbook for biographers than a prolegomenon to what might be called "meta-biographics." My autobiography is here, too, but only in the form of my habits of mind given freedom: that is, it is behind the lines, running loose in the framework, the architectonic.

CREATIVE CHARACTERS

The main thesis of this study is simple. Creative people, I argue, create whatever they create in the medium of, through the developmental lineaments and structures of, their characters. They have, consciously or unconsciously, an image of their characters, or, in other terms, of their general psychic (mind and body) organization, which they both aspire to—it is an idealized image—and project into whatever they create. This image, called here a "character-ideal," appears in their works, their social visions, their philosophies of nature, and also in their understandings of creative processes, their own and others'. Creators are their own border guards, charged with stamping their cipher—their psychic "character" in the graphic sense—on all departing products of their minds. It is not only *le style* of creations that is *l'homme* (or *la femme*) *même*.

The word *character* is normally used as though it were virtually synonymous with "individuality," but there are also, I argue, creative character-types given to corollary types of creativity, of work, of social visions, of philosophies of nature, and of understandings of creativity. This book is also a typology, a characterology, sketched with a range of philosophical, psychoanalytical, and biographical techniques.

I realize that it will strike many readers as strange to encounter a book about "character" written without methodological blushing, and just as strange to find one in which a typology is offered. Such notions as personality and self, motivation and creative intention, as well as all sorts of categorizing enterprises and epistemic systems, have recently been "problematized." The problematizing discourses of deconstructionism, post-structuralism, post-modernism, and their associated isms are not unfamiliar or unimportant to me, but I do not chart my course with these maps or anti-maps of recent years.

Since the late 1960s, when I was Hannah Arendt's graduate student, I have felt, rather, an emotional and intellectual affinity with the years immediately after World War II, in that brief interlude between the war and the Cold War. In those years, it seems to me, an atmosphere of passionate quest invisibly united intellectuals in all the lands—the better part of the planet—torn by the war; a quest to understand what had happened, how such loss of life and moral havoc and material devastation could have come about. Everywhere, in the pages of *Combat* and *Les Temps modernes*, of *politics*, of *American Imago*, of *Présence Africaine*, in Arendt's *The Origins of Totalitarianism*, *The Authoritarian Personality* by Adorno and his colleagues and the other volumes in the "Studies in Prejudice" series, Simone de Beauvoir's *Le Deuxième Sexe*, Sartre's *Ré-*

flexions sur la question juive. Fanon's *Peau noire, masques blancs,* Marcuse's *Eros and Civilization,* social and political theory was written with passionate urgency. There was a great effort at synthesis. Study of individuals, analysis of groups and historical contexts, construction of types were to merge: the merger realm was titled *Idealtypen,* in acknowledgment of Max Weber's contributions, or "representative figures." Notions of "social character" and linkages between "culture and personality" were debated. And the shared goal was collective portraiture of the anti-Semite, the white racist, the sexist, the classist.

It seems to me that much of this work, done in the shadow of a catastrophe, will echo again in the coming years, as it did to a certain extent in the late 1960s. In the wake of the Cold War, as prejudice is emerging again into public discussion from under the cover of superpower confrontation, it is being newly recognized as the old problem that refused to cease. Attention will focus on relations among types of prejudice—anti-Semitism, racism, sexism, classism, and so forth—and relations between prejudiced individuals and the societies and cultures in which they live and experience conditions conducive to prejudice.

But the approaches developed in the post-war years for examining individuals' conscious and unconscious thoughts, words, and deeds in relation to their characters, and for doing characterology can also be used to consider culture constructors as well as culture destroyers. This is what I have in mind with *Creative Characters.*

Introduction

There is an enormous library on the topic of creativity. People add to it all the time—creatively, they hope—and in America items are added at an accelerated pace whenever we reach a crisis of intellectual confidence. In the late 1950s, as the most ferocious A-bomb competition evolved into what might be called "the Sputnik crisis," social science researchers rushed to examine scientific creativity, which meant military technological creativity. The reason for this boom of interest was, as one researcher put it, that "we are in a mortal struggle for   our way of life". Artistic creativity was a compelling subject in the late 1960s and early 1970s, when some people feared that progressive education had destroyed the nation's schools and quite a different group wondered if mind-expanding drugs were going to cure the nation of the 1950s and make ordinary genius obsolete. "Gifted children" started going to special schools, not just to special tracks within conventional schools. Creative leadership has been sought more recently in books and political forums. Business executives are currently being coached to keep up with the overseas competitors threatening our national innovation and enterprise self-image, and a stream of self-help manuals offers individuals means to enhance their "creative potential" and live richer lives. The right and left hemispheres of many brains have responded to questionnaires and meditation has been learned by fast-trackers during the present cultural moment, wild as it is with both psychometrics and Westernized Eastern religions.

The emphases of creativity quests have changed over the post-World War II decades, but similar and similarly dire warnings have emerged all along: "An emotional disease, a paralysis of creative imagination, an addiction to superficials—this is the diagnosis I would offer to account

1

for the greater part of the widespread desperation of our time," wrote the psychologist Henry Murray in 1960. While this kind of anxiety stays constant, the national educational pendulum swings back and forth—not usually for educational reasons—between focus on group discipline and learning and focus on individual talent and thinking. At each arc of the pendulum, the most elementary insights into creativity are rediscovered and reapplied. This year, when it is obvious that the nation's public schools are in a grave state of crisis, educators have announced solemnly that young children learn at different rates and in different ways. Too much regimentation is harmful to their joy in learning and their creativity. But, coming full circle, educators note that it is also important to structure children's time, require regular and frequent skills exercises, supply supervision lacking at home.

The always growing library on creativity is divided into three parts. First, there are writings devoted to "the creative process" (to borrow the title of an often reissued 1959 anthology of reflections by literary, artistic, and scientific people on their own processes) or to "the act of creation" (the title of a huge study by Arthur Koestler). Products of creation are considered, but in light of their production, as results or effects of "the creative process." Such writings describe experiences of inspiration or the lack of it, conditions for composition, traits of creative mental activity (flexibility, spontaneity, curiosity, independence from authorities and conventions, etc.), varieties of activity and key cognitive processes within the process, like the "bisociation" that Koestler offers as the way ideas are combined to produce new ideas. Usually, these descriptions are fitted to some schematization of creativity's stages: a period of preparation is needed, then inspiration, then some baking time (often called "incubation"), and finally some revision or adjusting, testing or verification, before the result is served. Some theorists argue that there are different creativities for different fields (art and science, poetry and philosophy) and for different human activities (making, acting, laboring, thinking, willing, judging, to use Hannah Arendt's list). But much more frequently, portraits are drawn of a universal creativity that can fit itself to different tasks or a virtuoso creativity that can shine anywhere. Some compare creative processes from person to person, culture to culture, era to era, or even species to species (with help from primatology or zoology in general), while others go in pursuit of an ancient association between poetic manias and neurotic manias by asking about creative processes and psychopathological ones. Questions are often raised in this literature about whether the creative process, or exercise of imagination in a related way such as playing, is a necessity for us humans in evolutionary terms, and it is always obvious that these questions are raised to tell unimaginative, hyperserious people that the answer is yes.

A second territory of the library is devoted to creators or geniuses or eminences of some form of achievement. One social scientist has contrasted the two approaches from a point of view that assumes the centrality of "cognitive" elements in the creative process: "There have been two major types of approach to problem-solving and creativity. The first of these relates problem-solving to learning and thinking, as a type of 'higher mental process' or 'cognitive process,' to which problem-solving certainly belongs. The second approach, supplementary rather than contradictory to the first, sees creative problem-solving as a manifestation of personality and looks for social and motivational determinants instead of (or in addition to) the purely cognitive ones."

The social-scientific approach to personality depends upon tests and scales and interviews with living subjects. But outside of the academies where such scientists work, and where a science known as "cognitive science" has recently been born, personality is approached rather differently. Individual biographies study individuals, while an ideal-type of the Creative Person is encompassed by or built up from multiple biographies—for which individual biographies and encyclopedias of biography provide the material. The British, pioneers in biography writing and in biographical dictionary making, have also been innovators in collective study, with Sir Francis Galton's *Hereditary Genius* (1869) and Havelock Ellis's *A Study of British Genius* (1904) marking the extremes of British concern with the nature and nurture of genius.

In biographical study, individuals are sometimes held to be "representative men," and a great abstract Creative Person is sometimes held to be ideally incarnate in some individual, some Messiah of Creativity or Renaissance Man (like Leonardo). It is not just in British biographical studies of the genius or of geniuses that old questions about what contributions are made by heredity, temperaments, and natural gifts versus familial and social influences and acquired skills get old answers produced by new means. American longitudinal empirical studies of "life stories" reach, as Plutarch's *Lives* did, the unsurprising conclusions that nature and nurture both play a role in achievement, and that in chaotic times more of the best of both is needed. Lawfulness is desired

3

in this genre, but it is very hard to come by. Some say there is a correlation between measurable intelligence—which is not to be confused with intelligence—and measurable creativity—which is certainly not the only kind of creativity: and some disagree, citing various creative giants who failed algebra. This genre of study has a remarkable tendency to find every unexplainable genius proof for a rule of genius and to temper every rule or typical characteristic in a fire of exceptionality. Those who try to compass the mystery of creativity are also those who keep the shrine of that mystery—so the reasons for their research never disappear either.

A sub-division of this second territory of the creativity literature is concerned with social or social-critical conditions of creativity. Are there ideal family configurations for producing creativity—and dis-ideal ones for killing it? What educational and cultural and social and political conditions are conducive to creativity? Do material structures give rise to cultural superstructures (or vice versa), and do texts really have individual authors or only forces of production or institutional influences or intertextualities, which means that creativity is a false concept? Can a good man be good in a bad state (Aristotle asked), or a creative person creative in a totalitarian one? Do great periods of artistic production come before, during, or after political golden ages? Can creative people, who, like everyone else, do not work well on regularly empty stomachs, serve princes or churches or causes or national endowments without being corrupted? Can a person who teaches creative writing write creatively? Should anybody expect poets or scientists to be moral, or political? I've marked off this whole genre with questions because its answers are all ideological, generalizations for a purpose other than study of creativity.

There are, on the other hand, questions about social and cultural conditions of creativity that can be considered without having first to decide—to cite a recent example of ideological polemic—whether The American Mind is closing, opening, or defying such generalizations. These questions are the responsibility of a third kind of creativity study—not one acknowledged by most social scientists—that is focused on motivations, conscious or unconscious. Descriptions of creative people or the Creative Person do not necessarily get to the level of what moves a person to create or keeps a person creating, thus using gifts and flourishing in specific—or specifically experienced—social or cultural conditions. Similarly, descriptions of the creative process seldom get to the level of drive—particularly when such descriptions come from creative people, who often assume that they do what they do because they could not do otherwise. They are painters, they paint: it's their fate.

Inquiries into motivation are, in our time, psychological by common definition. They look for "personality." Anyone who announces that God instructed him to paint or that she was a vehicle for the Divine Voice will satisfy fellow believers but only invite further inquiry from psychology. Psychology, in its turn, invites further inquiry from creative people, particularly when psychology works with the two ideas most difficult for creative people to accept. The first is Freud's notion that a common psychic motivational source gives rise to creative products, to dreams, to fantasies, to parapraxes (Freud's term for slips of speech or writing, little everyday errors), and to neurotic symptoms. This idea seems to point no path for distinguishing between any of these things— particularly between a product and a symptom—or for distinguishing between a creative product that is good and one that is not. The second idea, developed differently in different schools of psychoanalysis, is that a single mechanism somehow connects motivational source and creative product or act. Freud himself wrote about sublimation of the sexual drive—the sexual drive aimed at, redirected toward, production rather than sexual pleasure—and noted sublimation as a mechanism that could be involved in fantasies, dreams, parapraxes, and symptoms as well. (The sublimation idea has been widely rejected in its bald form because it seems to imply that creativity and satisfying sexuality are somehow antithetical. Freud himself never viewed sublimation as a substitute for sexuality, and he stressed that sublimation and repression, which interferes with sexuality, are opposites.)

From within the psychoanalytic ranks, many ideas other than Freud's have been advanced to compass motivation. The psychoanalytic dissident Alfred Adler saw all creative acts and products as compensations for losses suffered or damages done in a creative person's life. Since Adler, many versions have appeared of the idea that creators seek restitution of a lost love, compensation for a physical stigma or defect, substitutes for a not-good-enough mother, a way to go home again, succor after religious disillusionment, and so forth. In a related vein, creativity has been seen as a mode of mourning and a variant on melancholia or depression, a capacity rising up out of splits and fissures in the creative psyche. Putting a different accent on these hypotheses, many psychoanalysts stress not the tragedies of the past but the riches in the past for the mining of which the creative have special night vision and tolerance of discomfort. Some of these writers followed Ernst Kris and spoke of "regression in the service of the ego" as the key mechanism of creativity. Others find Jungian ideas about universal archetypes in the collective unconscious more persuasive.

It is very interesting to note that the only dimension of artistic creativity the great Greek encyclopedist Aristotle thought worth analyzing in detail does not have a place in this three-part inventory of approaches to creativity. Aristotle's *Poetics* is not concerned with the creative process, the creator's abilities and conditions, or the creator's personality—though he makes occasional remarks appropriate to all three domains. His attention is focused on artistic products (specifically, tragedies and comedies) and the elements of which they are made. In his other work on "productive science," the *Rhetoric*, Aristotle analyzes types of public speeches, but he also pays a great deal of attention to types of audiences and to what we call communications (and what some contemporary specialists call "reader response theory").

For us, poetics and rhetoric are part of aesthetics or literary criticism, and in practice those fields may or may not intersect with study of creativity. They almost never intersect with study of character, so that aphorisms like Schopenhauer's about style—"Style is the physiognomy of the mind, and a safer index to character than the face"—have not been picked up for the epigrams to books. Indeed, there has recently been much effort among theorists like Michel Foucault to sever connections between various kinds of "discourses" and authors, to argue that obsession with authors and their biographies is symptomatic of a particular modern discourse—a psychologizing discourse—that makes it impossible for us to understand the power relations in which we are always entangled. As such theorists note, psychoanalytically informed literary criticism takes the opposite path and views the creator and the work together. Psychoanalytic critics usually set themselves in contrast to "New Criticism," in which the work was viewed in isolation from not just its producer but its social surround. This was critical study of the work for the work's sake, overlapping with creativity study only in "the creative process" form. But, to compound the matter further, certain trends within psychoanalysis itself also argue for separating producer and product. Otto Rank, for example, had the idea that a "new type of humanity" would evolve when people of creative power were able to "give up artistic expression in favor of formation of the personality." In recent years, Abraham Maslow has Americanized and given a sexist turn to this idea by distinguishing "special talent creativeness" from "self-actualizing creativity." The former is more common among men, but the latter is the birthright of everyone and the special province of women—which explains why they are not often great achievers.

Even less "self-actualizing-oriented" recent empirical studies of creative people quite often have no reference whatsoever to poetics, to what people actually produce. Their experiments rest on the odd assumption that what people produce for empirical creativity research—answers to questions, solutions to problems, explanations of phenomena—has some direct relation to what they produce at their desks, in their studios or laboratories, when they are doing what they do quite unresearched. To see what is the matter with the assumption, you have only to contemplate for a moment what André Gide once said about his products: "It is not so much what you say in a book that constitutes its value . . . [but] all you would like to say, which nourishes it secretly." An example of this problem is the often quoted article "The Personality Correlates of Creativity: A Study of American Architects," which has nothing to say about the architects' designs. A group of top architects was selected and ranked by two different panels of experts, and then two comparison groups were selected from among associates of the top group and from a directory of architects. The experts knew the top architects' work and felt ready to rate their creativity on a five-point scale, but the researchers felt no need to comment on the criteria for judging creativity. In other empirical efforts, using psychological tests designed to measure creativity, work is even less at issue: creativity is held to be a mental quality or a mental capacity, independent of any work, action or labor; it is the same in children as in adults, and the same in all adults who have it.

In general, it seems to me that there are two problems common to studies of creativity of all sorts. The first is that each type of study slights the others and there is no integrative perspective. Those who take up "the creative process" neglect their subjects' lives and the products of the creative process—they are without biography or poetics. Those who focus on creators—individually or in pursuit of some ideal type—neglect their work and often "the creative process," too. Reaching for the level of the creator's motivations, people usually simplify the work—it is, for example, a mirror of the contents of the unconscious—and treat "the creative process" only as a function of motivation.

Second, each of the approaches operates explicitly or implicitly with a goal that seems to me to wreak havoc: they are common-denominatoristic. There is "the creative process" (singular). Even if varieties or fields of creativity are noted, the goal is to find where their creative processes intersect and are alike. People who lament, in the manner of C. P. Snow, that there are "two cultures" (art and science) do so because a single one is best—or was better, in the better past. Creator study is guided by the idea that all creators share certain psychological or psychosocial traits, which means that a single creative type can be found or constructed out of what creativities in different fields and media have in common. Periodically, calls are issued to promote the scientific unifying of diverse types of creativity study: "The time has come," wrote two psychologists in 1974, "to develop a metatheory of creativity." But what this means, in practice, is that the time has come for one mode of creativity study to establish hegemony over all others, or for two modes to make a strategic alliance and absorb all others. The same psychologists noted that what was needed in 1974, for example, was a "framework by means of which the findings of psychoanalytic research . . . can be related to cognitive science."

The urge toward metatheory or a unified field theory is so strong that even those who assume that there are different sorts of creative personalities think that there is something deep which deserves a singular pronoun, like "*the* dynamics of creation." This is the title of a stimulating 1972 work by the British psychoanalyst Anthony Storr in which he argues that, although there are two very distinct creative personality types, both types are defensively structured and kept from psychopathology by the single means of defenses. A similar course of argument is followed by people—Jungians among them—who distinguish feminine creativity and masculine creativity and then marry the two types in a common or collective dynamic.

Having made all these complaints and criticisms, I would now like to borrow for my own purposes. I think that the great virtue of the "the creative process" approach is that it draws upon what creative people have to say about their own processes. It may well be, as Plato often said, that the poets have no philosophical idea what they are doing, that they are not, as Aristotle agreed, deliberators or analyzers (practitioners of "theoretical science," quite a different matter than "productive science"). But what they have to say in their own terms is certainly reveal-

8

ing—as is Plato's hostility toward them. Most revealing are the things creative people have to say about their creativity when creativity is not their topic, when they are not reflecting on how they do things but are just doing them in their characteristic ways. What creative people say about their creativity, that is, is best read with, not in isolation from, what they do all the time. This is the key problem with anthologies like *The Creative Process*, which contains snippets of writings generated in response to questions or yanked out of other contexts.

From studies of creators, much can be learned about what creative people have in common, but the traits that appear repeatedly do not explain themselves. Creative people, many researchers announce, are characterized by great ego strength. What is ego strength, and how does it develop, and is it the same for all egos? The creative are also characterized, the research consensus goes on, by their independence. From what? (For example, isn't it possible to be quite independent of your historical predecessors and your peers—usually experienced by men and often by women as paternal or fraternal—and quite dependent on your internal image of your mother?) Independent for what? Creative people are, most researchers who pay attention to this sort of thing relate, compounded of both masculine and feminine traits. Which traits are these (masculine and feminine being in many ways culture-bound notions), and how compounded, and how developed?

Raising questions about the characteristics said to be common to creators leads right to personality and motivational studies, to the domain of "depth psychology." What seems to me most valuable in this literature is the idea that creative people cannot be studied as either collections of traits or as abstract minds abstractly engaged in processes. They are ensembles—minds and bodies, common traits and particularities; they are individuals with histories, and their individuality is what is called "character," which is a much more complicated thing than a list of traits could illuminate.

In the chapters that follow, I will make reference to the current literatures on creativity that I have been surveying and characterizing, and I will make use of what seems to me valuable in them. But my own approach is built upon hypotheses and assumptions that are not reflected in any of these literatures, even though I make liberal use of psychoanalytic work on creativity, which is, I find, the most interesting and the least superficial. I think that Freud's notion of sublimation is very important, but I also think that sublimation is the key mechanism of creativity for only one type of creative person—a type of which Freud himself was one of the most deeply self-reflective examples. Other types of creative persons may sublimate, but sublimation is not the key to all doors in their lives and works.

In general, it seems to me that the scientific search for a model Creative Person, or for a creativity common to all creative persons, obscures the diversity of creative types. Within the history of characterology, the tendency to reductionism, while not so clear or simple, also dominates. There is a pluralist tradition, which goes back to the ancient Greeks, who assumed that there are four bodily humors and four corresponding types of temperaments—sanguine, melancholic, choleric, and phlegmatic. The basic principle of most pluralist characterologies has been that character reflects the predominance of one humor, one physiognomy, one passion, one trait. But there have also been more complex plural schemes, like Aristotle's, in which character is distinguished from physiologically based temperaments and viewed more socially as a blend of traits that reflect an individual's location between the extremes of age (youth and old age), birth (low-born and well-born), wealth (poor and rich), power (powerlessness and despotic power), fortune (unluckiness and luckiness). The most stable and dependable character is one blended from mid-way traits in all the categories, but most people are marked by a predominance of one trait stemming from a key disbalance or extremity in their situations. Aristotle's scheme stands behind the European literary tradition of characterology, in which Aristotle's disciple Theophrastus is the founding figure.

My own approach to character study is indebted to this pluralist tradition, particularly as it has woven into psychoanalytic theory, and my approach is also set against the other main tradition in European characterology, which is relentlessly dualistic. Large abstractions redound in this dualistic tradition: people are either of this character or that, either introverts or extraverts (one of Carl Jung's typologies), romantics or classics, Prometheans or Epimethians, Apollonians or Dionysians, intellectualist or sensualist, optimistic or pessimistic, dogmatic or skeptical, masculine or feminine. Behind these categories, it seems to me, there always lies a we-and-them mode, and a valuation—one pole of the polarity is always higher, better, stronger, more desirable. The we-and-them mode is particularly obvious when group characters—national, racial, ethnic, gender-based—are being asserted, offensively or defensively.

My central working characterological hypothesis is that there are three broad character and creative types, within which there are many variations. The types can be delineated in different ways, according to different principles, for different purposes, and in the chapters that follow I will sketch the types from many different angles, building up as I go—rather than announcing at the outset—answers to the obvious questions: why three types? And why just these three types?

Second, I work from the hypothesis that people of great creativity formulate theories—or, less formally, have images or notions—about creativity that reflect their own creative types, their own ways of being creative. And I assume that these theories will be similar to the works that the creative produce. The ground of the similarity is what I call "the character-ideal." I assume that creative people develop (usually unconsciously, but sometimes consciously) an ideal for the organization of their minds and lives, and that they project this ideal in their theories about creativity as they project it in their works, which may also represent their idealizing theories about human relations or societies, about nature or the order of the cosmos. To put the matter very summarily: what creative people wish for themselves, for the psychic order in themselves, is what they wish for their work, and also what they delineate when they talk about their way of being creative. That is, there are forms and styles of work as well as different types of creativity theories that lend themselves to, or are particularly suited to, are regularly taken up by, each type of character-ideal. Viewed under the aegis of "the character-ideal" or the self-wish, creative people are consistent, while in their lives as they actually live them and as others can observe them, there may be wild inconsistencies. They may also find the conditions of their social, cultural, and political lives conducive to their abilities to live up to their ideals or not, as they will have found themselves either supported by their milieus or not as they developed their character-ideals. Different social, cultural, and political environments, I will argue, have different predominating "characters" themselves, and creative people can run with these or against them. Such prevailing currents also, I will note, have great influence over who is deemed creative and who not—a type of judgment that has densely clouded the question of whether there is such a thing as "feminine creativity," a question which, in turn, has meant that no typology of feminine creativities, in the plural, has been explored. (In Chapter 9, where theories of social character come under review, I will criticize the notion that there is such a thing as a feminine creativity and explore the plurality of types.)

11

As I noted, Freud spoke of dreams as distorted or disguised representations of unconscious wishes, and he felt that the same governing wish that could be discovered deeply underlying a dream could be found behind daydreams or fantasies, parapraxes, symptoms, and works of art. I assume that creative people have a particular kind of wish—a wish for self-ordering, self-organization—which is expressed, sometimes fulfilled, in all facets of their lives and works. This wish may have infantile sources that can be explored in the psychoanalytic manner—I will consider this possibility at length below—but it is a wish that typically emerges in late adolescence, as adolescents are doing what the current generation of American adolescents calls "getting their acts together."

I am going to begin my presentation of three broad manners of getting one's psychic act together—or of imagining it getting together (in a theory about creativity), or of getting a product together, or of getting a product to reflect the history of its being gotten together—by turning to three ancient Greek theorists of creativity and then to three modern theorists of creativity. The couples for comparison that will emerge from these two discussions are Plato and Friedrich Nietzsche, Aristotle and Sigmund Freud, and the Stoic Zeno and Marcel Proust. In very different ways, each claims that a creator's character determines his (they spoke only of males) manner of working and works. They each operate with a definition of "character," and with what I want to call a "character-ideal," but I am going to let this multiplicity flow by without commentary.

After the three character-ideal types I hypothesize and present as *Idealtypen* (in Max Weber's term) have grown less schematic or abstract with familiarity, then questions of definition can be posed. My meaning-as-use procedure with the words "character" and "character-ideal" here reflects my expropriation of a very interesting passage in which Freud explained why he was willing to live with the obscurities he knew resided in the word *instinct* (*Trieb*):

> The true beginning of a scientific activity consists . . . in describing phenomenon and then proceeding to group, classify and correlate them. Even at the stage of description it is not possible to avoid applying certain abstract ideas to the material at hand, ideas derived from somewhere or other but certainly not from the new observations alone. Such ideas—which will later become the basic concepts of the science—are still more indispensable as the material is further worked over. They must at first necessarily possess

some degree of indefiniteness: there can be no question of any clear delimitation of their content. So long as they remain in this condition, we come to an understanding about their meaning by making repeated references to the material of observation from which they appear to have been derived, but upon which, in fact, they have been imposed. Thus, strictly speaking, they are in the nature of conventions—although everything depends upon their not being arbitrarily chosen but determined by their having significant relations to the empirical material, relations that we seem to sense before we can clearly recognize and demonstrate them. It is only after more thorough investigation of the field of observation that we are able to formulate its basic scientific concepts with increased precision, and progressively so to modify them that they become serviceable and consistent over a wide area. Then, indeed, the time may come to confine them in definitions. (14: 117–18)

I am also going to ignore the convention that seems to govern studies of creativity. They are supposed to start off with pages of effort to define "creativity," to get the elusive object of study into an observational cage. I prefer to procede by making and then clustering biographical vignettes and portraits of ideas in which I can show rather than try to define the "creativity" as well as the "character" and "character-ideal" that I have in mind. My main method of study is not the clinical observation Freud presumed for his science, but observation in the medium of biographical writing and artistic production; the (not very scientific) method of presentation is a kind of philosophical-biographical contour drawing.

No one, of course, can leap out of her or his own manner of doing things, her or his own type, in order to make a study of creativity, although it is certainly possible to avoid assuming that your own type is the only one, to pay attention to differences, and to acknowledge (even if you cannot do so in detail) that your cultural frame delimits you. My bent for conversion of concepts, observations, and experiences into spatial forms, and my conviction that people are knowable through *their* manners of conversion into forms—a "by their metaphors shall ye know them" conviction—are characteristic of a particular way of thinking and character. I have become aware of the particularities of this way in the experience of writing two biographies, trying to get close to two ways of life and mind, one quite like and one quite unlike my own, and also in the experience of reading widely in biographical literature to see how others have negotiated the problems of identifying with and disindentifying with biographical subjects. It was observing my own manner of being interested in the characters I wrote and read about that brought me to this study in the first place. I hear my own systematic way of thinking in this remark of Pablo Picasso's, which could be entitled "Making Good Use of Narcissism":

> There is nothing more interesting than people. One paints and one draws to learn to see people, to see oneself. When I worked at the painting *War and Peace* and the series of these drawings, I picked up my sketchbooks daily, telling myself: "What will I learn of myself that I didn't know?" And when it isn't me any more who is talking about the drawings I made, and when they escape and mock me, then I know I have achieved my goal.

Judging from the current scientific literatures on creativity, it is obviously not good form for researchers to state that they, like the people they study, have minds and life stories. Even the demurring admission, really too obvious to need making, that powerfully creative people create while lesser lights look on, which is a variant on the acerbic truth that "those who can write do, and those who cannot teach," does not seem to sanction the presence of a personality in creativity study. Psychoanalysts warn that they may be guilty of "countertransference" as they write, but they seldom say—as Freud refreshingly did in writing about Leonardo da Vinci—what brings them to their subjects, much less what they bring to their subjects. More narrowly scientific writers simply present themselves as "objective," as though "subjectivity" could be eliminated—ought to be eliminated—from study of other people's subjective experiences.

I take running true to characterological type as a necessity for any kind of thinking, and it seems to me that, among the diversity of ways of thinking, a particular bent toward spatialization or conceptual mapping is more useful than most for a project of typological survey, as it is more likely than most to want such a project in the first place. Further, turned into a topic, my own way of thinking serves me up questions and clues. I ask of myself, for example, why until recently my proclivity for mapping took me always outward, to others and other's ideas, as a biographer and an expositor; why being directly rather than by detour autobiographical felt dangerous and forbidden to me. The reason is neither belief in the possibility of "objectivity" nor modesty. It has much more to do with diverting a troublesome, threatening channel to fill another the fuller; with finding narcissism acceptable in disguise, in the form of regard for others. Everyone has consciously or unconsciously self-imposed conditions of creative work, and can have some capacity to adjust those conditions, grow through them. Although he is not of my creative type, I understand why the critic Walter Benjamin found it difficult as well as challenging to abandon his usual mode of work for an assignment to write "in a loosely subjective form" about Berlin, his hometown. He said: "If I write better German than most writers of my generation, it is thanks largely to twenty years' observance of one little rule: never use the word "I" except in letters."

My method of making biographical-philosophical drawings is, in effect, a way of listening to and then juxtaposing, organizing, patterning, statements about creativity, statements about motivation and character, ways of doing art analysis or poetics. Any biographer develops such an informal method of necessity. It is a way of querying people's statements about themselves and their work: How are they alike? How not alike? And are they familiar to me? Not familiar? The building blocks are, for examples, the two statements by Picasso and Benjamin just quoted above and the two that follow below, which are, I think, obviously of the same respective types. Picasso, who wanted to be always learning about himself, was notorious for his disdain toward biographers and art critics wanting to learn about him or to capture his art with their foolish explanations. He preferred to make the maps of his life and art with his own hand and to summarize them with, for example, this statement:

> If all the ways I have been along were marked on a map and joined up with a line, it might represent a minotaur.

Benjamin, the one reluctant to write "I," and famous for his labyrinthinely plotted essays on literary figures like Kafka, Proust, Baudelaire, who seemed to him to have entered into modernity and mapped it with their works, presented himself thus:

> I was sitting inside the Café des Deux Magots at St.-Germain-des-Pres, where I was waiting—I forget for whom. Suddenly, and with compelling force, I was struck by the idea of drawing a diagram of my life, and knew at the same moment exactly how it was to be done. With a very simple question, I interrogated my past life, and the answers were inscribed, as if of their own accord, on the sheet of paper that I had with me. A year or two later, when I lost this sheet, I was inconsolable. I have never since been able to restore it as it arose before me then, resembling a series of family

trees. Now, however, reconstructing its outline in thought without directly reproducing it, I should, rather, speak of a labyrinth. I am not concerned here with what is installed in the chamber at its enigmatic center, ego or fate, but all the more with the many entrances leading into the interior. These entrances I call primal acquaintances. . . . So many primal relationships, so many entrances to the maze.

For Picasso the minotaur, all the roads of the labyrinth were himself. For Benjamin the labyrinth, the "ego or fate" at his center—metaphorically, the minotaur—was to remain unspoken, split off, even from the "primal acquaintances" traveling inward.

No one will ever be able to *explain* great creativity in any individual or group, to answer "how?" in the face of a work or works of genius—it seems to me both a misunderstanding and bad taste to try. Typology, however, is a different kind of enterprise. It can celebrate diversity, enjoy the differences among people and productions, while looking for generalizations that do not do violence to the panorama or drop into the commonest mistakes: taking too narrow or exclusive an approach; attempting to reduce all creativity to a key ingredient or to one kind of thing; making character study mechanically and prejudiciously dualistic. I like to give myself instructions in the form of beloved aphorisms, and for this project of typology, I listen to the very serious Blaise Pascal—

> The more intelligent people are, the more originality they will discover in others. Ordinary people see no difference between one human being and another.

and the very funny Robert Benchley—

> There may be said to be two classes of people in the world: those who constantly divide the people of the world into two classes, and those who do not.

Chapter One

Characterology and Creativity

CHARACTER AND CREATIVITY AS AIMS

Inquiries into character have traditionally been made in the service of education or eugenics. When political leaders or philosophers decide that people of genius or "great eminence" (Sir Francis Galton's phrase) are needed to restore or maintain the health of their cities and states, they soon come to realize that to breed or cultivate people who are creative—either as innovators or as conservators of origins—it is not enough to make a catalogue of desired behaviors and select or proselytize for them. Neither Galton nor his imitators have been able to prove that creative abilities are heritable, and development of talents, even positivist psychologists know, is a deep matter, not one of "behavior modification." Writing in 1947, the American psychologist L. M. Terman echoed centuries of similarly urgent pleas for study of creativity:

> So little do we know about our available supply of potential genius; the environmental factors that favor or hinder its expression; the emotional compulsions that give it dynamic quality; or the personality distortions that make it dangerous! And viewing the present crisis in world affairs who can doubt that these things may decide the fate of a civilization?

Creative character seems to be just as elusive as moral character. Long before Freud suggested that the mechanisms and motivations of character stem from childhood and are largely unconscious, reformers lamented that bad people can go through the motions of good behavior, just as ugly souls can reside behind beautiful faces. Many characterologists have hoped that a simple formula like the physiognomical one *monstrum in fronte, monstrum in anima*—"ugly in face, ugly in soul," the

saying with which Friedrich Nietzsche loved to chastise Socrates—
would turn up for character judging, but they have been disappointed.
In a softer mood, Nietzsche lamented in his *Gay Science* how difficult it
is to judge by appearances:

> Why has nature been so stingy with human beings that it did not allow
> them to shine—one more, one less, each according to the plentitude of his
> own light? Why are great human beings not as beautifully visible in their
> rise and setting as the sun? How much more unambiguous that would
> make all life among men!

Divine insight into the real person behind a public persona has frequently been invoked as a check, a Last Judgment to correct less-than-
last and often mistaken human judgments confined to the level of appearances. "Character is destiny," said Heraclitus in a non-monotheistic
vein—and this means not just that a person will live and die as character
dictates, but also that character is more or other than what can be seen
of a person at a glance, in a short series of actions, or even in a pattern
of behavior. If not a light-bestowing Nature or an omniscient God, then
Time will tell.

Theories of creativity that try to grasp character rather than just
intellectual functioning or what is called "the creative process" also start
from distressing observations concerning people of great intellectual
gifts who came to nothing or collapsed into illness; people of highly
specialized talents who could not live well—*idiots savants* or *savants
idiotiques*, prodigies or absent-minded professors; people who suffered
from or with their abilities to such an extent that they could not use
them; or people who made their rare intellectual capacities into means
toward horrifying ends. Theorists of creativity think that something—
say, character—must subtend purely intellectual functions for creative
people to be more than precocious, pyrotechnical, sports of human
nature, fragile, and flash-in-the-pan. Or, looked at historically, evolutionarily, something—say, character—must make it possible for creative
people to leap out of the ordinary, perhaps to the advancement, perhaps
to the endangerment, of the ordinary rank, without succumbing to
unsurvival of the unfittest.

Theories of creativity have always been tied to views of what educational or eugenic methods are needed to prevent waste of gifts and
provide humankind with the maximum leaven of hard work, spirit,

wisdom—in whatever proportions the theorists think necessary under the historical circumstances. Within the European traditions, in the literature directly concerned with creativity, as well as in the various literatures about political education, cultivation of the soul (*cultura animae*, the Romans called it), spiritual exercise, and (in our day) self-help, there seem to be three recurrent images of maximally creative minds. First, there are images of minds in which great innate chaos submits to a higher and more beautiful form; second, there are images in which great energy is kept under strong but flexible control as the mind gradually evolves or matures; and third, images in which great encumbrances are dispatched to let the mind lighten and take wing, or refine and concentrate itself. Among the Greeks, from whom so much of our imagery of mental processes derives, the three possibilities are apparent in the works of—respectively—Plato, Aristotle, and the Stoics.

At these headwaters of our philosophical tradition, there was a good deal of debate about the relationships that should exist between creative artists and men of philosophical ability or wisdom, and about what the two types had mentally or spiritually in common. Plato is notorious for having offered both some of the most beautiful encomiums to divinely inspired poets and a complex rationale for excluding poets, no matter how divinely inspired, from the ideal city where philosopher-kings (or philosopher-queens) are to rule and pronounce upon moral rectitude. Aristotle, on the other hand, made no political objection to poetry and marveled uninhibitedly over the intellectual capacity poets and philosophers (all male) most obviously share—the capacity for seeing similarities in dissimilarities, the metaphoric capacity. The Stoic wise person (male or female) can be a philosopher or a poet or a politician or anything else—as long as his or her soul is properly organized and attuned to the world-soul.

PLATO: CRAFTING AND PROCREATING

Plato's theory of creativity was built up out of hierarchical distinctions, and his higher/lower drawings of the line were of basically two kinds. In the *Symposium*, Socrates' rendition of the instruction he received from the seeress Diotima is dense in such distinctions. She informed him that men desire immortality and that this leads them to desire offspring: either they want children to approximate eternity in the continuity of generations, or they want immortal glory which they win by conceiving and bearing things of the spirit. "And what are they? you ask. Wisdom and her sister virtues: it is the office of every poet to beget them, and of every artist whom we may call creative." Procreators of the spirit are higher than procreators of the body, and among procreators of the spirit there are, also, those who create educational or political or legal monuments of human wisdom (the highest of which is the wisdom called justice and moderation) and those special few initiates who are able to go further on to "true contemplation" of the beautiful itself, which is distinct from any bodily creature or spiritual creation in which beauty may be manifest.

Throughout his dialogues, Plato moves in this way: he distinguishes a realm of the false or unreal from a higher realm of the real and true, and then within the real and true realm he distinguishes a lower form and a higher—highest—form of life, of knowledge, of creativity. Those who reach the very highest plane are inspired by, or by a vision of, the eternal forms—the good itself, the beautiful itself. People who live in the lower two realms can physically procreate (as the *Symposium* notes) and also produce things, either as artisans or as imitators of things artisans have produced (as Plato points out in the *Sophist* and the *Republic*), but these activities are very far from the highest realm of truth. Such physical and spiritual procreators are trapped in and confined to looking at only what comes and goes, what is transient and changeable. They may aspire to immortality, but they produce only generations of mortals; they may aspire to immortal fame, but they produce only imitations of imitations. Creativity in the higher realm comes from the domain of the eternal, not from the created world.

In the middle class or lower part of the higher realm, people are properly inspired by eternal forms, but they register their inspiration in mortal materials—in education for youths, in poetry, in political institutions, in laws. From the *Symposium*:

> And I ask you, who would not prefer such [spiritual] fatherhood to merely human propagation, if he stopped to think of Homer, and Hesiod, and all the greatest of our poets? Who would not envy them their immortal progeny, their claim upon the admiration of posterity? O think of Lycurgus, Diotima went on, and what offspring he left behind him in his laws, which proved to be the saviors of Sparta and, perhaps, the whole of Hellas. Or think of the fame of Solon. . . .

On the other hand, the highest of the high are not, apparently, producers at all. They are purely lovers; the offspring of their souls is only the unwritten wise speech they bestow on those they would educate—like Diotima's speech, or like the speech about the ideal city (a city existing only "in speech") that Socrates makes in the *Republic*. Specifically, the very highest lovers are not associated with any type of production traditionally presided over by a god, as Apollo presides over oracles, Dionysus over tragic festivals, and the nine Muses over their nine genres and media. Thus Socrates distinguishes human inspiration or madness and divine madness in the *Phaedrus* and then indicates which of the divine madnesses is the highest—the one associated with Eros and Aphrodite, who were not gods of production:

> In divine [as opposed to human] madness we distinguish four types, ascribing them to four gods: the inspiration of the prophet to Apollo, that of the mystic to Dionysus, that of the poet to the Muses, and a fourth type, which we declared to be the highest, the madness of the lover, to Aphrodite and Eros.

But all the types of mad inspiration, the ones characteristic of producers (prophets, mystics, poets) and the one specific to contemplators or lovers, come from above—throughout the *Phaedrus* Plato calls inspiration "divine"—and all are imagined as spiritual impregnation.

> There is a . . . form of madness or possession of which the Muses are the source. This seizes a tender, virgin [*abaton*] soul and stimulates it to rapt, passionate expression, especially in lyric poetry, glorifying the countless glorious deeds of ancient times for the instruction of posterity.

The imagery of divine inspiration is more scientific in the more cosmological context of the late dialogue called *Timaeus*:

> And we should consider that God gave the sovereign part of the human soul to be the divinity of each one, being that part which, as we say, dwells at the top of the body, and inasmuch as we are a plant not of an earthly but of a heavenly growth, raises us from earth to our kindred who are in heaven. . . . He who has been earnest in love of knowledge and of true wisdom, and has exercised his intellect more than any other part of him, must have thoughts immortal and divine. . . . Now there is only one way of taking care of things, and this is to give each the food and motion which

21

are natural to it. And the motions which are naturally akin to the divine principle within us are the thoughts and revolutions of the universe. Those each man should follow, and by learning the harmonies and revolutions of the universe, should correct the courses of the head which are corrupted at our birth, and should assimilate the thinking being to the thought, renewing his original nature, so that having assimilated them he may attain to the best life which the gods have set before mankind, both for the present and for the future.

Inspiration here is a kind of ingestion of divine cosmic motions into the soul, which becomes shaped by these unchanging patterns and harmonies.

Plato's answer to the question, What kind of person is suited for such inspiration, suited to be either a producer of beautiful things or a non-productive lover of wisdom? is very simple (and a bit circular): the person who, by natural endowment and proper education, has attained the kind of character that can love the real, true, beautiful. As there are three realms, the lowest one and two higher ones, on the ontological scale, there are three character types. In the *Republic*, Plato presents them: (1) that in which appetites prevail and love of money is the norm, so common among the Phoenicians and Egyptians; (2) a higher type, which is marked by spiritedness and is common among northerners, Thracians and Scythians; and (3) a highest type in which reason prevails. This last, Plato concludes on a chauvinistic note, is "chiefly attributed to the region where we dwell." (It is interesting to note that if the poets were to be represented in this threefold scheme on the principles laid down in the *Symposium*, they would be in the middle, among the spirited. But, in his political work the *Republic*, Plato associates spiritedness with military ability, and, as we shall see, makes no place for the poets.)

People of these three character-types should, Plato thought, be engaged in pursuits appropriate to their types—acquisitive activities, military activities, and political-intellectual leadership. A good and just state is one in which this kind of order prevails, and people do not leap out of character in their occupations. In the ideal republic Socrates outlines, people should be bred for these types, and a person assigned to the artisanal lower class, the military middle class, or the leadership highest class should not only procreate to perpetuate his or her type, but never set hand to another type's work. Respect for order and for the laws that sustain order is to be everyone's "second nature," and no innovation in the laws should ever be considered once the just division of labor and good order are achieved. Good order does not get better, it only gets worse.

Plato offered a number of character-identifying schemes in the *Republic*. This one is quite simple:

> As people lead colts up to alarming noises to see whether they are timid, so these young men [with leadership potential] must be brought into terrifying situations and then into scenes of pleasure, which will put them to a severer proof than gold tried in a furnace. If we find one bearing himself well in all these trials and resisting every enchantment, a true guardian of himself, preserving always that perfect rhythm and harmony of being which he has acquired from his training in music and poetry, such a one will be the greatest service to the commonwealth as well as to himself. Whenever we find one who has come unscathed through every test of childhood, youth and manhood, we shall set him as Ruler.

But although Plato's full educational scheme for leaders, presented in Book VII of the *Republic*, is a good deal more complicated than this rough sketch from Book III, his characterology does not vary: leaders must have the virtue the lower classes most need, temperance to control their appetites; the virtue military people most need, courage; and also the virtue peculiar to the highest class, that prudence or moderation in counsel characteristic of mind inspired insofar as human products, which are formed by divine inspiration, can inspire. The leaders have minds into which "rhythm and harmony have sunk and taken strong hold."

But people whose characters are of the leadership type have to be further educated if they are actually to rule. Music and poetry are enough for initial youthful formation (up to age seventeen or eighteen, Plato suggests), but the leader needs further intellectual shaping if he or she qualifies for it. During the period now known as late adolescence (when, I will argue later, creative people form a "character-ideal"), Plato suggests that the young leaders study arithmetic, geometry, solid geometry, astronomy, harmonics—that is, not music but the soundless principles and elements that music manifests in its sounds. Finally, between the ages of thirty and thirty-five, they reach dialectic, that form of argumentation and definition-making which Plato describes as "the ability to see the connexions of things." Again, there are two upper stages of education, and only men and women skilled in the highest—dialectic—are strong enough for a period away from their studies in order to "take a turn at the troublesome duties of public life and act as rulers for their country's sake, not regarding it as a distinction, but as an unavoidable task."

Commentators on Plato's *Republic* have always been struck by the contrast between this high-minded character-shaping educational program—open to women as well as men, remarkably—and the diatribe launched against poetry in Book X. Some commentators solve the problem by saying that Book X is inauthentic, but this skirts the fact—obvious in Aristotle's work—that in the Academy debates about the worth of poetry were common. It seems much more likely that Plato was reacting defensively toward the chaotic Athenian political context, so dangerous, he thought, to philosophers—so deadly to Socrates. Book X concentrates on why poetry is politically dangerous.

In Book X, there is not a word about poets as inspired by the gods, divinely mad. Rather, artists are presented as "thrice removed from reality" because they offer images of people and events, which are, in turn, only appearances of the true and real. Homer represented generals and statesmen, but, Plato asks contentiously, did Homer know anything about war or statecraft? Do people acknowledge Homer as their chief of staff or their lawgiver? Did Homer found a school for teaching what he knew to future generals and leaders? It seems that these strange and tendentious queries were prompted by the contemporary opinion, which Plato later cites, that Homer was "the educator of all Hellas," to be consulted on all questions. Apparently, unnamed literary enemies held up the *Illiad* as a treatise on the art of war, hailing Homeric heroes as the very models of kings.

Plato reacted so strongly to the threat he perceived that he went right on to use his strange "thrice removed from reality" argument for banishing tragic poetry from the ideal Republic. He combines the argument with an appeal to the characterology he had developed: people, he reiterates, have conflicts in their minds between their lower (appetitive) and higher (reasoning) parts; different characters are marked by the dominance of one or the other part; drama is marked by its attention to the lower, and most of the people who go to the theater are also of the lower sort; so the dramatist's work can only strengthen the "element that threatens to undermine reason."

> As a country may be given over into the power of its worst citizens while the better sort are ruined, so, we shall say, the dramatic poet sets up a vicious form of government in the individual soul: he gratifies the senseless

24

part which cannot distinguish great and small, but regards the same things as now one, now the other; and he is an image-maker whose images are phantoms far removed from reality.

Dramatic poetry, Plato concludes, has such power that it can even corrupt a person of reason-dominated character. This is because people in the theater let their reason relax its vigilance; they enjoy the spectacle of excessive emotions or appetites—of lower characters in action—because they think that this excessiveness is far from them and that they could never themselves behave in the "womanish" way people do on the stage. But these reasonable people underestimate the danger, Plato says, because:

> Few, I believe, are capable of reflecting that to enter into another's feelings must have an effect on our own: the emotions of pity our sympathy has strengthened will not be easy to restrain when we are suffering ourselves.

A reasonable person's characterological balance can be upset by exposure to too much that is not-reason, and the result will be political corruption: "Pleasure and pain will usurp the sovereignty of law and of the principles always recognized by common consent as the best."

In the less politically defensive dialogues, while he was writing non-polemically and speaking positively of divine inspiration, Plato stressed what the poets and lovers of wisdom have in common; here, however, he focuses on "a long-standing quarrel between poetry and philosophy" and on the idea that reasonable characters will be made "womanish" and over-emotional by poetry. A gap opened. Plato had assigned the poets and philosophers to the two higher forms of life and knowledge, the productive and the contemplative, and set both over against those dwelling down in the lower realm of appetites and false knowledge. Here he drops the poets into that lower realm, and the second rank of the higher realm is left empty. There are only emotional-appetitive people and reasonable ones, the kind of stark "we-and-them" dualism that is typical (as I will note later in detail) of characterological classifications designed to conserve a threatened socio-political status quo.

The basic problem is that the creative character of the reasonable people, the leadership, is not incorruptible, not immune to change, devolution. (It is possible that Plato also thought that poets can change for the worse, too, by turning away from the divine realm, source of their inspiration, and imitating imitations in the lower realm—but he does not make this argument in the *Republic* or elsewhere.) Fear of corruption or fear that harmony once attained will be lost is typical of theories of creativity of the Platonic type, that is, theories based on an image of characters being beautifully fabricated, inspirationally shaped into a hierarchical ordering of parts. What has been constructed can be deconstructed. And it is very remarkable—as we shall see in a series of examples below—that the source of corruption in such theories is almost always something effeminizing or "womanish" in the subordinated part of the character. This is so, even especially so, when such a theory permits women a great range of creative activity and when the theory presents inspiration or self-shaping in obviously feminine terms as a form of pregnancy or reproduction.

Fabricated characters are vulnerable characters. But creative characters that have evolved organically, slowly reaching their true or perfect form by unfolding their potential for perfection, are grown to last. In theories of creativity built around images of creative characters evolutionarily made to last, the basic anxiety does not focus on the possibility of subversion or rebellion from the part of the character that is subordinated and controlled. The source of trouble for potentially creative characters as they are evolving is, rather, an unconducive, un-nourishing, growth-inhibiting environment. As Aristotle put the matter using moral-political terms: In a bad city, a good man has no forum to act well.

ARISTOTLE: EVOLUTION TOWARD TRUTH

About everything to which he turned his attention, Aristotle thought evolutionarily. The unformed everywhere seeks form, becoming is everywhere aimed toward being. The three basic types of human inquiry or science, which Aristotle called Theoretical, Practical, and Productive, all delineate histories: the history of philosophy and of individual humans' mental abilities; the development of ethical ways of life and political institutions; the evolution of genres of things produced by people. In each domain, individuals can recapitulate in their small stories the general movement-toward-form story of which they are a part or in which they participate.

In the *Poetics*, Aristotle offers a history of the genre tragedy that starts with the simple, pre-Aeschylean emergence of tragedy from the epic, goes forward into Aeschylus' own practice, and stops when tragedy attains its nature. Sophocles and Euripides wrote when the most important of the genre's elements, the arrangement of incidents into a plot, had been perfected. Aristotle shows that the plot is the end or *telos* of tragedy by remarking that "those attempting to produce tragedies are able to make exact diction and characters before they are able to construct the incidents." This applies to the pre-Aeschylean poets as well as to all poets starting out, learning their art.

Aristotle has very little to say about the poets in his *Poetics*, because his topic is the inner workings of the thing produced, not the producer. He is concerned with how-to, not who-does. But, in passing, he points out the key to a poet's ability to live up to requirements of fully developed tragic art. The poet should keep the action of his drama so clearly before his imaginative eye that he feels he is actually looking at it, and in this way he will be able to discover what is possible and not "forget the incongruities," which means those actions that might positively or negatively jar the spectator's expectations. The poet should "work out the incidents in gestures," that is, he should himself play all the parts:

> . . . for apart from nature itself [i.e., an actual instance of passion], those are most persuasive who themselves suffer the passions they are imitating. He who is himself distressed most truly distresses, and he who is most truly angry most truly enrages. On this account poetic science belongs to those either naturally well-endowed [*euphues*] or mad [*manikos*], for of these the former mold themselves well [to the passions required], the latter are ecstatic [*ekstatikos*].

Enactment is the poet's key ability, and the ability to enact a tragedy imaginatively is either a naturally given ability to become, say, an angry man or it is an ability to "stand outside of one's self," to range over all passions, the whole human stage. Aristotle does not further describe the ek-static state. In the *Rhetoric*, however, he says that poetry is inspired (*entheos*), which seems to imply that the mad poet reaches the realm of the Deity, who is, in Aristotle's system, the Unmoved Mover, the final cause that draws everything in the cosmos toward essential, perfect form.

In his earlier and more Platonizing lectures gathered under the title *Eudemian Ethics*, Aristotle had presented inspiration in terms like those Plato had used to extol inspiration (as he presented character in terms indebted to the Hippocratic theory of four bodily humors, including the heavy one typical of melancholics):

> As in the cosmos, so in the soul, the Divine moves everything. The starting point of reason is not reasoning but something greater. What, then, could be greater even than knowledge and intellect but the divine? . . . For this reason, those are called fortunate who, whatever they start on, succeed in it without being good at reasoning. And deliberation is of no advantage for them, for they have in them a principle that is better than intellect and deliberation. They have inspiration, but they cannot deliberate. . . . Hence we have the melancholic men, the dreams of what is true. For the moving principle seems to become stronger when the reasoning principle is relaxed.

But all that remained of this approach in Aristotle's mature work is the claim that poets do not deliberate as theoretical people do. However, although he stressed differences between the mental modes of poets and philosophers, Aristotle also carefully noted what they have in common: an eye for resemblances. Use of metaphors, Aristotle claimed in the *Poetics*, "is a sign of the naturally well-endowed [*euphues*] poet," and it is the one element of diction that cannot be learned or taken over from others. The poet's originality resides in his metaphors. In the *Rhetoric*, Aristotle saw no difference at all between poetical (or rhetorical) ability for metaphors and philosophical:

> Metaphors . . . should be drawn from objects that are related to the object in question, but not obviously related; as in philosophy, the producer will perceive resemblances even in things far apart. Thus [the philosopher] Archytas said [for example] that an arbitrator and an altar were the same, since both are a refuge for the injured.

Ability for enactment, for playing all the parts, and ability for metaphors are the only two abilities that Aristotle explicitly attributes to the naturally well-endowed poet.

In the *Poetics*, as I mentioned, Aristotle considers tragedy in and of itself, not at all in terms of the character of its producers or the functions it may serve in social or political context. But his approach is very different in the *Politics*, where he considers—in a profoundly un-Platonic tone—art in education, and education in the state. The discussion is crucially important, for it supports Aristotle's vision of life's highest aim—cultivated leisure. In cultivated leisure, people reach their perfect form, the way of life toward which they are drawn by the Divine.

All education, Aristotle thought, should ultimately aim at pleasurable occupation in *scholē*—a word that means leisure or recreation, but refers less to freedom from work than to freedom for cultural activity. Education should not be specialized, designed to promote one quality over others, as the Spartans, for example, promoted military and athletic prowess. (Or, Aristotle might have added, as Plato had suggested that education should be specialized, with each class performing one function in the state.) Nobility of character, Aristotle says in the *Politics*, is impossible for someone one-dimensionally or lopsidedly trained.

The psychology of character that underlies Aristotle's educational conviction is—predictably—evolutionary. Fully mature men (not women) are possessed of a lower soul or psyche, called irrational and concerned with basic nutritive functions, and also of a rational psyche that has a lower and a higher part. The higher rational part is reason (*nous*) proper, while the lower rational part consists of appetites and desire. If, in the course of maturation and education, appetites and desire become controlled by reason, they are rational; if not, they are connected to the irrational nutritive psyche. Control by reason—or, to say the same thing, moral virtue—develops over time by regular practice (habituation) following good models and following the general principle that extremes of behavior are to be avoided and a mean between extremes sought. A person whose reason is maximally developed is capable of both active and passive use of it. As there are poets who can mold themselves to passions as they imaginatively enact their dramas, and others who are ek-static, there are two capacities of reason, or *nous*, one for passively becoming all things and one for actively making all things, as light makes all colors actual. The second capacity of reason seems to be the capacity required for those poets who can be ek-static, outside of the self and spread over everything—like the immortal, separate, unmixed Divinity.

It is completely characteristic of Aristotle's mature way of thinking that he does not set the appetites and desire off from the rational domain as Plato did; the appetites and desire, rather, occupy the lower rank of the rational soul, where Plato had placed spirit, which predominates in the characters Plato called spirited and also (Plato implied in dialogues other than the anti-poetic Book X of the *Republic*) in the productively inspired poets. Appetites and desire are not opposite to reason, "other," as they were for Plato; they are the ground which potentially contains reason and out of which reason slowly evolves.

This distinction between Plato and Aristotle is obvious in Aristotle's attitude toward *musikē* and its role in education. Both in the course of producing well-roundedness and in preparing a gentleman (ladies were not at issue) for leisure, important roles were to be played by singing, dancing, theater, and all the fine performing arts (collectively called *musikē*). They did not threaten reason, they helped it mature into its controlling role, as Aristotle stresses in the *Politics*:

> It is not easy to define either what the effect of music is or what our object is in learning it. Is it for our amusement and refreshment, like taking a nap or having a drink? I hardly think so, because these things are not in themselves of prime importance, though they are pleasant and help us forget our worries, as Euripides says. Must we not rather regard music as a stimulus to goodness, capable of having an effect on the character, in just the same way as gymnastic training produces a body of a certain type, and so capable of forming men who have the habit of right critical appreciation? [Finally,] it surely has a contribution to make to the intelligent and cultivated leisure times.

Musikē is and serves all three modalities: amusement and relaxation, education, and leisure. But Aristotle was particularly concerned to elaborate on the second, education, for good use of leisure will follow from good education. He thought that *musikē* could teach men "right judgment and taking pleasure in good morals and noble actions" because it resembles reality. A disposition shaped by a resemblance to reality is very like one shaped by reality itself: "In *musikē*, moral qualities are present, represented in the very tunes we hear." People are "affected in a manner in keeping with the performance," in musical settings or in the theater. When people listen to music (in the narrow sense of the word *musikē*) their psyches become harmonious as the music is harmonious—an affinity connects the two; when they go to the theater and watch a tragedy, they are purged of fear and pity—they undergo a catharsis—and are left serene. These effects seemed to Aristotle so obviously beneficial that he recommended not just attendance for young gentlemen at musical and theatrical performances, but actual cultivation of musical skill. Political leaders should play the lyre.

Aristotle agreed with Plato's notion in Book X of the *Republic* that resemblances influence the psyches of spectators in performances, but he neither thought of resemblances as "thrice removed from reality" nor thought that their influence would be necessarily baleful because too emotional. On the contrary, he asserted that *musikē* draws people into harmony, inspires them, as the poet or musician is inspired by the Divine. When a poet or musician composes or enacts a piece of music or a drama, as when people hear or see the resulting product, their characters are drawn upward, perfected. Reason comes to prevail in them. And there are no warring claims to such reason between poetry and philosophy. But, should people be surrounded by *musikē* that is bad, of course, this result will not come about. Similarly, if they grow up in an environment lacking good models and the possibility for choosing the mean between extremes of behavior, the conditions of good habituation, they will never attain the full unfolding of reason. Creative character, in Aristotle's conception, depends upon education and social and political conditions conducive to creativity.

That city-state in which there are no characterological extremes will be the one best suited for producing balanced, harmonious characters. So in the *Politics* Aristotle recommends a political organization or constitution that is moderate in every way:

> In all states there are three sections of the community—the very well-off, the very badly-off, and those in between. Seeing therefore that it is agreed that moderation and a middle position are best, it is clear that in the matter of possessions to own a middling amount is best of all. This condition is most obedient to reason, and following reason is just what is difficult both for the exceedingly rich, handsome, strong, and well-born, and for the opposite, the extremely poor, the weak, and the downtrodden. The former commit deeds of violence on a large scale, the latter are delinquent and wicked in petty ways.

Aristotle goes on to detail the characterological shortcomings of the very rich and the very poor, noting, as he had in the full discussion of character-types in his *Rhetoric*, that people shaped by extreme social circumstances are unreliable and usually unreasonable. Neither masters nor mastered—neither the contemptuous nor the resentful—are capable of that equality and respectful friendship that obtains between moderate citizens who are partners in a moderate state.

Aristotle's conviction that people cannot fully actualize their potential except in the right conditions does not entail the Platonic idea—the

31

basic Platonic political anxiety—that good and reasonable characters can be corrupted. He notes in his *Nicomachean Ethics* that only the Spartans have really given public, legislative thought to "questions of nurture and occupations." But good people have been able to function elsewhere because their families have supplied what the state has neglected. Similarly, a person who has attained good character and then finds himself in a state that has deteriorated will not regress, his character will not be deconstructed. He simply will not be able to act well, since acting well depends upon being able to join his fellow citizens in the relations of equality and respect. So he will have to retreat to a more contemplative, non-public life. Retreat will not be a loss to the individual, however, but only to the state, for the contemplative life, which need not entail any public deeds, is the one that Aristotle presents in his *Ethics* as ultimately the best:

> Now he who exercises his intellect and cultivates it seems to be both in the best condition and most dear to the gods. For if the gods have any care for human affairs, as they are thought to have, it would be reasonable both that they should delight in that which is best and most akin to them [i.e., intellect] and that they should reward those who love and honor this most, as caring for the things that are dear to them and acting both rightly and nobly. He, therefore is dearest to the gods.

STOICISM: REMOVING OBSTACLES TO VIRTUE, FOR EVERYONE

Among the ancient schools of philosophy after Plato and Aristotle, the Stoic was the one most appreciative of poetry. The early Greek Stoics, starting with the founder, Zeno of Cittium, treated Homer as a philosopher, quoting him frequently in their own arguments, which they often presented in poetic forms. Poetry was purely didactic for them, the most effective medium of direct appeal to the human reason that they held to be universal—the same for poets as for spectators and hearers of poetry, the same for women as for men, the same for slaves as for masters, the same for citizens of a good state as for citizens of a bad state.

In the Stoic theory of language, words are imitations of reality, but this did not mean—as it did for Plato—that words are of a lesser ontological status, *mere* imitations related to reality only conventionally. The Stoics held that words are in a natural relation—originally, an onomatopoetic relation—to the things they name, and that grammar, relations among words, is in a natural relation to the relations among things in the cosmos. When a poet or a philosopher writes truly, he or she presents a microcosm of the cosmos—and he or she also *is* a microcosm of the cosmos.

For the Stoics, literary or language theory, psychology, and physics are just three different ways to inquire about the order of the same world. The world is one, it is not divided Platonically into a material realm and a realm of eternal immaterial forms, and it does not even evolve in the Aristotelian manner from formless irrational matter toward completely formed rational matter. No Divinity is posited who either shapes the world or draws the world upward toward Itself. Rather, matter and Divinity are part of a single continuum; the Stoic doctrine is monistic. The entire cosmos is one living organism, and it is entirely permeated with the Stoic Divinity, which can be called *logos* (reason, but also language), or *pneuma* (fiery life-breath) or *tonos* (vital tension holding all things coherently together). The cosmos and the Divinity, which are one and the same, reconfigure ceaselessly, without diminishing or losing shape—like a kaleidoscope. The vast cycle of intracosmic change goes from creation to destruction—or order to disorder, predominance of a heavy earthy element to predominance of the fiery one in a cosmic conflagration—and then goes back again. Each organism within the cosmic organism also has a cycle of ordering and disordering, coming to life and dying, in accordance with the degree of *logos–pneuma–tonos* it possesses. The portion of the divine *logos–pneuma–tonos* in a human being is that person's *hegemonikon*, or governing capacity, and it radiates out—like the arms of an octopus, like the water from a fountain, to use Stoic analogies—into the other human capacities: the five senses, speech and procreation. There is no mind/body dualism, no distinction between intellection in a realm of truth and perception in a realm of appearances, and no distinction between lower appetites and higher spirit and reason.

Creativity in the Stoic conception does not involve a higher part of the soul organizing the lower parts like an artist or a lower part unfolding or actualizing into a higher one. Rather, it involves the whole unitary microcosmic soul attuning itself to the cosmos. The best condition of the soul can be described physically as optimal tautness or tone, ethically as peaceable, well-ordered self-government, theologically as conformity to the cosmic Divinity.

A person whose soul is in proper condition cannot willingly make an error of knowledge or action. The person's hegemonic portion of divinity gives its assent to what the Stoics called a "mind-picture" (*phantasia*) arising in the process of sensation, and this assent will be correctly given if the soul is healthy, properly toned, carefully attuned to the picture, and intent or focused upon grasping it. The well-toned soul is, in short, attentive. Similarly, when impulses or appetites adumbrating a course of action to be pursued arise in the body, the reason can assent or refuse. There are courses of action or goals that are good, some that are evil, and some that are indifferent. The last are very typically Stoic—death, glory and disgrace, pain and pleasure, riches and property, disease. Good goals should be assented to, evil ones avoided, and indifferent ones judged according to their worth as positive or negative, advantageous or disadvantageous. Glory, pleasure, property, health are generally advantageous—but not always, and only in greater or lesser degree. Attention is, again, required as a person strips away from himself or herself everything that is not either good or advantageous. The ideal is self-sufficiency and stripped-down purity.

The Stoics called a person who is in the process of attaining the right tone of soul or virtue, with its clear knowledge of things good, things evil, and things either positively or negatively indifferent, a "probationer." They felt that a probationer finally attains virtue not piecemeal but all at once, in a moment, for virtue or right tone is a condition—you are in it, or you are not. Once attained, virtue is permanent and incorruptible. The Stoics optimistically held that virtue can be both attained and maintained under even the most adverse of circumstances.

The Stoics had neither Plato's fear of moral corruption nor Aristotle's desire for state-regulated public education. In comparison to Plato, they were egalitarians who did not attribute to a lower portion of humankind the capacity to infect the upper portion unless kept rigorously apart in a hierarchical arrangement. Everyone has the same inborn spark of the divine Reason. On the other hand, in comparison to Aristotle, they did not focus their attention on specific political constitutions for achieving political equality among free gentlemen because they thought of themselves and everyone, male or female, free or slave, as citizens of the cosmos, the cosmopolis, as they called the city-of-the-world.

Chapter Two

Creative Characters on Their Characters

MODERN PSYCHOLOGY AND CHARACTER STUDY

Many varieties of Platonists, Aristotelians, and Stoics have elaborated on the theories of creative character advanced by their respective founding fathers. In the Hellenistic period and afterwards, as Greek thought migrated around the Mediterranean and mingled with Hebraic and Christian traditions, many syncretistic versions of the three theories were also produced. Among the heirs of these traditions, there were virtuosos of self-reflection or introspection, like Augustine of Hippo. But the peculiarly modern, late nineteenth-century manner of self-study—the kind of self-experimentation that Sigmund Freud called "self-analysis"—was without antique precedent. It required a slow break with the idea that something external to an individual, a divine source of inspiration or evolutionary force, shaped or moved both specific thoughts and character as a whole. The great modern analysts of creative character looked upon themselves as self-contained products of their individual histories rather than as results of divine work. They were contained in themselves as chemical experiments are in laboratory flasks.

Modern self-analytical character study had its "history of ideas" origin in the "Introspectionism" that became a trend within German psychology after Immanuel Kant laid down a strict distinction between natural dispositions or temperaments and character. In the Platonic tradition, character is achieved as an individual with a given natural constitution is shaped to resemble mentally the divine, eternal models in the realm of the true. The fabricating agency, reason, is divine, as each individual's reason is a representative of the cosmic reason. Similarly, in the Aristotelian scheme, the ultimate force working upon a given irrational soul to draw forth the rational potential therein is the Divine Mover, and the Stoics imagined individual maturation as a piece of cosmic process. Kant was aware of these images, and he spoke in a quite Aristotelian manner about three human faculties—the sensuous faculty (source of inclinations, site of pleasures and unpleasures), a faculty of desire or willing, and a cognitive faculty consisting of three subdivisions: judgment, understanding, and reason. But Kant was also aware of the Greek medical tradition in which character is said to be the result of a preponderance of one or another of four humors—a matter of natural endowment that can be influenced by careful physical regime and education. Kant set his own characterology, however, on a quite different footing by arguing that neither Divine work nor physical nature is the source of character.

In his *Anthropology from a Pragmatic Point of View,* Kant started from the idea that people are born with "natural dispositions," on the basis of which they develop a temperament, turning into one of the four humoral types known to the Greeks. Humoral temperaments can be studied from a physiological point of view, in relation to the faculties of sense and desire. Character can then be considered simply as all the qualities defining a person, as a reflection of the person's temperament. But, Kant argues, this is not the proper use of the word *character*.

Character is a way of thinking, Kant insisted, a matter of reason supplying principles for action, which means that character study is a kind of ethics. From the ethical point of view, in which character is said to be good or bad, "it does not depend on what Nature makes of man, but what man makes of himself. What Nature makes of man belongs to temperament (wherein the subject is for the most part passive), and only what man makes of himself reveals whether he has character." A person can achieve character, by exercise of reason, regardless of his or her temperament; character gets the upper hand over nature, whether physically or divinely conceived.

With these clear strokes, Kant separated study of temperaments from study of moral character or ethics or philosophy generally. He made character a matter of conscious choice, entirely a work of reason, and not something cultivated through education or habituation on the basis of a given temperament. His view is summarized in the *Anthropology* with a beautiful passage, which contrasts with Kant's typically spare, abstract style and in which he writes like a biographer—or an autobiographer:

The person who is conscious of the character in his mode of thinking does not have that character by nature, but must always have acquired it. One may also take it for granted that the establishment of character is similar to a kind of rebirth, a certain solemn resolution which the person himself makes. This resolution and the moment at which the transformation took place remain unforgettable for him, like the beginning of a new epoch. This stability and persistence in principles can generally not be effected by education, examples and instruction by degrees, but can only be done by an explosion which suddenly occurs as a consequence of our disgust at the unsteady condition of instinct [or inclination]. Perhaps there will be only a few who have attempted this revolution before their thirtieth year, and fewer still who have firmly established it before their fortieth year. Wishing to become a better person in a fragmentary manner is a vain endeavor because one impression fades away while we labor on another.

What Kant proposed was an image of reason following principles and establishing governance over the realms of sensation and desire or willing. But this image, set forth by a man who had avidly followed in his newspaper the course of the French Revolution, was not of monarchical reason. Disgust (a matter of sensation) and resolution (a matter of will) make way for reason, which is more like a republican parliament than a king. Neither Plato's spiritual part of the psyche nor Aristotle's motive part, both of which were hierarchically higher than the appetitive or nutritive-perceptive parts but lower than reason, were agencies with a power like resolution. Both Plato and Aristotle held that if a man knew the good with his reason, his next lower spiritual or motive part would fall into line and pass reasonable orders on down the line to the appetites or nutritive-perceptive psyche. Doing followed knowing automatically. Correlatively, an evil person was one in whom the chain of command did not function, not one who rebelled against it. Rebellion presupposes an independent source of motion; it is disobedience to command rather than failure to obey due to mechanical problem or lack of habituation or education in the procedures of obedience. In Greek thought generally, there is no concept of the rebellious will. Not until St. Augustine spoke of an internally divided *voluntas*, which says at once "I will" and "I will-not," did the kind of irresolution Kant finds typical of the young come into the Western philosophical tradition.

Kant was well versed in the varieties of Christian search for a means to heal the will—by human agency or, more often, by divine grace—and his own reply was offered against the Christian background, against the famous image of St. Augustine sitting self-divided and self-disgusted in his garden and receiving divine guidance as he took up his Bible and read his salvation. Kant spoke, however, not of healing the divided will but of reconfiguring the faculties, establishing character. What prompts the reconfiguration is not God's intervention but, very modernly, the self-disgust.

German psychology after Kant went off in the two different directions indicated by his distinction between temperaments and character. A group known by its English and American heirs as "Behaviorists" focused on the dimensions of the self that can be observed, the phenomenal self, which Kant himself thought could be grasped by Newtonian methods of mathematical measurement and which have since been measured in every conceivable way. Others, known as "Introspectionists," were intrigued by the unobservable or noumenal self that can only be known by means of the internal conversion of moral experience—the inner self giving rise to and consolidating the moral revolution. Those influenced by introspectionism looked, each in his own fashion, and not many in Kant's own terms, for the hidden springs of human thought and action, the invisible—and certainly unquantifiable—substratum of daily human life. Schopenhauer came, thus, to Will. But throughout the nineteenth century the word that most often designated the pursued invisible domain was not the "noumenal" or the "Will," it was the "Unconscious."

During the nineteenth century, the idea that human thought has an invisible spring—the "Unconscious"—developed a corollary with similarly profound effects on philosophy and the history of ideas. That was, simply, that the hidden spring is not specific to an individual, but rather manifest more or less through all individuals. The Unconscious is the hidden spring of historical processes, of History, as well. The emphasis Kant had put on individual choice and resolution receded before various forms of determinism and various images of Progress. With this shift, much of the microcosm/macrocosm thinking that was typical of the Greeks returned—but with a difference. Aristotle had looked upon his predecessors as men whose reason was not fully actualized, whose philosophies were immature as the early forms of dramatic poetry were immature in relation to Aeschylus's achievement, but he had not taken this line of thought to the kind of sweeping conclusion that was typical of Hegel and his school: there is an Absolute Spirit operating unconsciously throughout history, progressing from the East to the Greece of the Golden Age, through the Christian centuries, and on upward until it reached Germany in Hegel's time, where it creates—for the first time in history—True Philosophy.

Searches for the metaphysical or depth-psychological foundations of human action and thought were routinely combined by the mid-nineteenth century with world-historical investigations, histories of ideas and histories of rises and falls of civilizations. In this context, characterological study became enormously complex, and portraits of creative character were always set in historical contexts, with the consequence that genius came to be thought of as the maximum individual mental attainment possible within the limits specified by a given stage of historical attainment. The Aristotelian idea that Aeschylus created tragedy from dramatic poetry was buffeted by ideas about what world-historical Spirit created Aeschylus. But, although the concentration on Progress was new, the three types of creative character held up as ideals by Plato, Aristotle, and the Stoics recurred in characterology toward the end of the nineteenth century.

Modernist versions of the Greek character-types and typologies are most obvious not in work by people who described themselves as either psychologists or metaphysicians, but rather in work by originators of new self-experimenting psychological methods, who were also themselves literary artists. Their work can be read as "Creative characters on their characters."

I will present three such innovators in biographical vignettes that focus on the creative moments in which their characterologies emerged—as self-reflections. We will follow Friedrich Nietzsche, as he analyzed and repudiated his own work as a "positivist psychologist." When he reached the last and most remarkable period of his philosophizing, Nietzsche, the arch-anti-Platonist, constructed a quite Platonic, self-artificing image of creative character. Sigmund Freud's characterology began to emerge at a key moment in his self-analysis. We can see it by looking at the one extended biographical study of creative character that Freud produced—his 1910 essay on Leonardo da Vinci—in which the approach is evolutionary. Finally, we can meet Marcel Proust, who had felt for many years encumbered and unable to write, as he turned Stoic, suffering through the death of his mother and launching upon his autobiographical masterpiece, *A la recherche du temps perdu.*

NIETZSCHE: SELF-CRAFTING AND MALE MOTHERING

Nietzsche took for granted the distinction between men of action and men of intellection—practitioners and theoreticians—that both Plato and Aristotle had drawn, each in his own way. Practitioners are active characters, internally harmonious and balanced; their instinctual drives are firmly under control and their controls are reflective of the life of their groups. Theoreticians are contemplative characters, Nietzsche says in his *Gay Science*. They are spectators and listeners but also creators (as the actors are not). Although they are internally divided and conflicted, the contemplatives' instinctual drives are freer—indeed, they win their freedom as self-experimenters—and they are solitaries, living as distinct from groups as possible. The contemplative type's creativity depends upon ceaseless self-transformation, self-overcoming, even self-attack: "In times of peace, the militant person attacks himself," Nietzsche declared in *Beyond Good and Evil*. But his times of peace are also important, for anarchy of internal instinctual drives is not the ideal. The multiplicity of drives submits like a group of servants or tools to a higher power, and self-discipline produces a "communal structure of drives and affects." Nonetheless, the creative person has to be able to resist the pressure all societies exert against self-transformative abilities and in favor of unchangeability and dependable, firm reputations. "Being at odds with 'a firm reputation,' the attitude of those who seek knowledge is considered dishonorable while the petrification of opinions is accorded monopoly on honor!"

Nietzsche experienced and described the internal division of the contemplative type—his own type—in the Platonic manner, that is, as self-formation or self-shaping of a lower material self by a higher one. As he said in *Beyond Good and Evil*: "In man creature and creator are united: in man reside not only matter, fragments, superfluity, clay, excrement, folly and chaos, but also a creator, a sculptor, a hammer-hardness, a spectator divinity and a day of rest." This claim about man as creature and his own creator echoes, although with more Biblical allusions, the terms of Nietzsche's first major work, *The Birth of Tragedy*, where he envisioned creative character as a balance of Dionysian and Apollonian elements. Dionysus, the spirit of music, the god of frenzy and instinctual freedom, comes gradually under the control of Apollo, the spirit of sculpture and the plastic arts generally, the god of freedom from wild impulses, the god of wisdom in tranquility, of the beautiful world of dreams. In Greek tragedy itself—as in the character of poets—the two divinities stake out domains. Dialogue is Apollo's domain, and it assumes—as Aristotle had indicated—a more important role in tragedy after Aeschylus, that is, in tragedies played by more than two actors. The chorus, singing and dancing, is Dionysus's domain.

Nietzsche's main images for presenting self–formation are drawn from the plastic arts: the frenzy and instinctual freedom of the Dionysian realm are sculpted by Apollonian reasonableness. But he, like Plato, switched easily into a second image system. The Dionysian element is female, the Apollonian male. The Dionysian is procreative: "The choral parts that interlace the tragedy in a sense form the womb of the drama proper." Among the contemplative creative characters, there are two subtypes, one imagined as female, one as male. Like Plato, Nietzsche spoke of spiritual gestation and birth of ideas, and he thought there were two ways to engage in such spiritual procreation—the feminine way and the masculine way. From *Beyond Good and Evil*: "There are two kinds of genius: above all, one which begets, and another which will gladly allow itself to become fertile and will give birth." Nietzsche told his friend Lou Andreas–Salomé, his first biographer, that he considered himself an example of the second type—a mother—even though it seems obvious that he was constantly struggling to become a genius of the more self-reflective and self-knowing male begetter type:

> Animals do not think about females as men do; they consider the female the productive being . . . The females find in their children satisfaction for their desire to dominate, a possession, an occupation, something that is wholly intelligible to them and can be chattered with: the sum of all this is what mother love is; it is to be compared with an artist's love for his work. Pregnancy has made women kinder, more patient, more timid, more pleased to submit; and just so does spiritual pregnancy produce the character of the contemplative type, which is closely related to the feminine character; it consists of male mothers.

Later in the work just cited, *The Gay Science*, Nietzsche notes—in the Platonic-Aristotelian manner—that the poets do not deliberate about what they do:

> Consider a continually creative person, a "mother" type in the grand sense, one who hears and knows nothing more except about the pregnancies and deliveries of his spirit, one who simply lacks the time to reflect on himself

and his work and to make comparisons, one who no longer has any desire to assert his taste and who simply forgets it, without caring in the least whether it stands, or lies, or falls—such a person might perhaps eventually produce works that far excel his own judgment, so that he utters stupidities about them and himself—utters them and believes them. This seems to me almost the norm among fertile artists—nobody knows a child less well than its parents do—and it is true even in the case, to take a tremendous example, of the whole world of Greek art and poetry; it never "knew" what it did.

The Gay Science was the text with which Nietzsche made his exit from a period in his life that was marked by adherence to a philosophical positivism and faith in science. The positivist period, from 1876 to about 1881, appeared to Nietzsche himself, in his retrospective autobiographical works, as a great and necessary detour during which he was working against, out of, his youthful phase. Charting his three-part "Way to Wisdom," he described this youthful phase, in which he produced *The Birth of Tragedy*, his adoring praise for "Schopenahuer as Educator" and for Richard Wagner, and also his notes for *Human, All-Too-Human*, as typical of a person who was

> worshipping (and obeying and learning) better than anyone else. Assimilating all things that are venerable and letting them struggle with one another. Putting up with every difficulty. . . . Courage, time of fellowship. (Overcoming wicked and petty inclinations. The most receptive heart: One cannot conquer without love.)

When he painfully broke off his relationship with Wagner, Nietzsche entered into the positivitist period he called "the second path":

> Breaking the heart of the worshipper when he is strongly committed. The free spirit. Independence. The time of the wasteland. Critique of all that is venerated (with idealization of all that is not venerated). The attempted reversal of evaluations (. . . natures such as Dühring, Wagner, and Schopenhauer have not even attain[ed] this level!).

This second path looked, in retrospect, then, like a departure from being female, dependent on males. When he had worked his way thoroughly through the positivist phase, Nietzsche saw himself alone on a mountain top, "the third path," from whence he telegraphed a third description:

Great decision whether suitable for positive attitude, for affirmation. No longer any God or man above me! The instinct of the creative person who knows where to set to work. The great responsibility and the innocence. . . . (Only a few: most people will perish even on the second path. Perhaps Plato and Spinoza succeeded?).

The exuberant youthful works, like *The Birth of Tragedy*, extolled genius as Nietzsche discovered it and worshipped it in others. Genius—not any way of individual or political life—was the goal of human development. Geniuses form

a type of bridge over the barren streams of becoming. . . . A giant calls out to another one through the desolate connecting rooms of time, undisturbed by the malicious, noisy dwarfs who crawl away, as highly intellectual conversations continue. . . . The goal of mankind cannot lie in its ends but only in its highest types.

But in his last phase, Nietzsche focused not on genius in others but on his own; he universalized himself. The three stages he could track in his own history became the universal path of genius, The Way of Self-overcoming. The kind of tripartite hierarchical thinking about the supremely well-ordered character that was typical of Plato became, in Nietzsche, tripartite historical thinking. To his own retrospect, his life unfolded dialectically: thesis–antithesis–synthesis. But that abstract formula does not catch the key psychological forces, which are apparent in both of the metaphors for creativity with which Nietzsche operated: chaos formation and procreation. As Neitzsche wrote in *Gay Science*, out of the grief and chaos of all human history, the hero will arise:

Anyone who manages to experience the history of humanity as a whole as his own history will feel in an enormously generalized way all the grief of an invalid who thinks of health, of an old man who thinks of the dreams of his youth, of a lover deprived of his beloved, of the martyr whose ideal is perishing, of the hero on the evening after the battle that has decided nothing but brought him wounds and the death of his friend. But if one endured, if one could endure this immense sum of grief of all kinds while yet being the hero who, as the second day of battle breaks, welcomes the dawn and his fortune. . . .

Such historical encompassing requires an overcoming of receptively creative character, the male mothering character; it is transformation of a man who gives birth into a begetter. The transition required withdrawal from male companionship ("the death of his friend" in battle) and rejection of any submissive worship of male creators. This is very like Plato's rejection of passive poetic inspiration as a philosopher's creative mode and of tragedy as a form capable of corrupting men of reason with "womanish" excess of feeling.

FREUD: EVOLUTION THROUGH SUBLIMATION

Within the psychoanalytic tradition, there are theorists whose emphasis on various aspects of creative character align them with the three Greek exemplars. In his many short writings on creativity and creative individuals, Freud himself stressed the evolution of creative character and the mutability or flexibility of the creative person's psyche. He thought in quite Aristotelian maturational terms. But later psychoanalysts took this perspective, in which the concept "sublimation" was central, and worked it in different directions. Phyllis Greenacre, more than any other, used biographical study of creative individuals to elaborate on Freud's views and to add an emphasis on what she called "splits in the self-representation." The creative person, she said, imagines that he or she has an ordinary, everyday self and a creative self, and struggles to let the creative self be free and able to shape the ordinary self. Her internally split creative character, as she describes it in "The Relation of the Imposter to the Artist," is a Platonic self-fabricator, a Nietzschean self-transformer. Lawrence Kubie, on the other hand, was distressed by the emphasis within the Freudian camp on how close to neurosis creativity lies; he wanted to show (as one of his book titles put it) "neurotic distortions of creativity." To Kubie, the creative character was one in which both the conscious mind and the preconscious borderland or buffer between the unconscious and the conscious mind were as free as possible of the *uncreative* unconscious. With its emphasis on disencumbering the mind, his educational program was reformative in the Stoic manner:

> What we need is to be educated in how not to interfere with the inherent capacity of the human mind to think. . . . My point is that education will continue to perpetuate a fraud on culture until it accepts the full implications of the fact that the free creative velocity of our thinking apparatus is continually being braked and driven off course by the play of unconscious

forces. Educational procedures which fail to recognize this end up by increasing the interference from latent and unrecognized neurotic forces.

Psychoanalytic theory, then, can describe creative characters of various types, but Freud himself consistently stressed only one type. When he presented creative character and its ability to reconfigure and sustain always new creative surges, he was proceeding as he always did—going in search at one and the same time for scientific truth and for self-description. He was a thinker who never ceased revising himself and his thoughts or theories, and he took this characteristic of his own as central to creative character. But he did so theoretically by finding the characteristic in a man for whom he felt a deep affinity—Leonardo da Vinci. "Like others I have succumbed to the attraction of this great and mysterious man," Freud wrote, "in whose nature one seems to detect powerful instinctual passions which can nevertheless only express themselves in so remarkably subdued a manner" (11:134).

Freud began his excursion into biography, "Leonardo da Vinci and a Memory of His Childhood," in 1909, two years after he had written his initial paper on character development, "Character and Anal Erotism." The paper links character to three basic libidinal stages through which we all travel—oral, anal, and genital—by exploring how the specific character-traits obstinacy, parsimony, and orderliness develop from fixation in or regression to the anal stage. But Freud was becoming aware that this characterological theory needed, in turn, to be linked to his idea that all people have a combination of feminine and masculine "mental sexual characteristics;" that all are, to some degree, bisexual. And, in the Leonardo study, he also began to question how these two characterological theories might be related to the type of love-choice he calls "narcissistic." The Leonardo study is, in short, a crossroads in which the diverse strands of Freud's thought about character come together—to coexist, if not to fall into systematic place.

Many factors brought Freud to Leonardo as a subject. In his own life, he was sorting out what his needs were for friendship and for protégés. His deepest friendship, with the Berlin physician Wilhelm Fliess, had ended, but that friendship was certainly being recalled as younger men enrolled in the cause of psychoanalysis. Freud traveled in America during September 1909 with the Swiss Carl Jung, the Hungarian Sandor Ferenczi, and the Welshman Ernest Jones, celebrating the international renown that their invitation to Clark University in Massachusetts represented. These were not men whom Freud, then fifty-three years old, had chosen—they chose him—but they did constitute a workshop, an atelier for psychoanalysis. Leonardo's atelier was a model with which to compare the psychoanalytic circle, and Leonardo's Oedipus complex, which had such determinative power over the company he kept, was one with which Freud could compare and contrast his own early life with a strong, adoring mother and an affectionate but ineffectual father. In the following passage, Freud's reflections on early object choice and masculinity and femininity in character formation meet with his first sketch of narcissism in adult operation:

> In all our male homosexual cases the subjects had a very intense erotic attachment to a female person, as a rule their mother, during the first period of childhood, which is afterwards forgotten; this attachment was evoked or encouraged by too much tenderness on the part of the mother herself, and further reinforced by the small part played by the father during their childhood. . . . Indeed, it almost seems as though the presence of a strong father would ensure that the son made the correct decision in his choice of object, namely someone of the opposite sex.
>
> After this preliminary stage a transformation sets in whose mechanism is known to us but whose motive force we do not yet understand. . . . The boy represses his love for his mother; he puts himself in her place, identifies himself with her, and takes his own person as a model in whose likeness he chooses the new objects of his love. In this way he has become a homosexual. What he has in fact done is slip back to auto-erotism: for the boys whom he now loves as he grows up are after all only substitute figures and revivals of himself in childhood—boys whom he loves in the way which his mother loved *him* when he was a child. He finds the objects of his love along the path of *narcissism*, as we say; for Narcissus, according to Greek legend, was a youth who preferred his own reflection to everything else and who changed into the lovely flower of that name.
>
> Psychological considerations of a deeper kind justify the assertion that a man who has become a homosexual in this way remains unconsciously fixated to the mnemonic image of his mother. By repressing his love for his mother he preserves it in his unconscious and from now on remains faithful to her. . . . [On] each occasion [when he is tempted to unfaithfulness] he hastens to transfer the excitation he has received from women on to a male object, and in this manner he repeats over and over again the mechanism by which he acquired his homosexuality (11: 99–100).

The analysis Freud set out in these passages remained the touchstone for all of his subsequent writings on male homosexuality, including the next case study he wrote, of Dr. Schreber, a paranoid with strong repressed homosexual desires. The passages also gave Freud himself a summary for use in his own self-analysis. He had once freely admitted to Fliess that "a certain almost feminine side" of his character had made him seek Fliess's friendship, just as he had told Fliess that his earlier friend, Joseph Breuer, had been unable to comprehend "what achievements can result from the sublimation of the androphile current in man." Like Leonardo, who surrounded himself with young reflections of himself whom he could mother as he had been mothered, Freud was attracted to men like Fliess and Jung who were, even if they had appreciable passive traits, active and assertive as Freud himself had been in his youth. More obviously passive men produced in him the reaction he confessed in a letter to Jung about a summer vacation tour of Italy he made in 1910 with Sandor Ferenczi:

> My travelling companion is a dear fellow, but dreamy in a disturbing kind of way, and his attitude toward me is infantile. He never stops admiring me, which I don't like, and is probably sharply critical of me in his unconscious when I am taking it easy. He has been too passive and receptive, letting everything be done for him like a woman, and I really haven't got enough homosexuality in me to accept him as one. These trips arouse a great longing for a real woman.

In America, Freud had established with Jung the habit of outlining his libidinal ups and downs, of noting, for example, what he described to Jung as "the Indian summer of my erotism" and the winter of his discontent on returning to Vienna for overwork and sexual abstinence. The Freud/Jung correspondence conveys the turmoil Freud felt. But it was Ferenczi to whom Freud confessed, while they were sorting out retrospectively their difficulties during the trip, that he had been reticent to meet Ferenczi's desire for sharing self-analyses as they apparently had on their America trip. He had also declined to elaborate on why he had been having dreams about Fliess while they toured Italy (as he explained in a letter cited by his biographer, Jones):

> You not only noticed, but also understood, that I no longer have any need to uncover my personality completely, and you correctly traced this back to the traumatic reason for it. Since Fliess's case, with the overcoming of which you recently saw me occupied, that need has been extinguished. A

part of the homosexual cathexis has been withdrawn and made use of to enlarge my own ego. I have succeeded where the paranoiac fails.

The Leonardo study was, in part, about why Sigmund Freud did not end up repressing his homosexuality and becoming paranoid like Dr. Schreber; it was also, in part, about why Freud did not end up an obsessional neurotic like the patient called the "Rat Man," whose case he wrote in 1909. The train of thought in the *Leonardo* dealing with homosexuality and narcissism was woven complexly with the train of thought dealing with anal erotism and obsessionality—a train which was also very intricately attached to Freud's relations with his young colleagues. While Freud, Jung and Ferenczi were traveling to and from America in 1909, they had discussed the obsessional neurotic "Rat Man." When Jung saw the manuscript of Freud's case study, he was, he wrote, filled with delight: "Every sentence is made to measure and fits reality to a T." With great candor, Jung acknowledged: "I regret from the bottom of my heart that I didn't write it." Freud was, in turn, delighted with how enthusiastically Jung identified himself with the case study and its method. He urged the younger man to make further psychoanalytical conquests by marching on toward mythology. "We must also take hold of biography. I have had an inspiration since my return. The riddle of Leonardo da Vinci's character has suddenly become clear to me."

In a letter to Jung, Freud summarized his argument as he had then worked it out. At an early age Leonardo

> converted his sexuality into an urge for knowledge and from then on the inability to finish anything he undertook became a pattern to which he had to confirm in all his ventures: he was sexually inactive or homosexual. Not so long ago I came across his image and likeness (without his genius) in a neurotic.

Freud saw this level of his subject's riddle first, and emphasized its inhibiting consequence rather than the potentiality it contained for continual renewal of productivity, which Freud saw later. In the final study, as he emphasized the active, renewing side of the urge to know, Freud moved from stress on Leonardo's passivity and homosexuality to stress on his activity—the side of him Freud found more attractive and to which he could "succumb" (11:134). Only during the writing did he come to the level where Leonardo and the "Rat Man" were kindred souls:

> From the slight indications we have about Leonardo's personality we should be inclined to place him close to the type of neurotic we describe as 'obsessional'; and we may compare his researches to the 'obsessive brooding' of neurotics, and his inhibitions to what are known as their 'abulias' " (11:131).

The Leonardo study, which Freud had finished by April 1910, was a campaign on the biography front, but also a necessary preoccupation for Freud himself who, as he noted to Jung, was in a period of sexual abstinence: "Quite against my will I must live like an American: no time for the libido." The biography became, he told Jung, "an obsession." The two men could joke in their correspondence about how the autoerotic joy of a period of intense study and thinking presaged a new piece of writing. As Freud said to Jung about Jung's mythology studies: "Autoerotic enjoyment is sure to be followed by exhibition—a development that I am eagerly awaiting." Jung had the impression, when he read the Leonardo study, that "the intellectual freedom in this work far exceeds that of its predecessors," and this judgment relays the intensity with which Freud had been able to merge himself with Leonardo: "I am all Leonardo."

As he was finishing it, the Leonardo biography fulfilled yet another function for Freud. It served as a record of Freud's depression over his oldest daughter Mathilde's illness, which kept her from visiting her parents' home for three months, and which had as a consequence her barrenness: "Analysis [of my depression] leads far afield to the distress which the state of my daughter's health causes me—I have been trying in vain to replace her. You will discern the note of resignation in *Leonardo*." The wound to Freud's narcissism that his daughter's illness represented—for she was thinking about adopting a child rather than turning out to be the perfectly healthy and happy mother of his grandchildren—taught him a lesson about the limits of his power to preserve from harm or loss to himself the objects of his narcissistic love. It was a lesson he had to learn again and even more agonizingly a decade later when the next eldest daughter, Sophie, died of influenza; then he told Ferenczi by letter: "Deep down I sense a bitter, irreparable narcissistic injury."

The lesson was about the difference between repression of losses—and the early loves to which they are connected—and sublimation, Leonardo's great gift. In his own life, Freud was able to make a place in his psyche for Fliess, whose loss had also been an irreparable narcissistic injury. Withdrawing cathexis for the enlargement of his ego meant ceding Fliess a place, rather than repressing him or the early loves to whom he was connected. The note of resignation in the Leonardo text marks this maneuver, which is accomplished by setting the limits of psychoanalytic biography: "We are left, then, with these two characteristics of Leonardo which are inexplicable by the efforts of psychoanalysis: his quite special tendency towards instinctual repressions, and his extraordinary capacity for sublimating the primitive instincts." Freud then cedes to Fliess part of this mysterious territory, which he designated "instincts and their transformations." Invoking his former friend's controversial theories about constitutional bisexuality as though they were accepted by biologists everywhere, Freud granted Fliess "the organic foundations of character":

> We are obliged to look for the source of the tendency to repression and the capacity for sublimation in the organic foundations of character on which the mental structure is only afterward erected. . . . The tendency of biological research today is to explain the chief features in a person's organic constitution as being a result of the blending of male and female dispositions, based on [chemical] substances. Leonardo's physical beauty and his left-handedness [considered as a "feminine" trait] might be quoted in support of this view (11:136).

As soon as he had thus divided the kingdom of character and mapped out the territory that was to be Fliess's, Freud turned to the future and pointed to his own realm: "We will not, however, leave the ground of purely psychological research." To anyone who objected to the results achieved on this ground, Freud was ready with a reply:

> But may one not take objection to the findings of an enquiry which ascribes to accidental circumstances of his parental constellation so decisive an influence on a person's fate—which, for example, makes Leonardo's fate depend upon his illegitimate birth and on the barrenness of his first stepmother Donna Albiera? I think one has no right to do so. If one considers chance to be unworthy of determining our fate, it is simply a relapse into the pious view of the Universe which Leonardo himself was on the way to

overcoming when he wrote that the sun does not move. . . . The apportioning of the determining factors of our life between the 'necessities' of our constitution and the 'chances' of our childhood may still be uncertain in detail; but in general it is no longer possible to doubt the importance precisely of the first years of our childhood . . . (11:137).

The character-type Freud portrayed in his Leonardo study (whether accurately attributed to Leonardo or not) was one permitting psychic control with comparatively little repression: the greater part of Leonardo's sexual instinct could be sublimated into a general urge to know, an urge that fed both artistic and natural scientific work; his great first love, of his mother, could be resurrected again in him as he worked—if not as he loved. Leonardo's character, despite his inhibitions of love and sometimes of work, was not authoritarian. To speak in the later language of Freud's structural theory, his ego did not have to quell rebellions of his id, it could commandeer id-energy by providing acceptable goals or channels for sublimation. It must have been enormously heartening for Freud, at fifty-three, surrounded by the younger men who would be his successors, to write about what this flexibility in Leonardo's character meant for the artist's sixth decade:

> At the summit of his life, when he was in his early fifties—a time when in women the sexual characters have already undergone involution and when in men the libido not infrequently makes a further energetic advance—a new transformation came over him. Still deeper layers of the contents of his mind became active once more; but this further regression was to the benefit of his art, which was in the process of becoming stunted. He met the woman who awakened his memory of his mother's happy smile of sensual rapture; and, influenced by this revived memory, he recovered the stimulus that guided him at the beginning of his artistic endeavours, at the time when he modelled the smiling women. He painted the Mona Lisa. . . . With the help of the oldest of all his erotic impulses he enjoyed the triumph of once more conquering the inhibition of his art (11:134).

Leonardo's character was one that could prevent psychic sclerosis, but it was also one that could protect the artist from external threats. When he wrote his *Leonardo*, Freud did not emphasize this protective function of the kind of character he recognized as creative, but he did put the stress on averting suffering and protecting from outrageous fortune in a 1930 statement about sublimation. The following text, from *Civilization and Its Discontents*, was written under the shadow of the international economic crisis precipitated by the 1929 stock market crash and of the deteriorating political situation in Germany:

> Another technique for fending off suffering is the employment of the displacements of the libido which our mental apparatus permits of and through which its function gains so much in flexibility. The task here is that of shifting the instinctual aims in such a way that they cannot come up against frustration from the external world. In this, sublimation of the instincts lends its assistance. One gains the most if one can sufficiently heighten the yield of pleasure from the sources of physical and intellectual work. When this is so, fate can do little against one. A satisfaction of this kind, such as the artist's joy in creating, in giving his fantasies body, or a scientist's in solving problems or discovering truths, has a special quality which we shall certainly one day be able to characterize in metapsychological terms. At present we can only say figuratively that such satisfactions seem 'finer and higher' (21:79).

Freud was so much under the dominance of his idea that creative productions represent aims that are "finer and higher" than directly sexual or libidinal aims—that is, under the dominance of his evolutionary idea—that he would have found strange a comment like the one Phyllis Greenacre made in "The Childhood of the Artist" (1957):

> It is . . . possible that in very gifted people a process comparable to sublimation in those of more average endowment does not occur, inasmuch as they possess much more mobility of libidinal energy, and change of aim and object is achieved with greater flexibility, although often accompanied by outer displays of disturbance.

PROUST: RELEASING *LE MOI PROFOND*

Greenacre's description may very well be more appropriate for a person of Nietzsche's creative type than for one of Freud's; for one who exalts in self-transformation more than for one who admires psychic suppleness and potentiality for growth, expansion. I will return to Greenacre's contribution in Chapter 8 below; here I will merely note that her hypothesis does not seem at all appropriate for someone obsessional in the manner of Marcel Proust, whose adolescence and early adulthood were spent trying—laboriously, unsuccessfully—to spiritualize or purify his family loves, especially for his mother, but also for his father and his younger brother Robert, a beloved rival. He wished to love in the medium of literature—a goal that his highly cultivated mother sanctioned and his physician father reluctantly and somewhat clinically approved. Proust examined in minute detail the pain his hope for a vocation cost him. "As in artesian wells, the deeper suffering has bored into the heart the higher the work of art rises."

Reflecting on his own experience, Proust viewed creativity as a matter of renunciation, an *ascesis*. Giving up a love, mourning, and then recreating the love in memory or in literature, was the only way to love lastingly, beyond the realm of suffering, betrayal, abandonment, jealousy. Proust worked for detachment in three ways. His greatest efforts focused on his parents, particularly after his father's death in 1903 and his mother's two years later. But he also withdrew slowly from society, from the salon *mondes* and the cafe *demi-mondes* of Paris and later from the fashionable seaside resorts in which the fin-de-siècle Parisian upper classes sought their own form of detachment. Finally, he withdrew from the authors and works of literature he had worshipped and translated as a young man. Proust's self-therapy involved giving up his identifications on all these fronts by putting himself in the service of universal truths, mysterious laws of human behavior revealed only to initiates. All his disidentifications he called giving up idolatry—and he made the quest for freedom from idolatry the quest of his narrator in *A la recherche du temps perdu*. His renunciations in the service of a higher cause were to bring their own rewards, as he explained in a passage about beloved authors:

> When you are in love with a work of art you would like to do something just like it. But you must sacrifice your love of the moment and think not of your taste but of a truth which never asks our preferences and forbids us to consider them. Only by following that truth will you sometimes fulfill your abandoned desire.

Proust withdrew with difficulty from his taste for the English critic John Ruskin, two of whose works he translated into French with urging and help from his mother and rough drafts prepared by his friend Marie Nordlinger, that is, as the center of an all-female translating atelier. Ruskin's slow, rich descriptive style taught Proust to attend to every detail and nuance of artworks, landscapes, emotions, to appreciate the universe as something of infinite value. His submission to Ruskin had

had a clear rationale and purpose: "There is no better way of attaining complete awareness of one's feelings than to try to recreate in one's mind the feelings of a master. . . . The attempt strikes deep into consciousness, with the result that not only one's own thoughts, but his as well, emerge into the light of day." In his apprenticeship period, Proust often presented himself in this way, as the creator Nietzsche called a "male mother," as a passive female being intellectually impregnated by a masterful male. He used Platonic clichés about books as children. But later he used his own idioms, as he did in *Swann's Way*, where he pictured the narrator Marcel, who has penned an ecstatic description of three steeples, as a hen that has laid an egg. Behind this maternal image from which the rooster has departed lay a deeper one. It surfaced in *The Past Recaptured*, where the artist narrator says he is like a dying mother who must still give care to her son.

This image was formulated in Proust's youth, probably even before his Ruskin period, as it is presented in a complex, confused form in a fragment (left undated and unpublished) called "Poetry, or the Mysterious Laws." Proust was developing an argument about the difference between a poet's—or his own—true, deep soul, the *moi profond*, and his superficial self, the self observable in society. (The distinction later became the centerpiece of a polemic against the criticism of Sainte-Beuve, who thought that a biography of the writer's social self could explain the writer's works.) The social self, growing decrepit, gives birth as it dies away to the deeper self, which contains the poetry or the "mysterious laws" of human nature, and which Proust likened to a seed or sperm, a microcosm of the whole human species. The deeper self then gives birth to a work of art while it dies away, as Proust explained in the fragment:

> The mind of the poet is filled with manifestations of the mysterious laws and once these manifestations appear, and grow stronger, and stand out strongly against the background of his mind, they aspire to come out from him, for whatever is to endure aspires to come out from whatever is fragile, decrepit and may perish this very evening or be no longer capable of giving birth to it. Thus does the human species tend at every moment, whenever it feels sufficiently strong and that it has an egress, to make its escape, in a complete sperm that contains it in its entirety, from the short-lived creature who this evening perhaps will die, will perhaps never again contain it so completely, in whom (for it depends upon him so long as it is his prisoner) it will perhaps never again be so strong. Thus, when it feels itself to be

sufficiently strong, the thought of these mysterious laws, or poetry, aspires to escape. . . . At that moment [the poet] has exchanged his soul for the universal soul. . . . [After] each one of the opportunities he has had to give birth to forms in which his sense of the mysterious laws has been deposited, he can die without regrets, like the insect that prepares itself for death, having deposited all its eggs.

There is less in this intricate image system of passive impregnation and gestation—Plato and Nietzsche's spiritual procreation—than there is of purgation, shedding a shell and releasing the true self and the true self's essence, the work of art. The dying mother is parthenogenic, the father has disappeared or has merged with the mother (she ejects a seed or sperm). The cosmic "mysterious laws" with which the artist's work merges are female.

Detachment from the superficial present with its superficial self and merger in—with—the past became Proust's life project and the theme of his masterpiece. Detachment meant for him training his *moi profond* for extreme and undistracted attention to objects and sensations, any of which might, at any moment, open a secret avenue to his past, which he thought of as lying in him entire but hidden and unrecoverable by any willed intellectual effort. The *moi profond* does not command or artistically shape the outer self, the social self; rather, it withdraws from the social self and from the world, retaining a special communication from a point where "as if in a telephone or telegraph booth, he can be connected to the beauty of the entire world." Similar images recur in Proust's novel:

It is useless for us to try to evoke our past; all our intellectual efforts are futile. It lies hidden beyond the reach of the mind, in some unsuspected material object (rather in the sensation which the material object would produce in us). And it depends entirely on chance whether or not we encounter the object before we die.

Instead of a carbon copy of the various facts of our life always at hand, memory is rather an abyss whence at moments an identical sensation allows us to draw up and resuscitate otherwise dead recollections.

When nothing remains of our remote past, after the people are dead and the things are destroyed, alone—more fragile yet longer lived, more immaterial, more steadfast, more faithful—the smell and taste of things persist, like souls, ready and waiting to remind us; over the ruin of all the rest they bear unflinchingly on their almost impalpable droplet the immense edifice of memory.

The social self, from which Proust said the *moi profond* must detach itself in order to be ready for the memories he termed "involuntary," is a collection of habits. The social self is what a person has become by force of habit or—to say the same thing—by weakness of the will. It is *l'homme* of which *le style* is simply the uninteresting replica unless an artist can achieve freedom from it:

> No less than a man's character, habits make the writer's style; and the author who has often been satisfied to achieve a certain charm in the expression of his thought sets once and for all the limits of his talent, just as by often yielding to pleasure, to sloth, to the fear of suffering, one sketches oneself, without possibility of retouching, the outline of one's vices and the limits of one's virtues.

But Proust's version of this rather conventional, Aristotelian notion about how habits accumulate to delimit character went further. He summarized its full consequence in *Cities of the Plain*: "By dint of supposing yourself ill, you become ill, grow thin, are too weak to rise from your bed, suffer from nervous enteritis. By dint of thinking tenderly of men, you become a woman. The obsession, just as in other instances it affects your health, may in this instance alter your sex." But habits can change, too, and a man who has altered into a woman can return to being a man, or assume a mixed mode. From his own detachment and in acute awareness of the circuitry of his own habits, Proust wrote a novel of people's precarious definitions being, in the flux of time, changed, eradicated. In Proust's novel the men—like Charlus, like Robert Saint-Loup—become feminine, and women—like Albertine, the narrator Marcel's lover—become masculine; heterosexuals become homosexuals; defiant people become submissive; people who submit to maternal figures come to submit to paternal ones; guilt, corruption, decay, and death are everyone's lot; borders between characters give way, differences vanish. There is a radical egalitarianism in Proust's vision, as all are moved by the "mysterious laws" of human nature. All combinations among people are possible, and as soon as one has been explored in the novel another is introduced, just as the habits of love move people from one lover to the next. People fall in love with the image of a person they contrive in their desire—"We build up an individuality, we create a

56

character"—and then they proceed to be disappointed, disillusioned, perhaps even instructed a little by the insufficiency of their understanding and thus the inevitability of their jealousy.

> In its early stage love is shaped by desire; later on it is kept alive only by anxiety. In painful anxiety as in joyful desire, love insists upon everything. It is born and it thrives only if something remains to be won. We love only what we do not completely possess.

All of the characters in Proust's novel also share their derivation from facets of himself. Each had a model or many models among his long and short acquaintances, but each was also himself. Proust reiterated, in *Within a Budding Grove* as well as in *The Past Recaptured,* that the great writer is not the cleverest or most learned or most aristocratic (in any sense of the word), but "the one who knows how to become a mirror" and is able to reflect not just life—the task Stendhal assigned the novelist—but his or her own face, faces, lives. The writer's narcissism is not of the sort that turns everyone and everything into the self; it expands the self, rather, by searching it for universal laws, examining it microscopically. Proust encouraged and expected his readers to find in his novel and its characters nothing but themselves:

> Every reader reads himself. The writer's work is merely a kind of optical instrument that makes it possible for the reader to discern what, without this book, he would perhaps never have seen in himself.

Creativity, for the writer as for the reader, is the elimination of barriers that separate people, that divide time, that mark off one world from another. It is the modernist artist's Stoic means of becoming the "universal soul."

In *The Captive,* Proust summarized his Stoic philosophy, in which paradise appears as the world before and after this one, the world of childhood and of after-death, and he set the summation as a eulogy for the great artist Bergotte—a eulogy, in advance, for himself, as he conceived of himself as a mother dying while still caring for his novel:

> All that we can say is that everything is arranged in this life as though we entered it carrying the burden of obligations contracted in a former life; there is no reason inherent in the conditions of life on this earth that can make us consider ourselves obliged to do good, to be fastidious, to be

polite, even, nor make the artist consider himself obliged to begin over again a score of times a piece of work the admiration aroused by which will matter little to his body devoured by worms, like the patch of yellow wall painted with so much knowledge and skill by an artist who must forever remain unknown and is barely identified under the name of Vermeer. All these obligations which have not their sanction in our present life seem to belong to a different world, one founded upon kindness, scrupulosity, self-sacrifice, a world entirely different from this, which we leave in order to be born into this world, before, perhaps, returning to the other to live once again beneath the sway of those unknown laws which we have obeyed because we bore their precepts in our hearts, knowing not whose hand had traced them there—those laws which every profound work of the intellect brings us nearer and which are invisible only—and still!—to fools.

Chapter Three

Comparative Character-Ideals

FORMS AND FUNCTIONS OF THE CHARACTER-IDEAL

The ancient Greeks took it for granted that the mind which either shapes itself, or actualizes itself evolutionarily, or purifies itself, exists as part of and is participated in by a world that is being divinely shaped, actualized, purified. The theater for creativity among the moderns is only intra-psychic: one part of the psyche, one self, molds, moves, or detaches from another. World-historical processes may provide the creator with a context, but they are not thought to participate directly in the creator's process. A creator's historical or evolutionary moment may set limits on his or her possibilities, but it does not make a genius a genius. Ontogeny may recapitulate phylogeny, but recapitulation does not produce creativity. Something more is needed.

What is the modern equivalent of divine agency? It seems to me that the three exemplary modern self-analyzers—Nietzsche, Freud, and Proust—agreed that the "something more" needed for creativity is an unconscious wish. The wish, most generally, is to be psychically organized, and such organization is, then, the condition for creation. They did not share Kant's belief that a person can, in maturity, after years of disorder, suddenly choose order and become ordered in the ensuing revolution. Although this belief reflects the Stoical view that psychic order involves indifference to what is indifferent and is attained at a stroke, Kant's confidence in rational choice marks him as a man of the Enlightenment. The modernists' wish is located in "the Unconscious." And I, as I explore the varieties of this wish, am going to assume the modern perspective and speak intra-psychically of what, in other ways of thinking, might be described as divine agency or attributed to conscious reason.

59

Despite the very clear historical differences among them, all of the thinkers I have considered assume that character theory and theory of creativity are of a piece, two sides of the same coin, because all assume that the mind must be organized, conditioned for creativity. Disagreements begin when descriptions and causal analyses of the necessary mental conditions for creativity are advanced, for these are (I assume, from my psychologistic viewpoint) autobiographical—perhaps the quintessence of autobiography. The three types of psychic ordering I have been describing reflect, I think, three different, largely unconscious organizational wishes, or what I will call "character-ideals."

The term *character-ideal* is modeled on the psychoanalytic term for conscience, which is *ego-ideal*. According to Freud, the partly conscious, partly unconscious ego-ideal, represented as the gaze of an internal witness or the voice of an internal commander, has the functions of self-observation and self-regulation. In his late works, Freud called the ego-ideal the "superego" (*Uber-Ich*) to convey that it guides and rules the ego. The ego-ideal is the ego's model both in the sense that it is aspired to and in the sense that it is corrective, modeling. Formed during the childhood "dissolution of the Oedipus complex," the ego-ideal is initially a collation of identifications with parental or familial figures, but it becomes more richly associated with other authority figures, mythic figures, and stories when children are old enough to understand storytellers or (more frequently in contemporary literate cultures) to read. During adolescence, it is influenced by introspection and conscious measuring against role models in the world.

But what I have in mind when I speak of the "character-ideal" is not the ego-ideal, though it may well be developmental successor to an ego-ideal. A person's character-ideal is his or her image of an ideal order to be aspired to: it presents either facets of the self or psychic parts (even called "personalities"), structures, forces, energies, in a configuration, usually in a harmonious configuration. This order is initially envisioned as an order for the self—a character-ideal—but it later becomes projected onto or enlarged up to social and cosmic dimensions. The creative individual's expansionist or projective tendency, if it is conscious, is imagined as—to borrow a phrase from Nietzsche's *Philosophy in the Tragic Age of the Greeks*—a "microcosm swelling up to the macrocosm." The character-ideal is crucial for self-fashioning—"Character makes character," as Goethe said—but it is also the projective means for social and natural philosophical vision.

The character-ideal takes visual form when it is projected in a work as a human figure acting. While an individual's ego-ideal may be represented in fantasy as a single static composite human figure looking at or listening to the individual as though it were outside, independent, the character-ideal involves a controlling or organizing human fantasy figure acting on or with something else, in a dynamic relationship to another material. A sculptor sculpting; a general commanding troops or an expert giving instructions; a porter setting down a heavy burden. The ideal psychic configuration is more like a narrative than a static portrait: in it, the controlling human figure's dynamic relationships are of greater consequence than any heroic proportions or prodigious legacy distinguishing the figure itself. Relationships define the figure; and the configuration, not the figure alone, matters to the individual who articulates for himself or herself a character-ideal.

When a creative person is at work, the character-ideal figure participates in the work in the same way—according to the same relationship with the medium of the work—that it has been felt to be acting intrapsychically. The work is made or drawn forth or revealed as the creator feels the order of his or her psyche has been. For example, this is Picasso (quoted from the wonderful collection of his remarks, *Picasso on Art*) talking on three different occasions about how his paintings evolved:

> One never knows what one is going to do. One starts a painting and then it becomes something quite else. It is remarkable how little the "willing" of the artist intervenes. It's uncomfortable always to have a "connoisseur" standing next to you telling you "I don't like this" or "This is not as it should be." He hangs on the brush, which becomes very heavy, very heavy. Certainly he doesn't understand a thing but he is always there. [Rimbaud] was right when he said, "Je est un autre."

> "I consider a work of art as the product of calculations," he said, "calculations that are frequently unknown to the author himself. It is exactly like the carrier pigeon, calculating his return to the loft. The calculation that precedes intelligence. Since then we have invented the compass, and radar, which enable even fools to return to their starting-point. . . . Or else we must suppose, as Rimbaud said, that it is the other self inside us who calculates."

> "I'm always saying to myself: 'That's not right yet. You can do better.' " It is rare when I can prevent myself from taking a thing up again . . . x number of times, the same thing. Sometimes it becomes an absolute

obsession. But for that matter, why would anyone work, if not for that? . . . It's always necessary to seek for perfection. . . . To me, it means: from one canvas to the next, always go further, further.

The other, the "connoisseur," the internal expert in Picasso set standards, urged him on, prompted him to perfect form, and he spoke the connoisseur's words to his paintings.

The character-ideal may, as noted, be a successor to the ego-ideal: the ego-ideal, composed of identifications, may come to be a facet of or the figure in the character configuration. But the character-ideal also usually incorporates a version of the adolescent sexual ideal or ideal way of being sexual. In Nietzsche's image system, for example, we noted a struggle between a "male mother" ideal and a male begetter; in Proust's, we observed works being mothered or nursed in the manner of the author's own passive desires. There are many variations on basic ideals, as we will see in detail below: sexual ideals range from potent possessiveness to asceticism, and notions about works as children take very different forms—children being birthed, children as narcissistic extensions of the self, children as gifts being received from transcendent sources. The character-ideal is a developmentally later product than the ego-ideal, but contemporary with the sexual ideal: it is formed not in the five-year-old's process of Oedipus complex dissolution and superego consolidation, but in adolescence or late adolescence, usually in association with both the adolescent's conscious versions of possible lifeworks or ways of life (which now are sometimes called "life styles") or life-plans (what Alfred Adler called *Lebensplanen*) and with his or her initial sexual experiences or rejections of such experiences. It has often been noted in psychoanalytic literature that a kind of reexamination and integration of the superego takes place in adolescence, and I think that the formation of the character-ideal is part of this process in creative people, people who are organizing themselves—or, one might say, to stress the predominant unconscious element, being organized—for creative efforts. They come to feel in retrospect about this consolidation something like what Charles Baudelaire expressed in his essay on Edgar Allan Poe:

All those who have reflected upon their lives, who have often turned back their gaze in order to compare their past with their present life, all those who have learned the habit of ready self-analysis, know what an immense share in man's definitive genius is due to his adolescence. It is then that things stamp themselves deeply upon the tender and responsive mind; it is then that colors are vivid, and the senses vocal with a mysterious tongue. The character, genius and style of a man are formed by the apparently vulgar circumstances of his youth. If all the men who have come upon the world's stage had set down their impressions of their boyhood, what an excellent psychological dictionary we would have!

With adolescents in general, as Freud noted, childhood memories assume new forms as they are consolidated in what Freud describes as "a complicated process of remodeling, analogous in every way to the process by which a nation constructs legends about its early history" (6:48). With creative people, however, these remodeling processes are not merely analogous, they are two movements in the same larger process of projecting and consolidating an individual story as a social story, a founding legend or an "origin and development" legend, for societies or for the cosmos conceived as an all-embracing society.

Different creative types share this propensity to read outward or project their character-ideals into larger contexts—social contexts, cosmic processes. They are, that is, geniuses in the sense of the word that Ralph Waldo Emerson employed in a famous passage from his essay "Self-Reliance": "To believe your own thought, to believe that what is true for you in your private heart is true for all men—that is genius. Speak your latent conviction and it shall be the universal sense; for always the inmost becomes the outmost." From Emerson's modernist point of view, creativity is sweeping in this way—outward, embracingly.

Theoretical people like Emerson express the tendency of geniuses to characterological projection in theoretical terms. But the same tendency can be presented graphically, as it was by Leonardo da Vinci, according to an anecdote recorded by the sixteenth-century biographer Vasari in his *Lives of the Artists* and then cited by Freud in his study of Leonardo:

> [Leonardo] often had a sheep's intestines cleaned so carefully that they could have been held in the hollow of the hand. He carried them into a large room, took a pair of blacksmith's bellows into an adjoining room, fastened the intestines to them and blew them up, until they took up the whole room and forced people to take refuge in a corner. In this way he showed how they gradually became transparent and filled with air; and from the fact that at first they were limited to a small space and gradually spread through the whole breadth of the room, he compared them to genius (11:127).

The form this blowing-up and embracing tendency of creative characters takes is tied to the type of self-organization or self-rule or self-purification the character aims at.

The character-ideals of highly creative individuals can be read in many ways, through many media, but they are easiest to see as traces in philosophical and literary works, and they are most obvious in the works of people with more than the usual adolescent proclivity for philosophizing. In their theories of creativity, you can often see the character-ideal as it is being projected onto societies—even to the extent of the human society as a whole—and onto the natural world, the cosmos. Before the development of modern science required stricter methods for investigating the origins of human societies and natural world, thinkers regularly projected their character-ideals as founding legends for their societies and as creation myths for the cosmos. People of our scientific age more frequently treat their projections as social utopias and hypotheses or "as if" natural histories or evolutionary sagas. This difference does not mean, however, that the original process of projection has become any more a matter of conscious, rather than unconscious, mental maneuver. Only the types of truth claims made for existing projections are different.

THREE TYPES OF CHARACTER-IDEALS

Because the fundamental structures in a person's theory of creativity, the fundamental ingredients in his or her social-political vision, and the guiding assumptions of his or her natural philosophy, have the same psychic sources and follow the same metaphoric patterns, it is possible—to speak simply—to line them up like specimens of handwriting and see that they were all penned by the same person. They are the characters—in the orthographic sense of the word—of a character; and their inconsistencies and idiosyncracies reveal as much as the general forms that make them recognizable.

For example, if the outline developed in the first chapter of Plato's theory of character, which is a theory of creativity, is put together with the social and cosmological ingredients of his system, a composite emerges. Plato presented a model of the man of creative reason, the philosopher, whose psyche was a harmonious relationship of a hegemonic reasoning part and two other parts, one spiritual and allied with reason, and one appetitive, not allied to reason. In the *Timaeus,* Plato suggests that these parts are housed in three regions of the body: reason in the head, spirit in the thorax, and appetites in the genitalia. The ideal republic Plato imagined has a hegemonic reasoning class—the philosopher-kings—and two subservient classes—the spiritual guardians and the appetitive artisans and laborers. For the cosmos, Plato used a different kind of tripartite model (and this mixture of modes is revealing about him): all things were modeled by a chief constructor, the Demiurge, after the model of the eternal ideas and out of a third ingredient, matter. This image characteristically has two higher elements—Demiurge and ideas—set over against a lower element—matter, and the relation between the Demiurge and the ideas could be understood as a relation between source of inspiration and inspiree. But this would mean, in effect, that the Demiurge is not the philosopher-king of the cosmos, he is only the middle-place poet or spiritual artist.

Plato's systematically tripartite construction is not, obviously, evolutionary as Aristotle's was. A composite of Aristotle's theories is much more dynamic—and more internally consistent, systematic. In his *Politics,* Aristotle shows that societies evolve from chaotic small-village simplicity toward harmoniously balanced city-state complexity, as he shows in his *Physics* that the cosmos evolves from formless matter with potential for form toward perfectly formed matter. In a very revealing metaphor, Aristotle notes in the *Physics* that matter longs for form as a female longs for a male and the ugly longs for the beautiful. His ideal human being is a man who has evolved from childhood lack of reason (a lack children share with women) to perfect rationality. In the psyche, in societies and in the cosmos as a whole, the end—the controlling, rational *telos*—is inherent, drawing the evolving entity forward (from potentiality to actuality) as an exemplary leader draws his people. In the cosmos, the commanding *telos* is the divine, the Unmoved Mover, as Aristotle calls it. The harmonious Unmoved Mover's relation to what is below him—or before him, to speak temporally—is analogous to the relation between psychic and social perfection and what precedes that perfection. As Aristotle noted in his *Politics* (Book 7):

> Also life as a whole is divided into business and leisure [*skole*], and war and peace, and our actions are aimed some of them at things necessary and useful, some at things noble. In this matter, the same principle of preference that applies to parts of the soul must also apply to the activities of those

parts: war must be for the sake of peace, business for the sake of leisure, things necessary and useful for the sake of things noble.

Within the European tradition, the political imagery used in different ways by both Plato and Aristotle appears very commonly in the character-ideals of reflective people, both theorists and activists. They envision a political configuration in which a leader relates to his people in some manner or another: as a tyrant, as an aristocrat or a timocratic member of an elite, as an inciter to revolution or new order, as a restorer of old orders, as a democrat. The followers, usually represented metaphorically as the emotions, the passions, the body, the appetites, the drives, or simply the irrational, usually take their orders from above. But there is also obviously a great difference between the Platonic and Aristotelian imagery modes. Aristotle's leadership element draws the troops onward and upward to their inherent destiny; Plato's leadership element crafts the troops into a static perfect order.

The difference is apparent even in the modern instances in which a thinker conceives of the troops bringing the leadership into being or constituting it in the grass-roots manner. Freud always struggled— not always successfully—against Aristotelian teleological constructions when he imagined the psyche developing. The allure of teleology is obvious every time Freud speaks of normal courses of sexual development, setting "normal" as a *telos* and viewing "perversions" as failures of form rather than alternative courses. On the other hand, his freedom from teleological thinking is apparent in the "structural theory" sketched in *The Ego and the Id,* where the history of the id's loves brings the ruling ego into operation. The ego is a collection of the remnants of the id's loves, a product of sublimation, built up from the bottom like an archeological site.

Nietzsche, for another example, envisioned the psyche in the Platonic crafting manner, but with creative power—the power for self-transformation—in the hands of the material, the troops. In *The Gay Science,* Nietzsche sketched his idea of good psychic governance:

> *Non ridere, non lugere, neque detestari, sed intelligere!* [Not to laugh, not to lament, nor to detest, but to understand!] says Spinoza as simply and sublimely as is his wont. Yet in the last analysis what is this *intelligere* other than the form in which we come to feel the other three at once? One result of the different and mutually opposed desires to laugh, lament, and curse?

Before knowledge is possible, each of these instincts must have presented its one-sided view of the thing or event; after this comes the fight of these one-sided views, and occasionally this results in a mean, one grows calm, one finds all three sides right, and there is a kind of justice and a contract; for by virtue of justice and a contract all these instincts can maintain their existence and assert their rights against each other. Since only the last scenes of reconciliation and final accounting at the end of this long process rise to our consciousness, we suppose that *intelligere* must be something conciliatory, just and good—something that stands essentially opposed to the instincts, while it is actually nothing but a *certain behavior of the instincts toward one another.*

The Platonic pattern employs political imagery, but it reveals—particularly in its theory of creative inspiration and on its cosmological level—a character-ideal that is more artisanal than political. It involves not images of a psychic polity with leaders and followers but a psychic workshop with an artisan and a material shaped and molded or somehow transformed by the artisan. Usually, in character-ideals of this type, one facet of the self or one part of the psyche works on another, as Plato's Demiurge, inspired by the ideas, worked upon the unformed cosmic matter. But we have also noted an important version of (or variation on) the artisanal type that presents an act of impregnation, often involving a father self and a mother self, but sometimes involving only the combinatory figure Nietzsche knew as the "male mother." The act leads to some form of miraculous birth—a child of the soul, as Plato's theory of creative inspiration has it.

Within the European tradition, this artisanal character ideal in both its creative and procreative forms is frequently associated, when it is combined with a social and a natural philosophical projection, with magic. People who have this kind of character-ideal imagine societies coming into existence and being organized by a Founding Father (either coupled with a Mother or by male mothering) and they imagine the cosmos as the result of magical fabrication. The world is verbally commanded into being *ex nihilo* or from "formlessness and void," crafted from precious arcane substances with a powerful tool, ejaculated into being as all-containing seed by a solitary Onan figure, magically gestated and/or delivered, and so forth. The human figure in the character-ideal is, in short, the Creator, or a Prospero–Merlin with a magic wand, or a Zeus with Dionysus sewn in his thigh, Athena born full-blown from his head.

The third type of character-ideal appears less frequently in the European tradition, except among the Stoical types of Christians represented well by the great Roman convert Constantine. But it appears very commonly in those Eastern traditions where ascetic spiritual discipline is stressed. Like the artisanal-sexual ideal, this is also a self-creating ideal; however, it involves not the making of a product but the unmaking of one already made. The self is stripped of everything that is not its essence, everything that is accidental, material, changeable, mortal. The essential self appears from behind the veil of the inessential in a practice of attentive attunement (as the Stoics said) or detachment or *askesis* or the Vedantic liberation path (*moksha*) or whatever the spiritual discipline of true self-revealing is called. The essential self is, then, known to be the same as and at one with the essence of the cosmos, as Atman is to Brahman in the Vedantic tradition or *tao* to the cosmic *tao* in Chinese taoism, or, in the Greek Stoic tradition, as the fiery psyche of the microcosmic individual is to the fiery psyche of the macrocosm. When there are cosmogonic stories associated with these microcosm/macrocosm theories, that is, when they do not envision an eternal sameness, an ahistorical part-whole relationship, the cosmogonic stories generally involve some form of emanationism: a cosmos pours out of a surround, unfolds, settles into order and then, after a period—which the Stoics called the Great Year—it is rolled back, returned into the surround from whence it came.

In most traditions where the character-ideal is ascetic in this self-stripping way, there is no specific corollary societal image, no intermediary step between individual and cosmos; rather, there is a notion that the cosmos is a *macropolis* or *cosmopolis,* the true world-state beyond any borders of national, racial, or ethnic, gender or class particularity, a state in which accidental individual differences matter not at all. The controlling figure in this character-ideal is a mystic or a saint.

THE ORIGINATION OF CHARACTER-IDEALS

The political, artisanal, or ascetic figures in these character-ideals, who may be imagined on the basis of one or more identifications with real persons, are not the same as what sociologists and psychologists call a role model. An individual's character-ideal need not be related directly at all to his or her type of work, and it does not necessarily supply specific images of how to do things, how to behave, how to fulfill a role.

It supplies, rather, images of psychic order—of the ideal ordering of conflicting forces or selves. There may be more types than the three I have sketched. But these three are very clear, not because they obviously relate to broad types of work—politics, art, or spiritual training—but because they appear in theoretical works on creativity, in the works of creative people, and in characterological studies. They also stand out in comparative studies of social visions (reformist or utopian) and in creation stories or what might more generally be called cosmic ordering stories.

Later I am going to take up the question of why three types, these three types, appear recurrently, but I want to focus first on their origination. Ideals of order are as clear as caricature in cosmic ordering stories that picture a chief who calls unformed matter or chaotic elements to order in a political way; a creator/procreator who either molds the elements as an artist does or conceives a product-child; or a figure who emanates a world out of itself and then draws the world back into itself or withdraws from the world. The simplest way to understand such cosmogonic images is to see them in the Emersonian way as an inmost-turned-outmost, a projection of unconscious thoughts or convictions. But this kind of interpretation closes off any questions about the origins of thoughts or convictions. The question of origins is more open if we speak of ideals or images of psychic order being projected, or of psychic order as it exists being projected. The second possibility is the one Freud took up.

Freud's many remarks about projection stemmed from an insight he advanced first to his friend Wilhelm Fliess in a speculative, tentative paragraph of a December 12, 1897, letter:

> Can you imagine what "endopsychic myths" are? . . . The dim inner perception of one's own psychic apparatus stimulates thought illusions, which of course are projected onto the outside and, characteristically, into the future and the beyond. Immortality, retribution, the entire beyond are all reflections of our psychic [internal] world. *Meschugge?* Psychomythology.

Apparently convinced that his psychomythology idea was not *meschugge,* crazy, he wrote it out for his public in *The Psychopathology of Everyday Life* (1901):

> A mythological view of the world, which extends a long way into the most modern religions, is nothing but psychology projected into the external world. The obscure recognition (endopsychic perception, as it were) of the psychical factors and relations in the unconscious is mirrored—it is difficult to express it in other terms, and here the analogy with paranoia

must come to our aid—in the construction of a *supernatural reality,* which is destined to be changed back once more by science into the psychology of the unconscious (6:258).

Confronted with a mythological view of the world, the psychologist reads back through it to "the psychical factors and relations in the unconscious" that the view mirrors. The psychologist is able to "transform metaphysics into metapsychology."

What this kind of reading or deciphering generally consisted of in Freud's practice was something that might be called "Oedipal poetics." In the characters and plots of myths or of literary works, the psychologist can find, more or less disguised, the characters and plots of the creative person's unconscious Oedipal drama or the record of a creative person's repressions. The creator's endopsychic perception is always of this story, and, as this story is held to have universal elements, "thematic generalization" (to use the psychoanalyst Ernst Kris's phrase) is natural. "The best-known coincidence between myth or great narrative and individual fantasy," Kris wrote in his *Psychoanalytic Explorations of Art* (1952), "concerns accounts which have the hero of miraculous descent, separated from his original parents, adopted by foster parents up to the day when he splendidly emerges." The most consistently discovered underlying story of myths and literary works is the idealizing story Freud called "the family romance."

But, as I have been arguing, unconscious material of the sort mirrored in "family romance" stories (and also involved in the ego-ideal formation) is reworked in adolescence, and the character-ideal, with its projective social and natural philosophical forms, reflects the reworked story. This story is not simply a matter of unconscious Oedipal wishes and *dramatis personae.* What the projector of a character-ideal has perceived endopsychically is a dynamic relationship between parts or forces in the psyche, making up the psyche. This is what Freud himself seemed to imply in his 1897 formulation to Fliess of endopsychic perception as perception not of thought-contents or family romances but of "one's own psychic apparatus." The projector is "seeing" his or her mind at work, which work includes relating to the unconscious part of the mind or the unconscious self.

The character-ideal is based upon, idealizes from, an endopsychic perception of the psyche's intersystemic relations (how conscious and unconscious relate, or, in later psychoanalytic terms, how id, ego, and superego relate) and intrasystemic relations (how the psyche's activity and passivity, love and hate, masculinity and femininity are distributed). The conscious mind (ego) and the unconscious mind (id)—usually called reason and unreason, reason and nature, mind and body, etc.— both have roles as such in the character-ideal, which expresses the endopsychically perceived state of affairs changing in the direction of desired order. Or, to say the same thing, the character-ideal expresses what is and what is wished for on the basis of what is. In the political character-ideal, for example, consciousness, personified or associated with a human figure, leads or commands the emotions, the irrational, the will—or whatever the unconscious mind is called. This ideal grows out of a perception that there is a psychic agency trying (not yet successfully) to exert such control. In the artisanal ideal, it is sometimes the conscious mind, personified as some form of demiurge or begetter, who shapes or gestates the unconscious, and sometimes, as for many Romantics, the unconscious is felt to be doing the shaping or impregnating. Here the ideal grows out of the perception that there is a recalcitrant psychic material or sexual presence in the psyche that is being crafted or pursued, not yet successfully. And in the spiritual type, the conscious mind strips away from itself all that it is not, leaving itself as vibrantly pure attention or thought or intellectual vision. This ideal grows out of a perception that the psyche is weighted down, burdened, sullied, riven with guilt, and struggling to free itself.

The character-ideal is, as noted, a developmental step beyond the projected Oedipal drama; it has a greater degree of abstraction about it, for it involves translation of Oedipal *dramatis personae* into organizational agencies, into versions of structural theory. To explore the character-ideal developmentally, then, this late adolescent process of translation should be the focus—and I will try shortly to show this tactic in operation in a series of illustrative biographical vignettes.

SOME SIGNS OF THE TYPES

The biographical vignettes offered in the next chapter will provide material for pursuing a developmental inquiry into character-ideal formation and taking up the "why three?" question, but they will also show two other facets of the character-ideal that I will note here—as part of the legend for this characterological map. The first is that as people measure themselves against their character-ideals, their senses of themselves come to include the sum of the self-reproaches the measurement produces: people are—in their own eyes—a lesser or paler or in some way noncongruent version of the character-ideal. The self-reproaches are, like the self-reproaches of a melancholic, unconsciously partly directed at themselves and partly directed at the character-ideal, which they hate to the extent that they suffer by comparison. The self-reproaches may even lead to a split in the character-ideal, or retention of the unsatisfiable, hated type of ideal along with acquisition of another. Such a split may lie behind Plato's fluctuation between political and artisanal ideals: the artisanal ideal, the philosophy of beauty and divine inspiration, was vulnerable to rebellion from the appetites, and the political ideal, the tyranny of reason, firmly excluded the appetites and the artists. On the other hand, the character-ideal can also offer the standard by which a person can be modest—and thus put a check upon ambition or exhibitionism.

The second thing that the biographical vignettes show is that many people have not only a character-ideal but what might be called a negative character-ideal, a crystallization of all they wish either to overcome in their present endopsychically perceived constitution or to avoid becoming in the future, an anti-order. The positive character-ideal and the negative character-ideal may recreate the object-poles of early childhood or Oedipal love and hate (ambivalence), or reflect childhood libidinal stage preferences retained or overcome; but they also gather to themselves facets of later loved and rejected loved ones, and to a greater or lesser extent in different individuals, facets of positive and negative ideals common to the surrounding culture. Projected onto the socio-political realm, the negative character-ideal becomes a regime detested, a form of government felt to be the worst, what a feared revolution would bring in its train, a "national character" felt to be despicable, an "evil empire," and so forth. On the cosmic level, echoes of the negative character-ideal take the form of a theory or an actual state of affairs that is equivalent to primal chaos—and a version of the condition that preceded cosmic ordering is also often imagined as an apocalypse. In the sexual variation on the artisanal ideal, primal chaos often takes the form of a sibling or generational struggle of the sort that Hesiod catalogued in his *Theogony* or that is related in the Biblical story of Noah's ark and the covenant assuring two-by-two sexual order.

Whether the world ends in an individual's imagination with a bang or a whimper or in some other way is to a great extent a matter of what image of psychic destruction or negation-of-order an individual entertains. Creation and destruction stories for the self and the cosmos follow the same courses, as has been apparent to psychoanalysis since Freud's studies in 1910–14 of the psychoses and their relation to narcissism. As he noted with regard to "the mechanism of symptom formation in paranoia," the rule is that "internal perceptions, or feelings, shall be replaced by external perceptions" (12:12). Like highly creative people, psychotics seem to experience themselves, their society and the cosmos as homologous. But they lack the capacity for self-control and ordering through idealization. They experience the homology as a matter of dreadfully threatening fact. (I will return in Chapter 8 to this similarity between creative people and psychotics—and to the many forms of dissimilarity.)

Because character-ideals are creations of adolescence, the human figures in them often reflect the cultural surround of that period—that is, they incorporate translations of general cultural ideals from the events, books, entertainments, and so forth, available to adolescents. When the culture, as is the case currently in Western Europe and America, is indiscriminately available to adolescents, the character-ideals do not have the kind of specificity of social reference that is typical of more traditionally age-divided, generationally articulated cultures with initiation rites into adulthood. The character-ideal may also reflect a specific social or cultural coloration on the latency child's "family romance," the adoption story that Ernst Kris noted as so cross-cultural. This is quite common with boys who once modeled themselves on the rich, powerful, or handsome "fathers" by whom they are adopted in the romance; their character-ideals echo the patriarchal exercise of power typical of such figures. For reasons that we will have to explore, the legacy of the "family romance" idealized patriarchal figure is strongest in the artisanal character ideal (and in its sexual or procreational variant). But the tie between "family romance" figures and the figures in character-ideals for girls is more complicated in cultures where females seldom appear as powerful figures—that is, in most cultures. As I will note in more detail in Chapter 9, the frequency with which late adolescent girls project the spiritual or ascetic character-ideal is influenced by their social surroundings as well as by their intra-psychic developmental histories. In the biographical vignettes offered in the next chapter, all the examples of the ascetic character-ideal are female; but male examples will be presented further along, as will female examples of the other two character-ideal types. The idea that there is a single or essential "feminine" (or "masculine") type of creativity seems to be mistaken. But women do frequently manifest the ascetic character-ideal type, for psychological as well as cultural reasons, and these can be explored.

The controlling figures in character-ideals have two distinct—though not usually completely distinct—sources other than their legacies from the ego-ideal and "family romance": model characters who exist only in history or fiction or religious ritual, and model characters who are living and nearby, even in the immediate family. They are available, that is, in mediated or unmediated forms. The mediated forms require of an individual a greater expenditure of imagination for appropriation, but they are less "present," and thus less able to actually participate in the individual's judgment about how far he or she falls short of the character-ideal. If the controlling figure in the character-ideal is or is very like a parent, for example, the parent can, with praise and criticism, become involved in the individual's self-reproaches. The character-ideal also, then, tends to stay very close to the ego-ideal or superego, to be consonant with it—even speaking, as it were, in the same voice. But a historical or fictional or religious figure is a different matter: not involved in the measuring process, and not necessarily close to the superego. Such a figure is generally more challenging.

This is important because the character-ideal has to be continually challenging, which is the same thing as unattainable, and to fulfill this need it may have to evolve over time—not to change fundamentally, at its structural level, but to adjust to the individual's growth and capacities as well as to external circumstances. If it could be attained, the character-ideal would lose its psychic organizational function. When an individual takes stock and measures his or her inevitable shortfall, self-reproach follows; but the self-reproach also means that no blurring of the boundaries between actual self and ideal order has taken place. If the individual goes too far, comes too close to perfection, a compensating or atoning act may take place. In moments of over-achievement, many highly creative people speak poignantly about their botched works or their broken lives; a well-intentioned, hard-working, near-miss of a failure may please them more, or they may have to confine themselves to certain limited spheres of perfection in order to avoid full perfection. It is not modesty that makes people stand outside their personal characterological pantheon, looking up and in at great models of self-leadership or self-artistry or self-uncovering.

Chapter Four

Illustrations, in Three Manners

THE RISE AND FALL OF CHARACTEROLOGY—BRIEFLY

In their political lectures and writings, Plato and Aristotle both advanced characterologies based on a simple idea: each type of character is dominated by a specific character trait. The same principle governed the characterologies of the Greek medical writers in the school of Hippocrates: each type of character is dominated by one of the four humors, blood, black bile, yellow bile, and phlegm. People are, then, sanguine, melancholic, choleric, or phlegmatic. Some medical theorists went on to associate a physiognomic type with each of the character types, stipulating that melancholics, for example, are thin, stooped, and long-faced, while phlegmatics are rotund, saggy, and round-faced.

Aristotle's classifications, which were more elaborate than the three-fold one with which Plato contrasted the appetitive Egyptians and Phoenicians, the spirited Thracians and Scythians, and the intellectual Athenians, unfolded along basically social lines, as his emphasis on the social forces involved in individuals' maturations would lead one to expect. *Ethos* or character is relative to extremes of age (youth and old age), birth (low-born and high-born), wealth (rich and poor), power (impotence and despotism), and fortune (unlucky and lucky). All of these social conditions have their effects and character is the sum of the effects. The best—most balanced and steady—character is the one that registers midway on each of the scales, but most people are marked by a predominance of one trait, which stems from a key disbalance or extremity in their social situations.

Aristotle's remarks about character became staples among rhetoricians, and over the centuries political commentators—particularly those adhering to the middle class, socially and politically—have been fond of such as these:

> Rich men are given to luxury and ostentation . . . because, like the rest of mankind, they give their time and thought to what they love and admire, and because they think that everyone else is keen for the same things they are. . . . To sum up, the character resulting from wealth is that of a prosperous fool.
>
> The wrongs, if any, that are done by men in power are not petty misdemeanors, but crimes on a large scale.
>
> In general, [good fortune] makes men more arrogant and less judicious; yet it is attended by one very excellent trait: the prosperous are god-fearing. They maintain an attitude of reverence, trusting in the divine power because of the goods that come from luck.

The Aristotelian method of drawing social characters was inherited by his discipline Theophrastus, author of *Characters,* who was, until the Renaissance, the most widely cited practitioner of the art of predominating-trait-to-type characterology. And, even though the Theophrastian characters were replaced in the Enlightenment by more complex types and by more simple types among nineteenth-century "ethologists" who studied "ruling passions," the basic idea that characters are determined by the predominance of a trait lived on into the twentieth century. But we moderns do not really have characterologies of this sort, and neither do we have a branch of literary or philosophical study devoted to character.

Psychoanalysis, which does include a strand of the old dominant characteristic sort of characterology—the idea that characters are determined by fixations or regressions to a libidinal stage—is otherwise so theoretically multifaceted on the topic of character that no clear coordination of traits and types has survived its advance. In character study conducted psychoanalytically, the predominating libidinal stage has to be considered along with (1) the interplay in a person of mental sexual characteristics (masculinity and femininity), (2) the history of his or her identifications, which compose the superego and influence the ego, and (3) the type and importance in the person of narcissistic traits. But there is no encompassing theory that indicates how these dimensions work together, how they interrelate, influence each other; and there is no developmental theory that links the dimensions over time.

The sheer number of dimensions psychoanalysis has proposed for investigation has virtually eliminated characterology—even psychoanalytic characterology, although there have been recent analysts, like David Shapiro in a book called *Neurotic Styles,* who have wished for a psychoanalytic characterology. Instead of literary or philosophical characterology, and instead of psychoanalytic characterology, we have, on the one hand, novels and biographies, and, on the other hand, huge shelves of self-help and popular psychology books detailing personality types (the "the addictive personality" and "the dependent personality" are the most recent constructions). These genres are the ones left with the old Theophrastian task of teaching readers what kinds of people they will meet in the world and how to recognize them. The whole history of characterology, of course, informs fiction and biography, as does psychoanalysis, the method that effectively destroyed characterology as an independent endeavor. But fiction and biography and "pop-psych" are not genres that carry on the old aspiration to a theory of types or a theoretical principle for constructing types. Characterological generalizations do not flow from them; they do not practice what might be called "comparative characters."

We can be grateful that the nontypological arts of fiction and biography have, in their flourishing, kept off the field of comparative characterology such efforts as the one made at the turn of the century by one G. M. Gould, who attempted to show in a six-volume treatise called *Biographic Clinics* (1903–07) that all creative geniuses have in common one feature—their poor eyesight and consequent eyestrain! On the other hand, characters can, I think, be compared, and fiction and biography can be used to suggest and support such comparisons. In the illustrations that follow, I am going to construct biographically, in three different ways, vignettes that focus on the three varieties of character-ideal that I set out in the last chapter. These biographical studies can, then, in subsequent chapters, be the focus of a comparative inquiry along developmental lines.

A FREUD PORTRAIT: THE POLITICAL
CHARACTER-IDEAL

In judging human character, Sidmund Freud said, "Actions, above all, deserve to be placed in the front rank." The explorer par excellence of the hidden world of dreams and fantasies had a perfectly Aristotelian view of how character should be judged; one drawn from the realm of action, the social and political realm. Freud spoke as an ethicist—not as a psychoanalytic theorist of character—but he also spoke in the mode of his own character-ideal, which circulated around an amalgamation of historical figures who had been political leaders. Not surprisingly, Freud's assessment of his own historical place reflects the same privileging of a process in which character has been achieved by effort over time and submitted to judgment in the public realm. In a letter to Arnold Zweig, he wrote of himself that "insofar as achievement is concerned, it was less a result of intellect than of character."

In his youth, the controlling figure in Freud's character-ideal had a number of sources—it was a composite of Hannibal, Napoleon, Napoleon's Jewish general Messena, Garibaldi, the leaders of the French Revolution. Freud indicated autobiographically that when he was an adolescent a slightly older contemporary, Heinrich Braun, later a prominent socialist leader, lent him a library of political histories and inspired his admiration personally. When he was a grown man, contemporary figures were assimilated to the ideal, as Kolomon Szell was during the Hungarian crisis of 1898. But, given the role that Rome played in Freud's imagination, it seems that Hannibal had a kind of pride of place among the exemplars. For Freud to visit Rome meant direct emulation of the conquistador's greatness—and Freud had to avoid for years making what felt like such a naked display of ambition. In his later adult life, Freud's character-ideal was more and more frequently associated with Moses.

About the controlling figure in Freud's character-ideal, we can say—generally—that he is a thoroughgoing independent, a rebel who does not stop short of his goals or his establishment of himself as the authority second to no other man, even if—like Moses—he must overcome great personal weaknesses to succeed. In him there are no unresolved questions about obedience to other authorities, including the parental (specifically, paternal) one. Furthermore, he leads without having to subdue his followers; they follow in deference to his charisma, and when they do have a period of rebelliousness against him, his charisma deters them—and he is able to be restrained and in authoritarian control over his emotions until it does. He is Moses as Freud described him in his essay on Michelangelo's statue of Moses in Rome: "The giant frame with its tremendous physical power [is] a concrete expression of the highest mental achievement that is possible in a man, that of struggling

78

successfully against an inward passion for the sake of a cause to which he has devoted himself" (13:223).

It is in relation to self-control that the politically constructed character-ideal seems to have been most important for Freud. The leader behaves toward the people as reason or a strong ego should behave toward the id. The human figures in the ideal character rule (as Freud said of the French revolutionaries) "by their sheer force of intellect and their fiery eloquence" (5:497). Or, as Freud said in his *Group Psychology and the Analysis of the Ego* of the ideal leader: "His intellectual acts were strong even in isolation, and his will needed no reinforcement from others." The leader is a man of "masterly nature, narcissistic, but self-confident and independent." In his later years, it seems to have become important to Freud that his ideal character-figure—who was then Moses—be an outsider, not a product of his group but someone who brought the group a redemptive vision from elsewhere. The ability to live as an outsider, a pariah, and to bear scorn and hatred had become crucial in the character-ideal. Again and again, Freud noted that his Jewish heritage was not a theology but a character—a phylogenetic heritage for enduring pariahdom.

The development of the character-ideal figure from earlier "family romance" figures is signaled by the fact that Freud imagined that his father—a man not heroic, without a masterly nature—looked, as he lay flushed and red-faced on his deathbed, like Garibaldi (4:228, 247). He related to his father through the medium of the idealized father figure, who was the human figure of his character-ideal. The character-ideal was also tied to an earlier sexual ideal. The character-ideal's figure is a ruler of people, but he must also have a history of sexual preparation for such greatness. As Freud said in general, not just of political figures: "A man who has shown determination in possessing himself of his love object has our confidence in his success in regard to other aims as well. On the other hand, a man who abstains for whatever reasons, from satisfying his strong sexual instincts, will also assume a conciliatory and resigned attitude in other paths of life, rather than a powerfully active one" (9:198). This passage presents the typical form of character-ideal measuring: the ideal is set out—it is possession, success—and then ("on the other hand") the failure is envisioned—lack of possession, unsuccess.

Freud as an adolescent had every reason to find himself headed for unsuccess when he failed to approach, much less possess, his first love, a girl named Gisela Fluss. To his friend Silberstein, the sixteen-year-old

Freud gave a literary account of his interior obstacle, a premonition of the account he would later give of Shakespeare's Hamlet as a character caught in an unresolved Oedipal dilemma: "This sentiment for Gisela appeared like a nice sentiment in spring, but my nonsensical 'Hamlethood,' my shyness, prevented me from indulging in conversation with the partly naive, partly educated young lady." Ten years apparently passed between this episode and his next sexual adventure. Then he had every reason to find his arduous, prolonged, but ultimately successful courtship of Martha Bernays a much more satisfactory augury for the future, and he told his fiancée repeatedly that she was his salvation from a life with no meaning.

It is hard to think that this story of salvation is not reflected in Freud's description of the kind of narcissism characteristic of males. The sexual instincts are at first attached to the satisfaction of the self-preservative, nutritionally focused ego-instincts, Freud argued, and they carry this attachment into later loves or object-choices. So men attach themselves continually to versions of the woman who nourished them (and, to a lesser extent, of the father who protected them):

> Complete object-love of the attachment type is, properly speaking, characteristic of the male. It displays the marked sexual over-valuation which is doubtless derived from the child's original narcissism and thus corresponds to a transference of that narcissism to the sexual object. This sexual over-valuation is the origin of a peculiar state of being in love, a state suggestive of a neurotic compulsion, which is thus traceable to an impoverishment of the ego as regards libido in favour of the love object (14:88).

A second kind of narcissism, moving a person to seek continually a version (an idealized version) of himself or herself in lovers, often combines with narcissism of the attachment type, but it can also predominate over the attachment type—particularly in women and male homosexuals, Freud argued. In Freud himself, both kinds of narcissism seem apparent, with the attachment type taking the upper hand in the period when he courted Martha Bernays.

The narcissim mixture in Freud is also revealed in his career plans. After his adolescent "Hamlethood" episode with Gisela Fluss, who was so much a creature of Freud's narcissistic fantasy and so little a real girl, Freud made two decisions. He gave up his goal of preparing himself with a law degree for a political career, and he gave up the possibility of an artistic avocation. The check he decided to put on his artistic and speculative imagination soon meant turning away from speculative philosophy as he encountered it in the classroom of Franz Brentano. But the refusal of an artistic self-ordering seems also to have been crucially tied to his sexual experience. When Gisela Fluss married, Freud joked elaborately with Silberstein about this girl they called "Ichthyo-saura" as though she were prehistoric, a dinosaur:

> Herewith this period ends, here I submerge the magic wand that has contributed to its organization: a new time may commence without secretly active forces, a time that does not need poesy and fantasy. Nobody may search for a principle [a girl] in the alluvium or diluvium or elsewhere but in the present, nowhere but among the children of human beings but not in the grisly primordial past.

Poesy and fantasy, associated with this ill-fated affair, were ruled out—as was what I have called the artisanal character-ideal.

Ruled in as careers were natural science (as presided over by Goethe) or medicine. The difference between artists and scientific people was, then, built in autobiographical terms into Freud's theory of sublimation. As he noted in an essay entitled " 'Civilized' Sexual Morality and Modern Nervous Illness":

> In the vast majority of cases, the struggle against sexuality eats up the energy available in a character, and at the very time when a young man is in need of all his forces in order to win his share and place in society. . . . An abstinent artist is hardly conceivable; but an abstinent young savant is certainly no rarity (9:197).

What the abstinent young savant Sigmund Freud could not do without for the development of his scientific career, was authority figures. Freud attached himself to a succession of male protective authority figures, chief among them the physiologist Ernst Brucke, who, as Freud much later dramatically proclaimed, "carried more weight with me than anyone else in my whole life" (20:253). Consciously, Freud turned political leadership over to these figures, but unconsciously he converted his own self-leadership ambitions into another field—science. Brucke was an emulatable leader in the manner of Freud's ideal, a real-life Garibaldi; he dreamt of Brucke's "terrible blue eyes by which I was reduced to nothing" (5:422).

It is possible to see Brucke as an ego-ideal, or what the analyst K. R. Eissler calls an "ideal superego figure," a corrective image to Freud's weak father, but it is also important to see him as a leader, the head of an institute bearing his name—that is, as fit to influence the figure in Freud's character-ideal. Freud's ego, his reason—to speak nontechnically—was to have dominion in his psyche, not as an artistic or magical Prospero with a wand, but as a political figure, an authority, commanding obedience without resorting to violence. In the more abstract terms of the character-ideal: reason (the ego) was to rule over unreason (the id) without ever rebelling against destiny or against what cannot be influenced because it is—like death—beyond our control. Reason's ally in exerting control, operating like the agency Picasso called "the connoisseur," was to be psychology, as Freud later (in a May 25, 1895, letter) told his friend Fliess:

> A man like me cannot live without a hobby horse, without a dominating passion, without—to speak with Schiller—a tyrant, and he has come my way. And in his service I know no moderation. It is psychology.

The social vision in which this character-ideal was projected outward also featured instinctual life undergoing a slow devolution in the process of civilizational evolution. Explicitly, Freud viewed the microcosm of the individual and the macrocosm of society as sharing a story—but in the manner common among his contemporaries, he claimed that the microcosm recapitulates the societal story: ontogeny recapitulates phylogeny. The ancients and primitives, Freud thought, were both more instinctually uninhibited and worshiped the instinctual:

> The most striking distinction between the erotic life of antiquity and our own no doubt lies in the fact that the ancients laid stress upon the instinct itself, whereas we emphasize its object. The ancients glorified the instinct and were prepared on its account to honor even an inferior object; while we despise the instinctual activity itself, and find excuses for it only in the merits of the object (7:149).

Freud's ideal became to avoid despising the erotic instinct by sublimating it—controlling it without repression. He thought of the result as a special type of civilized character, while, in general, he viewed the emergence of character-types as a phenomenon of civilization. "The differentiation of the individual character, which is so marked in our day, has only become possible with the existence of sexual restriction" (9:196).

The particular way in which Freud conceived of the voice of the controlling ego or reason is obvious in his texts. People of genius who create literary texts, and over time an oeuvre, project their character-ideals into their style or their form or their choice of genre or their working method, as well as into a social vision or a natural philosophy. In Freud's case, what this means is that his texts, singly and in relation to each other, are dialogic in a particular sense: they present a leader, the main voice in the texts, and other voices—specific dissenting theorists, propounders of anticipated objections, or choruses of unnamed critics. As the text unfolds, the opposition is given its say and then stilled while what is valuable in the oppositional views is peacefully assimilated to the dominating view—Freud's psychoanalysis. Like the Roman emperors, Freud gave citizenship in his empire to willing former opponents and banished the unwilling to outer darkness. The dialogue is quite fore-grounded and theatrical in the late work called *The Question of Lay Analysis,* but it operates everywhere in Freud's oeuvre, frustrating readers who find that their criticism has already been anticipated and defeated.

The opinions Freud banished were ones he thought too simple, either in the sense that they were reductionist attempts to find a single key to a complex mystery, or in the sense that they were based on a simple denial, usually of the pervasive influence of sexuality. Superficiality was the central complaint in Freud's negative character-ideal as well. In his youth, Freud's negative character-ideal had a human figure who was an amalgam of historical and contemporary people who had one thing in common—their aggressive unseriousness, their determined frivolity, their superfluity or lack of productivity. The model figures were Euro-pean royalty and aristocrats, who did not so much lead as enslave their entourages and peoples, often sadistically, usually without any intrinsic claim to merit. During the early years of his psychoanalytic practice, when Freud saw so many female hysterics and spent such energy on trying to analyze his own hysterical tendencies and somatic symptoms, an amalgam of hysterical characteristics seems to have accrued to the negative character-ideal. The misogynistic tone that sometimes (particu-larly in the "Dora" case of 1905) marks Freud's comments about women seems to me to point to the flighty, unserious negative character-ideal, which, in his later life, was routinely associated not with hysterical women but with the Americans as a group.

The Americans were, in Freud's view, the creators of "anti-Paradise," as he said in a letter to Arnold Zweig. This meant that they revealed themselves historically as a people quite incapable of producing heroes. America, he explained in *Group Psychology,* was a place where "leading personalities fail to acquire the significance that should fall to them in the process of group formation." The masses were not unified by a masterly nature, the land was chaotic, like an id so unruly about work and money as to make even the pleasures of sex unsatisfying. The Americans were not dedicated to lasting achievements, they were dedicated to wealth: they did not husband their energy for great purposes, they rushed around at a terrific pace, in a fury of sheerly utilitarian, materialistic, usually faddish activities. "Can an American live in opposition to public opinion, as we are prepared to do?" Freud asked Ernest Jones. As examples of an immature and anal-sadistic "national character," the Americans represented both the most hated and the most feared; they were the worst-organized self, the lower depths, which have to be overcome if the good political order of the best self is to be actualized.

Like most negative character-ideals, Freud's had about it something comical: it protested so much that it became a caricature. Among the prerequisites for creative comedians, it seems to me, is that they be conscious to a rare degree of their negative character-ideals and that they develop a capacity to conform to them occasionally. They are able to play their own worst enemies. Freud, although witty and fond of jokes, was no comedian.

A GROUP PORTRAIT: THE ARTISANAL/SEXUAL CHARACTER-IDEAL

Freud's political negative character-ideal, which he projected to embrace a group, contrasts sharply with the negative ideal typical of creative characters of the artisanal type. A craftsperson or poet who fails in the work of self-shaping or social-shaping or who deals with a completely recalcitrant material is the human figure in such a negative artisanal ideal. Among Freud's contemporaries, the politically conservative British esthetes of the turn of the century, for example, typically set Byronic heroes—Manfreds or Giaours—as the human figures in their negative character-ideals. These democratic adventurer figures destroyed themselves as they revolted against social values, or withered, corroded from within by a secret or a shame, or simply found themselves overmastered by enemy forces too strong for their self-crafting powers.

The positive artisanal character-ideal common in this group centered, on the other hand, on a figure who was in complete control of his well-crafted self. He could obey the well-known charge issued by Oscar Wilde: "Create yourself; be yourself your poem!" The biographer par excellence of this generation, Richard Ellmann noted in his aptly titled *Yeats: The Man and the Masks:*

> The measure of the greatness of the Wildean hero is the extent to which he has altered the raw material of his life into something quite different. So far as his passions emerge they are ignoble and uninteresting, part of an unpleasant, irrelevant reality, a subject for the naturalist and not for the true artist.

Wilde did not—like Kant—imagine character as rising above natural disposition or temperament; he imagined character as replacing nature, and he exalted the completely artificial self.

Among the British esthetes, it was the word *personality* that came to denote the crafted self, which in the Platonic tradition had been known as the *ethos,* or character. The crafted self or personality, however, was the product of the lower self, in the grass-roots modern manner we noted before as typical of Nietzsche. Self-crafting was not of the lower self by the higher self, as Plato imagined it, but the inverse, as Richard Ellmann noted in his Yeats biography:

> The implication of the esthetes' conception of the artistic personality is that a man is really two men. There is the insignificant man who is *given,* whether by God, by society, or simply by birth; there is the significant man who is *made* by the first. One evidence of this split, which goes beyond literature, is the verbal distinction that becomes common toward the end of the nineteenth century between personality and character, the former as in some way the conscious product of the later. In literature the splitting up of the mind is accomplished near the end of the century by two books, *Dr. Jekyll and Mr. Hyde* (1885) and *The Picture of Dorian Gray* (1890). . . . The last decade of the century is thronged by extravagant *poseurs* like Lionel Johnson and Aubrey Beardsley; even James Joyce, growing up in this atmosphere, says he felt compelled to construct "the enigma of a manner." The attempt to achieve a rarefied, synthetic self is implicit in Pater's extreme

preoccupation with style, his method of rewriting innumerable times so that his finished phrase would resemble as little as possible the one that had come initially into his head.

Yeats, as Ellmann shows, was well suited for internal division and quite able to exploit his state by virtue of his childhood revolt, "which could only be a half-revolt, against his father and his father's world." As a late adolescent, he adopted the notion of himself as two beings and began to write from it, with it. Then, when Yeats associated himself with the magical adepts in the Order of the Golden Dawn, his vision was projected outward, as Ellmann shows:

> From the attempt to achieve personal transmutation it was only a brief step to the attempt to achieve a more general transmutation. The Order taught that its doctrines should affect daily life. Many members of the Golden Dawn felt that they had the additional obligation of becoming "a perfect instrument for the regeneration of the world."

Yeats, thirty years old, but still an adolescent, shy and sexually quite inexperienced, expected socio-political Armageddon and envisioned a "civilization about to be born." Crafting a self and conjuring a civilization into being were two ranges of the same character-ideal in action.

For men at the turn of the century, both the political character-ideal evident in Freud, analyst of the "Oedipus complex," and this artisanal ideal went under the aegis of father-son struggle: they are ideals of conflict stilled by political authority or artistic skill triumphant over the "given," the self tied to the past and to paternal authority or precedent. But the father-son conflict is most obvious in the artisanal ideal, because it involves not just an image of authoritative control assumed, but one of construction—and construction entails destruction, violence wrought. The divided self can be at once father-identified and parricidal—even if, as in the Daedalus and Icarus story, the parricide has to be disguised, so that the artificer father survives rather than dying himself. "Who doesn't desire his father's death?" Ivan Karamazov asked—and he clearly meant no question at all. Yeats's concurrence was expressed first in an unpublished play he wrote when he was turning twenty, again at the age of thirty-eight in "The Death of Cuchulain," and on through two different translations of Sophocles' *Oedipus Rex* and a play involving parricide written shortly before his death in 1939.

But the specific forms that the political and artistic character-ideals can take in males are clued not just to the specific forms of Oedipal conflict; they call for a more complex reading along what psychoanalysts call "developmental lines." The Wildean *poseur,* for example, artistically defends himself as an obsessional does—his character is like a fully lived-out obsessional ceremonial, a ceremonial turned into a way of life, a childhood lack of control and a fear of passivity turned into active self-shaping.

With others, the self-shaping imagery may relate more to self-gestating than to fabricating. Character-ideals presenting one part of the self or psyche raising and educating another, or one part giving birth to a work of art that represents a facet of the self, or one part tied to a "civilization about to be born," are rooted in very early childhood experiences but reactivated with adolescent envy for pregnant women. Goethe's envy of his younger sister's pregnancy is an example that has been biographically studied. As much as Wilde abhorred Byron and Byron's heroes, Goethe had admired the English poet's "true poetical power" and his capacity to bear and rear his works naturally. The Platonic tradition of relating divine inspiration or madness and impregnation is echoed in the apostrophe to Byron recorded in Goethe's conversations with Eckermann: "With [Byron] inspiration supplies the place of reflection. He was obliged to go on poetizing; and then everything that came from the man, especially from his heart, was excellent. He produced his best things as women do pretty children, without thinking about it or knowing how it is done."

Among the late nineteenth-century British esthetes, one of the most explicit and sustained presentations of psychic procreation and male mothering (to use Nietzsche's phrase) was crafted by Gerard Manley Hopkins. His poem, dedicated to his friend, the poet Robert Bridges, can stand as a representative of the sexual corollary of the artisan character-ideal projected into a work:

> The fine delight that fathers thought; the strong
> Spur, live and lancing, like the blowpipe flame,
> Breathes once and, quenched faster than it came,
> Leaves yet the mind a mother of immortal song.
> Nine months she then, nay years, nine years she long
> Within her wears, bears, cares and combs the same:
> The widow of an insight lost she lives, with aim
> Now known and hand at work now never wrong.

Sweet fire the sire of muse, my soul needs this;
I want the one rapture of an inspiration.
O then if in my lagging lines you miss
The roll, the rise, the carol, the creation,
My winter world, that scarcely breathes that bliss
Now, yields you, with some sighs, our explanation.

FOUR SKETCHES: THE SPIRITUAL CHARACTER-IDEAL

Inspiration can be thought of as the divine spur to self-crafting, as it can be thought of as spiritual impregnation. But it can also be experienced and conceptualized quite differently, as a process of unburdening. People with character-ideals of the ascetic or spiritual type speak as T. S. Eliot did in "The Use of Poetry and the Use of Criticism" about what inspiration feels like:

> . . . a disturbance of our quotidian character which results in an incantation, an outburst of words which we hardly recognize as our own (because of the effortlessness). . . . [To] me, it seems that at these moments, which are characterized by the sudden lifting of the burden of anxiety and fear which press upon our daily life so steadily that we are unaware of it, what happens is something negative: that is to say, not "inspiration" as we commonly think of it, but the breaking down of strong habitual barriers—which tend to reform very quickly. Some obstruction is momentarily wisked away. The accompanying feeling is less like what we know as a positive pleasure, than a sudden relief from an intolerable burden.

Disburdening, or what I have called self-stripping, is the action of the ascetic or spiritual character-ideal. Stoical or sexually over-strict religious traditionalists of Eliot's sort often project such an ideal. But stripping the self of all its accidentality or materiality, revealing the essential self in its purity, can serve many purposes, and not the least among them is escape from psychic and social conditions in which being female seems a limitation, an inadequacy. I will consider later women whose creativity was tied to political and artisanal character-ideals, but for the moment I want to illustrate the quite disparate varieties of the ascetic ideal with female subjects. (This seems to me the most common female creative character-ideal type, and in Chapter 9 I will consider the reasons.)

In her biography of the French philosopher Simone Weil, Simone Petrement described her subject as a *lycée* student:

As for the plans she had already formed, her whole conception of what she wanted to do with her life, it was—as she herself later said—a great misfortune to have been born female. So she decided to reduce this obstacle as much as possible by disregarding it, that is, by giving up any desire to think of herself as a woman or to be regarded as such by others. . . . Her parents called her "Simon," "our son number two," and "our *cagne* boy." When Simone wrote to her mother while at Henry IV [her *lycée*], she even went so far as to speak of herself in the masculine gender and to sign her letters "your respectful son."

Simone Weil gave up her femininity for the gender she regarded as generic: she joined, as it were, mankind.

But her project also had a quite specific purpose within her family context, in the shadow of her astoundingly precocious mathematician brother André and in the atmosphere of her mother's contempt for feminine frailties and silliness. In her "Spiritual Autobiography," Weil recalled that:

At fourteen I fell into one of those fits of bottomless despair that come with adolescence, and I seriously thought of dying because of the mediocrity of my natural faculties. The exceptional gifts of my brother, who had a childhood and youth comparable to those of Pascal, brought my own inferiority home to me. I did not mind having no visible successes, but what did grieve me was the idea of being excluded from that transcendent kingdom to which only the truly great have access and wherein truth abides. I prepared to die rather than to live without that truth. After months of inward darkness, I suddenly had the everlasting conviction that any human being, even though practically devoid of natural faculties, can penetrate to the kingdom of truth reserved for genius, if only he longs for truth and perpetually concentrates all his attention upon its attainment. He thus becomes a genius, too, even though for lack of talent his genius cannot be visible from the outside. Later on, when the strain of headaches caused the feeble faculties I possess to be invaded by a paralysis, which I was quick to imagine as probably incurable, the same conviction led me to persevere for ten years in an effort of concentrated attention that was practically unsupported by any hope of results.

The sibling rivalry, the competition for prowess as a penetrator into a romanticized kingdom of truth, the stress on her own "invisible" equipment, give this passage all the marks of the Freudianly defined "masculinity complex," but what is important in the context I am developing is Simone Weil's solution: paring her self down into an ascetic, rarified attentiveness. The purity does not come, as with Oscar Wilde, from self-shaping—rarification or transformation by constant reworking—but by elimination, purgation.

A person of this character-ideal type would be likely to describe her writing style with words like these:

> I try to eliminate what isn't essential, and I try not to give in, as I did in my youth, to the temptation to add ornament. Back then I thought it was necessary to round off each sentence. Now I look instead for the sharpest possible sentence, the simplest images, and I don't try to be original at all costs. In fact, I don't try anything at all; my writing is the way it is.

This woman, cited from a collection of her interviews appropriately titled *With Open Eyes,* is the Belgian-born novelist Marguerite Yourcenar, the first woman ever to be initiated into the Académie Française. She was speaking of the style she had first worked for in *Alexis,* a *récit,* or monologue, penned by a young man explaining to his wife that he is a homosexual and cannot continue in their marriage. Yourcenar published the book when she was twenty-six, in 1929. Later she declared that she hoped to be like the central character in her novel *The Abyss,* Zeno, who is a mystic pursuing a goal typical of the self-purifier: to "die a little less besotted than he was born."

Near the end of her life, at the age of eighty-three, Yourcenar told an interviewer about the character-ideal she had had since her youth—even before she had produced a collection of male literary characters to present the ideal, and before she had achieved a lean, graceful prose style to announce it.

Yourcenar: "I don't mean to say that I will be fundamentally different—whatever I am I have probably been all my life—but I shall at least have gotten rid of a lot of excess baggage, or so I hope."

Interviewer: "For you, then, life is primarily a matter of divestiture."

Yourcenar: "Yes, certainly, but it is also a matter of enrichment. One sheds one's clothing in order to be bronzed by the sun's rays."

For Yourcenar, the spiritual discipline that lets an individual being (*un être*) understand that he or she is an essence (*l'être*) was a matter of course in much of the ancient world, in the Stoic quarters of Greece and Rome that she knew well as an amateur classicist, and also in the East:

> Generally speaking, one must try against considerable difficulty to achieve what Hindu sages describe as a state of "attentiveness," in which you get rid of three-quarters or nine-tenths of what you seem to think but really don't. Ordinarily, a person merely assembles bits and pieces of pre-existing ideas. All these must be eliminated and one's thought focused on nothing; the effect is quite salutary.

In Marguerite Yourcenar's social vision, all human particularities and differences were to be eventually overcome. Men and women will know themselves as humans; homosexuality and heterosexuality will become, simply, expressions of sexuality; people will come to respect animals and plants as fellow creatures, citizens of one world. The corollary to Marguerite Yourcenar's cosmopolitanism is a spiritual feeling for the cosmos that is almost pantheistic. Her assault upon egoism, which she equated with lack of perspective on the oneness of creatures and nature, is most intense in her two-volume autobiography, one volume of which provides a history of her mother's family and one a history of her father's family, and neither of which take her own story past her first month of life. She is embedded in, undifferentiated from, her people, their land.

In comparison to Simone Weil and Marguerite Yourcenar, Gertrude Stein, who was born in 1874, some twenty-five years before them, conceived of the process of stripping the self down to its essentials in temporal rather than spatial terms. She eliminated past and future and focused her attention only on the present. Having encountered William James's characterology when she was a student at Radcliffe, she concluded that every individual has a character—she called it (without intending any pun) "the bottom nature"—that never varies. This means that the present is the past being repeated and the future is what the present will be when it repeats itself. In her dualistic characterology, people are either of the "independent dependent kind" or of the "dependent independent kind," and the words and deeds of people within these two types are endlessly, infinitely repeated. Or, as she said of the book called *Three Lives,* in which she first embodied her vision of psychic order:

> In that there was a constant recurring and beginning there was a marked direction in the direction of being in the present although naturally I had

been accustomed to past present future, and why, because the composition formation around me was a prolonged present.

The literary language for expressing this temporal alinearity or amorphousness was to be a language, she concluded, stripped of sentence structure and burdensome rules: "The question is, if you have a vocabulary have you any need of grammar?" Similarly, the meditative condition in which the writer is to write is one in which personality and appearance in the world have given way to pure tenseless perceptive consciousness. As Stein said in *A Novel of Thank You:* "I am not any longer what I see. This sentence is at the bottom of all creative activity. It is just the opposite of I am because my little dog knows me."

In Gertrude Stein's image of psychic order there was also—not surprisingly—no structure, no division; she completely rejected Freud's theory of the unconscious. As she firmly said of herself (in the third person singular, writing the *Autobiography of Alice B. Toklas*): "Gertrude Stein never had subconscious reactions." Similarly, she claimed that there are no differences between people who want no differences between them: she insisted as she wrote Alice B. Toklas's autobiography that she and her friend were one, and then she went right on to insist that she could write the autobiography of America—a book called *The Making of the Americans*—or even *Everybody's Autobiography*. Her social vision was an expanded version of her character-ideal, which was an ideal of a singular psyche, without fixed order, stratification, structuration, or differentiation.

Stripping the self down to essentials, purifying it, can be accomplished in spirits as different as Simone Weil's—self-castigation or rebuke; and Marguerite Yourcenar's—ecstatic nature worship; and Gertrude Stein's—self-congratulation. It can also be undertaken for quite different purposes, by quite different psychic means. Anna Freud offered a classic description of one such means in a quite autobiographical passage on "altruistic surrender" in her 1936 book *The Ego and the Mechanisms of Defense*. "Altruistic surrender," which is a means of stripping the self of forbidden wishes by making over the wishes to others, can also translate easily enough into a social vision, as Anna Freud herself noted during an informal discussion of her idea that was recorded in *Analysis of Defense:*

> If you can't get what you want yourself and enjoy it yourself because it's prohibited by internal conflict, well at least somebody else can get it, and

you can enjoy it there through what you call vicarious enjoyment—which is certainly worthwhile. But that isn't all. At the same time the process liberates, or creates an outlet for, aggression. What I meant was that originally the individual wants to pursue his or her instinctual aims aggressively. "I want it, I'll have it, I'll fight anybody who won't give it to me." This aggression becomes impossible and forbidden when the fulfillment of the wish becomes impossible and forbidden, but now with the altruism you can fight for somebody else's fulfillment of the wish with the same aggression, the same energy. So you have both your libidinal vicarious pleasure, and you have an outlet for your aggression. It's surprising that not more people are altruists!

Many democratic and anarchistic social visionaries, of course, have conjured a harmonious world in which there would be no divisions among masterful leaders and followers, people-shapers and peoples shaped, in which all people would do unto others as they wish others would do unto them, or in which each would get according to his or her needs. But Anna Freud was able to imagine what non-hierarchical social harmony would actually require psychologically—that is, that all people find appropriate others whom they can help to do what they once wished to do for themselves but could not. In such a world, there would not be philanthropists and recipients of philanthropy, do-gooders and possibly quite resentful gooders-done-to—another form of hierarchy—but rather altruism that would be as universal as the universality of forbidden wishes. Each person would give according to his or her psychological need, and each would get an outlet for forbidden wishes and aggression. A paradise for mystical bookkeepers, accountant saints!

Chapter Five

Character-Ideals and
Libidinal Types

FOUR DIMENSIONS OF FREUDIAN CHARACTEROLOGY

By drawing one extended portrait of Freud, one group portrait of the British fin-de-siècle esthetes and one quaternary made up of four women who were quite unrelated in national background or profession, I have tried to show three types of character-ideals being formed and being projected into works and social visions. My three sketching techniques were meant to suggest different ways of biographically exploring the character-ideal. But I did not in any of the three sketches make more than a nod at the types of developmental histories and adolescent susceptibilities to cultural contexts that might underlie them. This developmental inquiry needs its own framework, an aerial survey map, and I want to suggest one in this chapter, before elaborating it in the next chapter and then offering another series of biographical studies. The framework will also open a way to question why there are three character-ideal types, and just the three I have been sketching.

The framework I want to offer depends upon Freud's work, but grows out of it at the point where I think Freud turned away from characterology. To show this point, I want to review Freud's approach to character, which has, as noted before, four dimensions—at least.

Freud first envisioned a characterology in the tradition of the ancient Greek medical characterologies: a correspondence theory of one predominating trait to one type. He spoke of oral, anal, urethral (or, in later variations, phallic or phallic-narcissistic) characters, and implied an ideal type, a fully mature genital character. Each is rooted in ("fixated" to) or commonly regresses to a specific libidinal stage. There are also characters fixated to or regressing to the component instincts, sadism and masochism, exhibitionism and scopophilia, and characters fixated to or dominated by specific early loves or by traumatic experiences. But these possibilities are secondary in comparison to the possibilities represented by libidinal stage domination. Freud's initial idea was that as each type of neurotic or psychotic symptom complex is rooted in a specific libidinal stage, so is each character-trait complex. The difference between a symptom and a character-trait is a matter of degree. Thus a trait like cleanliness is a less ego-threatening ("ego dystonic," to speak technically) matter than a symptom like compulsive hand-washing. The difference of degree or intensity is also linked, however, to a difference in attitude. Adults (though not small children) often feel their symptoms as painful and anomalous afflictions, but they feel that their character-traits, even when painful, are like their faces: they are given, immutable. Further, they mostly comprehend their character-traits in the mirror of other people's reactions, where they are distorted by the mirroring person's own character-traits.

Freud's first vision of character as primarily a function of libidinal stage domination came to him as he considered a particular set of character-traits—cleanliness, orderliness, parsimony, and obstinacy—in relation to anal erotism. In 1908, while he was in the process of analyzing the patient known as the "Rat Man," Freud noted that:

> anal erotism is one of the components of the [sexual] instinct which, in the course of development in accordiance with the education demanded by present civilization, have become unserviceable for sexual aims. It is therefore plausible to suppose that these character-traits of orderliness, parsimony and obstinacy, which are so prominent in people who were formerly anal erotics, are to be regarded as the first and most constant results of the sublimation of anal erotism (9:171).

The key concept here is obviously "sublimation," by which Freud meant redirection of instinctual energy. Those once passionately interested in feces become those passionately interested in money; lovers of dirt and messing become lovers of soap and showering; those once dedicated to retaining their stools, for the pleasure of a grander defecation later, or for the pleasure of thwarting parental wishes, become those retaining control over things and people by obstinacy.

Freud never felt the need to alter this basic insight into the "anal character," and it remains one of the most unchallenged and consistently obvious clinical features of analytic experience, although it is not clear in the psychoanalytic literature how a person develops an over-neat "anal character" rather than the related trait-complex typical of people who can only long for cleanlines, parsimony, and obstinacy as for salvation. They are disorderly and disheveled, unable to get or hold onto money, and so skeptical about the value of any wish that they have no convictions and are dedicated to being polemical deflators of others' beliefs. (We will return to this trait-complex below, in the person of Dr. Samuel Johnson, whose uncouth, bedraggled appearance and filthy quarters made his acquaintances marvel when they heard him say, for example, "Every man of any education would rather be called a rascal, than accused of deficiency in the graces.")

Although Freud felt that his insights into the "anal character" were secure enough, he never did feel satisfied with his understanding of how character-traits are formed through "sublimation," which he regarded as a term marking a mystery. Two decades after he had ventured an exploration of sublimation in his "pathography" of Leonardo da Vinci, Freud reiterated his puzzlement in *Civilization and Its Discontents* (1930):

> The development of civilization appears to us as a peculiar process which mankind undergoes, and in which several things strike us as familiar. We may characterize this process with reference to the changes which it brings about in the familiar instinctual disposition of human beings, to satisfy which is, after all, the economic task of our lives. A few of these instincts are used up in such a manner that something appears in their place which, in the individual, we describe as a character-trait. The most remarkable example of such a process is found in the anal erotism of young human beings. Their original interest in the excretory function, its organs and products, is changed in the course of their growth into a group of traits which are familiar to us as parsimony, a sense of order and cleanliness— qualities which, though valuable and welcome in themselves, may be intensified till they become markedly dominant and produce what is called the anal character. How this happens we do not know, but there is no doubt about the concreteness of the finding (21:96–7).

In addition to this "how this happens we do not know" libido-to-character formulation, Freudian psychoanalysis also has a second characterology based on "mental sexual characteristics," or what is now known as gender. These characteristics are "masculine" and "feminine" when a person has achieved the genital stage of sexual development, but they rest on a prior dichotomy between active and passive aims for the instinctual drives, which appears most obviously in the anal stage: "Activity is supplied by the common instinct of mastery, which we call sadism. . . . The passive trend is fed by anal erotism, whose erotic zone corresponds to the old, undifferentiated cloaca" (12:322).

That last baffling clause presupposes Freud's belief that ontogeny recapitulates phylogeny. In the remote phylogenetic past, genitalia and excretory organs shared an antechamber, "the old undifferentiated cloaca," which is still undifferentiated in reptiles, birds, amphibians and many fishes. This earlier anatomical state of affairs is retained, Freud thought, in every human being's unconscious memory, from whence it is reflected in dreams and in children's sexual theories. The unconscious memory influences the sexual receptivity that he considered essential to the mental sexual characteristic "desire for passive pleasure," which Freud designated feminine. While Freud started out (in 1905) claiming that females desire both passivity and activity while males desire only activity, he later changed his mind and said, much more logically, that both females and males can have both sorts of desires. Both sexes, in other words, are bisexual, both feminine and masculine, in mental sexual characteristics as they are in physical sexual characteristics. (Freud could not specify the physical characteristics in detail, as hormone chemistry, for example, was not available to him and the embryology he based himself upon was rudimentary and often just wrong.)

In females, the basic dichotomy between active and passive pleasure aims combines with another anatomically based set of characteristics— those associated with the female's lack of a penis. According to this most controversial part of Freud's theory, when girls discover that they lack and will not get a penis, their shock and disappointment "will leave ineradicable traces on their development and the formation of their character which will not be surmounted in even the most favorable cases without a severe expenditure of psychical energy" (22:125). One possibility for later development is neurosis or sexual inhibition; another is "change of character in the sense of the masculinity complex" (that is, development of a character marked by desire for a penis sublimated toward different aims); and a third is "normal femininity," which presupposes overthrow in a "wave of passivity" of the better part of a girl's desire for activity, her masculinity. In general, however, Freud thought of women's characters as much more marked by bisexuality than men's, and he also generally attributed character-traits like shame or modesty to "concealment of genital deficiency" (22:132). Finally, he thought of women as much more prone to characterological narcissism than men—but this brings us to a third dimension of Freud's evolving theory of character.

After 1914, when Freud began distinguishing two forms of libido, narcissistic (self-loving) and object-related (other-loving), the second of which can but need not develop out of the first, it became possible to speak of characters in which one or the other form of libido predominates. Tentatively, Freud argued that the development of object-love from original narcissism is less characteristic of femininity than of masculinity, and among women "to be loved is a stronger need for them than to love" (14:88–89; 22:132).

By the early 1920s, then, Freud had offered two types of dualistic characterologies, one on masculinity/femininity lines, one on narcissistic/non-narcissistic lines, on top of his first pluralistic libido-stage characterology. All three lines of thought merged into a fourth scheme that was articulated along with the so-called "structural theory" of id, ego, and superego. This theory, announced in the 1923 text *The Ego and the Id*, brought Freud very close to the manner in which the ancient Greeks and their Christian heirs had anatomized the human character. The troika of faculties that Kant had assumed—the sensual, the volitional, and the intellectual, for example—had its roots ultimately in Plato's *reason–spirit–appetites* hierarchy, and also had more immediate debts to the *appetitus–voluntas–ratio* division that was clear to Augustine. The id is Freud's sensual and pleasure realm; the ego is equivalent to *nous* or *ratio;* and the superego, like conscience, is the agency that directs the will's activity or inactivity. But Freud, in distinction from his predecessors, assumed that the ego and the superego are outgrowths of the id, and that they remain partly unconscious, like the id.

Developmentally, the ego is older than the superego. The ego's initial function is to represent the requirements of the external world to the id, which is all bent on pleasure. Freud located the "essence of a neurosis" in the fact that the ego can be too feeble, "not able to fulfill its function of mediating between the id and reality" (20:261). The mediating ego is made up of remnants; it is a collection of leftovers from all the early sensual, perceptually based loves that a child has abandoned, whether these be parts of the child's own body or its body products, parts of other people (like the mother's breast), or other people as wholes.

> When it happens that a person has to give up a sexual object there quite often ensues an alteration of his ego which can be described as a setting up of the object inside the ego, as it occurs in melancholia; the exact nature of this substitution is as yet unknown to us. It may be that by this introjection, which is a kind of regression to the mechanisms of the oral phase, the ego makes it easier for the object to be given up or renders the process possible. It may be that this identification is the sole condition under which it can give up its objects. At any rate, the process, especially in the early phases of development, is a very frequent one, and it makes it possible to suppose that the character of the ego is a precipitate of abandoned object-cathexes and that it contains the history of those object-choices (19:29).

This process, by which the id's love-pursuit can be directed toward the identifications that make up the ego rather than toward the external world—this process of creating narcissistic libido—was given by Freud the name of the great mystery, "sublimation." The early record of subli-mation, he argued, can be read in a psychoanalysis because it appears in the form of the ego's resistances to letting the story of its loves become conscious. The later story, as a child develops through the Oedipal period, can be read in that "precipitate of the ego" that Freud called the ego-ideal or the superego, which is specifically built from the child's identifications with its mother and father. The initial character of the superego is constituted by these "two identifications in some way united with each other." "The ego-ideal is therefore the heir of the Oedipus complex" (19:36) and it represents the surrounding social world in the psyche, as the ego represents the surrounding felt or perceptual world.

Character, in Freud's three-part structural scheme, was the sum of the characters of the id, the ego, and the superego, as manifest in the various relations that can exist between and among them and the external world. To put the matter another way, using the language that Freud's daughter Anna elaborated in *The Ego and the Mechanisms of Defense* (1936), a person's character, made up of a net of these relations within the psyche and between psychic structures and external world, is the sum of its defenses. The ego defends itself against the drives of the id, the ego defends itself against the demands of the superego, the ego defends itself and its partners against the pressures of the external world, and so forth. Some defenses become fixed and others retain a certain flexibility or mutability. If one type of relation or defense dominates in a character organization, it can draw into its service the better part of a person's instinctual drives. To choose an obvious example: single-defense dominance can be seen in people whose chief character-trait is shyness, for they are one-time exhibitionists who have transformed themselves, turning a drive into its opposite through a defense known as reaction-formation. (The adolescent Sigmund Freud had called the resulting state "Hamlethood.")

Freud's maps of these four ways in which character can be considered—in relation to libidinal stages, mental sexual characteristics, narcissism, and psychic structures or defenses—evolved as his insights into clinical phenomena evolved. As he said in a 1916 essay called "Some Character-Types Met with in Psychoanalytic Work":

> When a doctor carries out a psychoanalytic treatment of a neurotic, his interest is by no means directed in the first instance to the patient's character. He would much rather know what the symptoms mean, what instinctual impulses are concealed behind them and are satisfied by them, and what course was followed by the mysterious path that has led from the instinctual wishes to the symptoms. But the technique which he is obliged to follow soon compels him to redirect his immediate curiosity towards other objectives. He observes that his investigation is threatened by resistances he may justly count as part of the latter's character. . . . What opposes the doctor's efforts is not always those traits of character which the patient recognizes in himself and which are attributed to him by people around him. Peculiarities in him which he had seemed to possess only to a modest degree are often brought to light in surprisingly increased intensity, or attitudes reveal themselves in him which had not been betrayed in other relations of life (14:311).

With the effect of making his complex characterology even more complex, that is, Freud offered the idea that much of a person's character may lie, like the proverbial iceberg, under the tip that is visible outside of the analytic situation.

Freud himself never tried to systematize the insights he had reached in the four dimensions of his work on character. Possibly Freud felt that systematic characterology was simply not feasible. This conclusion seems implied by his response to a system offered by his younger colleague, Paul Schilder, during a 1926 meeting of the Vienna Psychoanalytic Society, as reported by Robert Waelder in his *Basic Theory of Psychoanalysis*. Freud commented that, listening to Schilder, he felt like a sailor who has hugged the coast all his life and now watches others sailing out onto the open ocean. He wished Schilder well, but had no inclination to go with him: "I am an old hand at the coastal run, and I will keep faith with my blue inlet."

The blue inlets of characterology that Freud added to his run in the 1920s and 1930s were chiefly two. The first, growing out of the "mental sexual characteristics" line of thought, focused on feminine character, to which Freud dedicated many remarks in the first group of essays he dedicated specifically to female development (1925, 1931, and 1933). The second was national character, especially Jewish national character, which he considered in *Moses and Monotheism.* The connection between individual "deformities of character" and national ones was a topic toward which Freud had pointed in 1916 only to turn away: "Nor do I propose to go into the obvious analogy between deformities of character resulting from protracted sickness in childhood and the behavior of whole nations whose past history has been full of suffering" (14:315). But *Moses and Monotheism,* among its many other functions, was designed to elaborate just this theme.

Although Freud never went on an ocean voyage of characterology—and, in fact, left the four dimensions of his characterology uncoordinated, as he never reviewed them from the perspective of his late work—he did offer one typology in 1933, five years after Schilder's systematic paper. Freud's essay, just three dense pages long, is called "Libidinal Types," and it contains a reflection on the early libidinal-stage characterology in light of the structural theory. Although this very abstract, abbreviated synthetic effort leaves out major components of Freud's own characterology as I have just sketched it, "Libidinal Types" is, nonetheless, very suggestive, and I want to try to make a bridge between it and the character-ideal types that I have been sketching. The intricacies of the four dimensions of Freudian characterology will reappear in the next chapter to give this bridge developmental traffic.

ON LIBIDINAL TYPES AND CHARACTER-IDEALS

Freud suggested that there are three basic libidinal types: people who are dominated by their ids, whom he called "erotic," those dominated by their egos, called "narcissistic," and those dominated by their superegos, the "obsessional" type. People seldom come in such clear types, however. Much more common are combinatory types: erotic-obsessionals in whom the superego restricts the id's pursuit of pleasure; erotic-narcissists in whom id and ego pursuits are equally strong, or, one might say, locked in compromise; and narcissistic-obsessionals in whom ego and superego pursuits are complementary, with the ego's hand being strengthened by the complementarity.

Freud developed this scheme of libidinal types on the foundation of his structural theory and in the context of the ideas he published in *Civilization and its Discontents* (1930). In that book, Freud had noted the great diversity of ways in which civilized people seek pleasure or seek to avoid unpleasure, either looking to the external world for satisfactions or feeling that they must—and can—change the external world to suit their wishes.

> The man who is predominantly erotic will give first preference to his emotional relationships to other people; the narcissistic man, who inclines to be self-sufficient, will seek his main satisfactions in his internal mental processes; the man of action will never give up the external world on which he can try out his strength (21:83).

In this preliminary sketch of the traditional types known in the Aristotelian tradition as the hedonist, the contemplative, and the man of action, one of Freud's libidinal types, the obsessional, dominated by his superego, is obviously missing. The man of action is in his place. The scheme in "Libidinal Types" is based entirely on dominance by a psychic structure, not on reference to the external world. Freud seems to have come to think that desire to change the world can be found in each of the various types of characters, taking different forms. Some world-changers are revolutionary, some conservative; some act for love in the sense of bringing benefit to themselves, others in the sense of benefiting their worlds, and so forth.

Before he returned to the libidinal types in his little 1933 essay, Freud had also thought further about the self-sufficiency he attributed to the narcissist, who, he had claimed, finds satisfaction neither in being lovingly attached to the world nor in trying to act upon it. As he confessed in a footnote to the text in *Civilization and Its Discontents:* "We require to know what being essentially self-dependent signifies for the economics of the libido" (21:84). This must have been a question of very great personal importance to Freud, who often pointed out his own narcissism, and he worked his answer intricately into "Libidinal Types."

Libido is, he noted at the beginning of the essay, "predominantly allocated" to one of the "provinces of the mental apparatus." In erotics, it is allocated to the id; in narcissists, to the ego; and in obsessionals to the superego. "The pure types, marked by the undisputed preponderance of a single mental agency, seem to have a better chance of manifesting themselves as pure characterological pictures," Freud remarked. The erotic is the one for whom life is loving and especially being loved; and for whom the chief anxiety is loss of love. Of obsessionals, Freud writes:

> People of this type are dominated by fear of their conscience instead of fear of losing love. They exhibit, as it were, an internal instead of an external dependence. They develop a high degree of self-reliance; and, from the social standpoint, they are the true, pre-eminently conservative vehicles of civilization.

The action of the obsessional is not to bring novelty into the world, but to keep the world as it is. Changing the world has now become the lot of the narcissist, who in *Civilization and Its Discontents* had been presented as a contemplative. The narcissistic type is predominantly concerned with self-preservation, Freud says in "Libidinal Types":

> He is independent and not open to intimidation. His ego has a large amount of aggressiveness at its disposal, which also manifests itself in readiness for activity. In his erotic life loving is preferred to being loved. People of this type impress others as being "personalities"; they are especially suited to act as a support for others, to take on the role of leaders and to give a fresh stimulus to cultural development or to damage the established state of affairs.

While the obsessionals will be particularly valuable within a culture because they value the culture's attainments, the ideals that it has generated based on its glorious past achievements, narcissists are valuable as innovators. Or, to put the matter another way, using a remark Freud made in *The Future of an Illusion*, whatever cultural narcissism obsessionals have is satisfied by their pride in what has already been satisfactorily achieved, while the cultural narcissism of narcissists requires more challenge (21:13).

The evolution in Freud's typology between 1930 to 1933 is very revealing, and it seems to have stemmed from his ongoing self-analysis as conducted in the shocking cultural and political context of the Nazi takeover in Germany and Austria's peril. He came to feel that he had slighted the aggressiveness of people who take pleasure in their own mental processes—which aggression leads them to the world, to think of changing the world in a cultural or political way, and even to action. Freud, that is, had almost fallen into the self-blindness typical of intellectuals: they slight their own aggression—while they remark very stridently the aggression they see in others. Freud had corrected for this in the later versions of his own instinct theory, but it remained difficult for him to follow his own correction. He had also slighted the conservativism of men of cultural or political action, the extent to which they are— even as revolutionaries—restorers, regainers of a lost ideal past, people pulled upon by the past through the medium of their superegos, their internalizations. Mythologization of the past, the "Aryan" volkish past, was obvious among the revolutionary National Socialists. But the problem of the past had been as clear to Karl Marx as it was to those liberals who, like Freud, watched in horror the conservative anti-Communist revolution going on in Hitler's Germany. As Karl Marx said in his "Eighteenth Brumaire" about the French revolutionaries:

> Men make their own history, but they do not make it just as they please; they do not make it under circumstances chosen by themselves, but under circumstances directly found, given and transmitted from the past. The tradition of all the dead generations weighs like a nightmare on the brain of the living. And just when they seem engaged in revolutionizing themselves and things, in creating something entirely new, precisely in such epochs of revolutionary crisis they anxiously conjure up the spirits of the past to their service and borrow from them names, battle slogans and costumes in order to present the new scene of world-history in this time-honored disguise and this borrowed language.

Among the three libidinal types Freud noted (erotic, obsessional, and narcissistic) and among the three combinatory types (erotic-narcissistic, erotic-obsessional, and narcissistic-obsessional), it seems implied that the erotics are the least often creative as producers or originators of actions. The predominantly erotic types might very well, however, be political actors, thriving on the love coming to them from their comrades or their followers, and they would be well structured for performance-creativity. Acting in the theater or dancing or playing music—insofar as these activities are modalities of loving and being loved (or what Madame de Staël called "self-love *à deux*")—are the erotic's modes. Erotic expression in performance is especially alluring to women, for whom performing has been so much more permissible historically than product-oriented and action-originating creativity. (Freud would have put the stress the other way around and argued that women, so much more inclined to being loved than to loving, thrive on being the applauded actress, the worshipped diva, the all-providing mother or hostess, the belle of the ball, and fear loss of love as they fear loss of beauty, loss of being the center of attention.) Women of other character-types have also often used what might be called the art and politics of eroticism as their creative field because no other fields were open to them. Great creativity in domestic arts, home-making and people-managing has been theirs as much for social reasons as for characterological ones.

To say that more purely erotic types are not the ones dedicated to cultural conservative or revolutionary production does not mean, of course, that product-creativity involves no eroticism or has no debt to eroticism's power. In Freud's evolutionary terms, which express Freud's character-ideal of id-forces under ego-leadership, erotic energy is sublimated into artistic and other kinds of creativity. But others have conceived the relation of love and these kinds of creativity differently. Poets and philosophers of the most diverse sorts have echoed Empedocles of Acragas and informed us that *philia* and *neikos,* Love and Strife, move all things. Freud, too, invoked Empedocles as the father of the notion that a force leading to union (Eros) and a force leading to dissolution (the death instinct) rule all (23:245). Other theorists of love as a cosmic force have spoken not of how love can be sublimated or directed to aims other than erotic ones, but of how erotic are all aims. All aims serve Love in Empedocles' image of Love mixing fire, air, earth, and water to make a cosmic imitation of the Strifeless precosmic period when "Aphrodite was queen," when Love reigned unchallenged. The Greek's image, a blend of artisanal and political ingredients, is less well known than Shakespeare's, but perhaps was not unknown to Shakespeare—or, at least, to Ovid, Shakespeare's Roman Muse.

> Hail Sovereign Queen of secrets, who has power
> To call the fiercest Tyrant from his rage;
> And weep unto a girl; that hast the might
> Even with an eye-glance, to cloak Marsis Drum
> And turn th'allarm to whispers, that canst make
> A cripple flourish with his Crutch, and cure him

105

Before Apollo; that may'st force the King
To be his subjects' vassel, and induce
Stale gravity to daunce.

But whether a theorist holds—at the level of grand theory, at the cosmic level—that all aims are served by sublimations of love or that all aims serve love, it is still a common opinion that those whose lives are made of loving and being loved are not the creators. Political character-ideal types, like Freud, invoke images of civilization rising above, evolving beyond, the great dance of libido. But the common opinion when it is held by people of self-shaping character-ideal takes the form that Plato gave it in the *Symposium:* while the vast majority give themselves up to procreation, the elite few dedicate themselves to spiritual procreation, children of the soul. People of the self-shaping character-type who tend to the sexual variant of this type—that is, to images of themselves as spiritual procreators or (among men) male mothers—very often come to the conclusion that love and creative work are simply irreconcilable. So Yeats famously sang (in "The Choice"):

The intellect of man is forced to choose
Perfection of the life, or of the work.

The conclusion is often a near neighbor, too, to the idea that creative work only comes when love has been lost or proven unrequited. It is not only romantics who agree with Yeats (in "Meditations in a Time of Civil War") that:

. . . only an aching heart
Conceives a changeless work of art.

Among people of the spiritual self-stripping type, the opposition between love and creativity usually takes a different form. Love's distractions are emphasized; love pulls against the refined attentiveness that is desired by this type. Physical love is sometimes rejected, with vows of chastity or ascetic practice, but as often physical love is viewed as spiritually perfectible. In the volume called *First and Last Notebooks,* Simone Weil asked herself, for example, whether love could be defined as feeling "with one's whole self the existence of another being." She replied with a vision of loving purely, so that the beloved is indistinguishable from the cosmos, or so that the beloved is the lover's cosmos as the womb is all for an unborn (pre-sexual) child:

But only if there is no desire and, strictly speaking, no sensuous pleasure. Certainly it is not like that for anyone, so far as I know. . . . Joy, not pleasure. . . . Certainly this would be the only pure form of physical love. And it must be at least theoretically possible for physical love to be pure. . . .

To live within a universe which is [the beloved]. It is by chance (a providential chance) that this profound aspiration, which has its roots in infancy (gestation), coincides with the instinct called sexual—which is alien to love, except in so far as there is thought of children. That is why chastity is indispensable to love. It is outraged as soon as need and desire, even reciprocal, enter in.

This attitude toward physical love had as its corollary Weil's equation of creative use of the mind with "supernatural love."

The intelligence cannot control mystery itself, but it possesses perfectly the power of control over the roads leading to mystery, those that mount up and those that lead down again from it. Therefore it can recognize, while remaining absolutely loyal to itself, the existence within the soul of a faculty superior to itself and which conducts thought onto a higher plane than its own. This faculty is supernatural love.

As Simone Weil's writings indicate very starkly, a degree of obsessionality, which implies a strong superego that can translate into a strong self-organizing character-ideal figure, seems to be a prerequisite of creativity in producing and acting. But the combinatory types in which obsessionality figures are very different from the purer erotics.

In the scheme of pure and mixed libidinal types that Freud offered, Weil seems a nearly pure obsessional type, or one shading off toward narcissistic self-sufficiency. The contrast with an erotic-obsessional is apparent in the contrast between her religious asceticism, replete with ceremonies of self-criticism and self-purification, and the rites of submission to divine authority and comfort that Gerard Manley Hopkins engaged in to craft his rebellious self—or let God craft it—to his Christian vocation. He writes in his "Carrion Comfort" series of the Patience ("it" in the first line below) needed:

We hear our hearts grate on themselves: it kills
To bruise them dearer. Yet the rebellious wills
Of us we do bid God bend to him even so. . . .
Soul, self; come, poor Jackself, I do advise

107

You, jaded, let be; call off thoughts awhile
Elsewhere; leave comfort root-room; let joy size
At God knows when to God knows what; whose smile
's not wrung, see you; unforseen times rather—as skies
Betweenpie mountains—lights a lovely smile.

By contrast with both pure obsessionals and erotic-obsessionals, obsessionals closer to narcissism take more pleasure in their mental processes. They do not flagellate themselves as Weil did or write of themselves as Hopkins did (in the same series of poems), "I am gall, I am
heartburn." Such narcissistic-obsessionals are much more likely to say
that they have lived to think or feel in their medium, such is their
vocation, and their thoughts or feelings have evolved naturally and
exuberantly or in bursts, spurts—not without pain, certainly, but also
not in the medium of pain. Each detail of their work has a meaning to
them as a contributor in the overarching thrust of their ideas, in their
great *esprit de système,* even if they cannot at any moment say what the
meaning is. Thus two statements from *Picasso on Art,* which might,
without a sense of the narcissistic and obsessional elements of character
uniting them, look contradictory:

> Basically I am perhaps a painter without style. Style is often something that
> locks a painter into the same vision, the same technique, the same formula
> during years and years, sometimes during one's whole lifetime. One recog-
> nizes it immediately, but it's always the same suit, or the same cut of the
> suit. There are, nevertheless, great painters with style. I myself thrash
> around too much, move too much. You see me here and yet I'm already
> changed, I'm already elsewhere. I'm never fixed and that's why I have no
> style.
>
> Why do you think I date everything I do? Because it is not sufficient to
> know an artist's works—it is also necessary to know when he did them,
> why, how, under what circumstances. . . . Some day there will undoubtedly
> be a science—it may be called the science of man—which will seek to know
> more about man in general through the study of the creative man. I often
> think about such a science, and I want to leave to posterity a documentation
> that will be as complete as possible. That's why I put a date on everything
> I do.

If Freud's libidinal types were translated into a diagram, they would
configure in these ways:

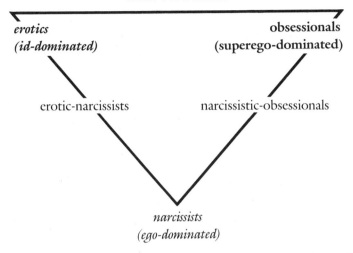

Libidinal Types

erotic-obsessionals

erotics
(id-dominated)   **obsessionals**
                                    (superego-dominated)

erotic-narcissists   narcissistic-obsessionals

narcissists
(ego-dominated)

The character-ideal types that I have tried to outline and then call up again quickly with quotations from Weil, Hopkins, and Picasso, correlate to parts of this scheme. The artisanal character-ideal is typical, I think, of erotic-obsessionals; the spiritual character-ideal is typical of obsessionals shading off in the direction of narcissism; and the political character-ideal is typical of narcissists shading off in the direction of obsessionality. Thus, for simplicity's sake:

ARTISANAL CHARACTER-IDEAL
erotic-obsessionals

erotics
(id-dominated)   **obsessionals**
                                    (superego-dominated)

                                        spiritual
                                        character-ideal

erotic-narcissists   narcissistic-obsessionals

                                        political
                                        character-ideal

narcissists
(ego-dominated)

Those who are governed by an artisanal or self-shaping character-ideal are people in whom, as Freud said of erotic-obsessionals, "the preponderance of instinctual life is restricted by the influence of the superego," not by the seat of narcissism, the ego. Such erotic-obsessionals are both dependent on their present love-objects and still dependent on earlier parental and authority figures identified with or internalized to make up the super-ego. Among the British esthetes, the erotic's fear of loss of love and the obsessional's fear of conscience, the voice of the predominantly paternal superego, were typically in vibrant equipoise. Also in equipoise were their early mother-love and their father-love retained in a balance manifest in either bisexual or homosexual object preferences. The split in their character-ideals—the expression of these ideals in either artisanal or sexual terms—means, in effect, that they follow their self-creating ideal in either a masculine or a feminine mode, actively begetting or passively giving birth (as what Nietzsche called a "male mother"). They are examples of what the analyst Lawrence Kubie called "the desire to be both sexes" (although Kubie puritanically tended to see this desire as inevitably pathological or pathogenic, rather than as a desire that can, like any other, turn pathological or be pathogenic).

Freud seems to have viewed himself as a person of the narcissistic-obsessional type. His description of the type contains a clue, also, to why his structural theory, with its notion of the ego-ideal or superego, took so long to supplant his earlier theoretical scheme featuring a two-party battle between id and ego:

> There is no tension between ego and superego (indeed, on the strength of this type one would scarcely have arrived at the hypothesis of a superego), and there is no preponderance of erotic needs.

This type is the one, he said, "which is most valuable from a cultural standpoint; for it adds to independence of the external world and a regard for the demands of conscience a capacity for vigorous action, and it strengthens the ego against the superego." In males, and less frequently in females, this is a type made for sweeping originality and leadership, and for having (in my terms) a political character-ideal.

As indicated, I think that the political character-ideal is associated with the narcissistic-obsessional libidinal type weighted, so to speak, toward its narcissistic component, or closer to the pure narcissistic type. The spiritual character-ideal, on the other hand, is associated with the

narcissistic-obsessional type weighted toward its obsessional component, closer to the pure obsessional type.

In females, it seems to me, the narcissistic-obsessional libidinal type
often underlies a spiritual divestment character-ideal in which the central
figure, the essential self, is felt to be masculine. Among the women
sketched in the last chapter, this was certainly the case for Simone
Weil and Anna Freud, and most likely the case for Gertrude Stein and
Marguerite Yourcenar. A woman whose creativity is bound up with an
ideal in which the self is stripped of materiality or erotic wishes or
differentiations of any sort often has in her development a crucial,
determinative identification with a male figure—often her father—who
is allowed command over her female body with the help of the character-
ideal. She may imagine herself divested of feminine physical desire, and
to at least some extent desexualized, asceticized; or she may actively
divest herself, in Simone Weil's manner; or she may imagine that she
was born with very little desire. It seems to me that when this libidinal
type and character-ideal combine in highly creative women—as I think
they very often do—they are peculiarly difficult for both men and
women of other types to understand: they are unexpected, beyond a
certain conventional sexual pale, beyond even the point where concepts
like homosexual, trans-sexual, and transvestite are meaningful, and thus
they are seldom the subjects of good biographical study.

In males, the central figure in the spiritual divestment character-ideal
is often female, and also often maternal. She cares for the self, comforts
it—as Proust imagined a dying mother caring for her child—by protecting it from the distractions and pollutions and temptations of the
world. The man of spiritual character-ideal is as difficult to comprehend
as his female counterpart, but he is often even more aggressively critical
than she of the world that others hold dear. The *contemptus mundi* of
philosophers and spiritual adepts is only reverenced or admired by
worldly people to the point where they find that they themselves are
encompassed by the attitude of rejection—and that they cannot imitate
it. From the point of view of the spiritually disciplined one, the incom-
prehension of others makes perfect sense, as the Russian spiritual teacher
Father Yelchaininov said plainly and typically:

> Nervousness is in a certain sense the psycho-physical condition of holi-
> ness; a refined body—transformed by tears, fasting, sickness, work—be-
> comes more susceptible to the influence of beneficent spiritual forces. But

at the same time it grows morbidly sensitive to the world of gross material objects, and its reaction toward this world is nervousness.

A saint, minus his saintliness, is a neurotic. (Striking words of a doctor who had visited Mount Athos: "Well, they are all neurasthenic in there.")

The saint who has fallen and lost his sanctity becomes an easy prey to demons; this is why the Fathers of the Church assert that the condition of one who has drifted from spiritual discipline is more dangerous than that of an unspiritual person. Here is the danger of fasting, asceticism, when not regulated by an experienced director and when emptied of the content of prayer.

In general, people have trouble understanding libidinal and character-types other than their own, and this trouble constitutes that danger for biographers that Jean Paul Richter captured in an aphorism: "A man never reveals his character more vividly than when portraying the character of another." This is a bookish danger, however, in comparison to what happens when people set out not just to portray another type but to model themselves on another type. Dr. Johnson, who was so expert (as we shall see further below) in matters of *mauvaise foi,* offered the corresponding aphorism: "Almost all absurdity of conduct arises from the imitation of those whom we cannot resemble."

Usually, people of one character-type view all other types as simply "the other," the opposite, often by assimilating them to their own negative character-ideal. The rare spiritual type provides striking examples of misunderstanding, but the most common sort of misunderstanding and disparagement is of erotics by culturally creative types. When these creative ones are male, they very often come to the conclusion that the majority of the erotic population is female. "As the faculty of writing has been chiefly a masculine endowment," Dr. Johnson noted, "the reproach of making the world miserable has been always thrown upon the women." Spiritualists like Father Yelchaininov are ready with the other-worldly equivalent:

> Woman has been called a "vessel of infirmity." This "infirmity" consists especially in her enslavement to the natural, elementary forces within and outside herself. Result: inadequate self-control, irresponsibility, passion, blind judgments. Scarcely any woman is free of the latter; she is always the slave of her passions, of her dislikes, her desires. In Christianity alone does woman become man's equal, for then she submits her temperament to higher principles and develops sound judgment, patience, logic, wisdom. Only then does friendship with the husband become possible.

A more complex case arises when a person turns his own character-ideal inside-out as he creates his opposite group, his "other." The Spanish philosopher Ortega y Gasset, for example, was a man of the character-ideal type I have called artisanal or self-shaping, and this is how he constructed his opposite:

> The woman possesses a theatrical exterior and a circumspect interior, while in the man it is the interior that is theatrical. The woman goes to the theatre; the man carries it inside himself and is the impresario of his own life.

Another limit of understanding is suggested by Freud's struggle to keep his own libidinal type clearly in his scheme of libidinal types. I think it is very rare for people to understand their own libidinal-character type economically (that is, in terms of what truly gives them pleasure), though they may understand it very well in other dimensions. "Not all those who know their minds know their hearts as well," is how La Rochefoucauld expressed this problem. The unknown heart marks their limit as biographers, or psychologists, of people of their own type, too.

Chapter Six

Developmental Stories

PRELIMINARY ORIENTATIONS: SYMBOLS, BEHAVIORS, EGO MECHANISMS

To point toward libidinal types as correlatives of character-ideal types is to open a door—certainly not the only one—on the much more complex question of how libidinal and character types develop. Characterology after Freud has a labyrinthine quality to it, as I noted before, both because Freud pointed to so many dimensions of character and because he did not try to relate those dimensions systematically. His most general schematization, the three libidinal types, does not have a developmental base: he speaks in terms of mental structures—id, ego, and superego—dominating, interacting, but he does not relate the different types of dominance to his theory of libidinal stages or to the classification of people by mental sexual characteristics ("masculinity" and "femininity"). The libidinal types scheme does overlap with his distinction between narcissistic and non-narcissistic characters, but Freud never did explore in any detail how the narcissistic or ego-dominated character is formed.

I want to continue looking for ways to discuss developmentally the libidinal types, and also the correlations that I am proposing of libidinal types and character-ideal types. One such way is to recapitulate over this particular developmental topic the historical layers of Freud's characterology, which extend from the simple to the complex. There are few libidinal stages, and their sequence is usually quite regular, just as there are few instincts (Freud said two, erotic and aggressive) and few component instincts (Freud noted two pairs and a derivative in the phallic stage: love of looking and exhibitionism, sadism and masochism, and then an instinct for research or curiosity). There are two poles of mental sexual characteristics, "masculine" and "feminine," as there are two basic libido positions, self-directed and other directed. On the other hand, the number of defenses (Anna Freud said ten, others have extended the list) and the variety and possible combinations of defenses and sorts of superego formations are very great. The instincts and their stages are what we all share, in varying degrees; it is the differences in ego and superego development in relation to those stages that are responsible for human variety and character differentiation.

How a person becomes a particular libidinal type or combinatory type, the story of his or her libidinal and then character formation, will be very complex. Perhaps complex beyond the reaches of an analysis, much less a biography. But the story may be approachable by a simple strategy: locating which associations of instinctual strivings or wishes and ego mechanisms seem to be typical of the person. And this strategy can be helped considerably by the fact that certain associations of instinctual wishes and ego mechanisms appear frequently and are recognizable outside of an analytic context. Using primarily work done by Anna Freud and her associates at the Hampstead Clinic in London, I am going to make a brief catalogue of such frequent associations. (Anna Freud's *Writings,* my main source, will be cited below by volume and page.) In my catalogue, I will pay particular attention to associations involving the ego mechanism Freudians call sublimation. Within the Freudian scheme, this association should be a key one—singly or in combination with others—sustaining creativity. In Chapter 8 I will turn to theories of creativity that do not focus on the sublimation concept.

There are basically three different ways in which associations between id or instinctual strivings and ego are manifest. The first is a group of common symbols or translations of unconscious content into dreams and other symbol systems, like works of art. The most universal of these are male or phallic symbols (snakes, pens, weapons, etc.); female symbols (all kinds of enclosed spaces or interiors, from rooms to bottles); symbols of sexual intercourse, like flying, mounting stairs; symbols of siblings or small children, like little animals, insects; and parental symbols, like kings and queens. If such symbols recur in creative work, they can be clues to a creative person's preoccupations. But they should not be treated like elements of a code that can be deciphered to provide immediate access to the unconscious, as they often were in the early days of psychoanalytically inspired literary and art criticism. Interpreted as code elements, without their contexts—in dream interpretation, without the dreamer's free associations, for example—symbols usually say more about interpreters than about what they purport to interpret. The painter Georgia O'Keeffe, who was often treated as though she were an illustrator specializing in genitalia, was certainly justified in complaining through an exhibition catalogue statement:

> Well—I made you take time to look at what I saw and when you took time to really notice my flower you hung all your associations with flowers on my flower and you write about my flower as if I think and see what you think and see of the flower—and I don't.

Second, regular associations of id and ego are manifest in behaviors, attitudes, and symptoms. Typical behaviors regularly signal a single unconscious or instinctual configuration in children, while in adults such pictures becomes tangled with additional elements. Anna Freud offered a list based on her work with children: "character trends such as ambition (based on urethral urges), undue interest in the misfortunes of others (repressed aggression), buffoonery (based on a specific fate of the phallic urges); behavior symptoms such as homesickness (based on ambivalence toward the parents), boredom (rooted in masturbation conflicts), oversensitiveness to 'bad treatment' by other children, colleagues, etc. (warding off passive trends), vegetarianism as a food fad (repression of oral sadism) . . . " (4:137). Certain anxieties and fears are regularly correlated with symbols or symbolic actions: fears stemming from the very early period when children are quite defenseless and completely dependent, for example, are associated with darkness, noise, strangers, solitude; separation anxiety is associated with annihilation, starvation, loneliness; fear of loss of love with punishment, rejection, desertion, earthquakes, thunderstorms, death, etc; castration anxiety with operations, mutilation, doctors, dentists, illness, poverty, robbers, witches, ghosts, etc. (7:176).

Such specific associations of id and ego in the medium of behaviors, symptoms, and symbols are clues. They cannot, in and of themselves, provide anything more than directions for investigation of a developmental story. But the characteristics of the buffoon (or imposter) and the bored man might well, for example, set off an inquiry into the life of Charles Baudelaire, whose famous prologue poem to *Fleurs du mal* celebrates *ennui,* and whose draft for a preface addressed to scandalized critics reads in part:

> But I have one of those happy characters that takes pleasure in hatred and glories in scorn. My diabolical taste for the ridiculous permits me to take peculiar pleasure in the travesties of slander. Chaste as a blank sheet of paper, sober as water, prone to devotion as a young girl at communion, harmless as a sacrificial lamb, it does not displease me to pass for a debauchee, a drunkard, a blasphemer and an assassin.

The third kind of association is as much richer and more informative as it is more difficult to interpret than the first two. The erotic and aggressive strivings of a particular stage link with a particular range—not the full range—of ego mechanisms. The earlier stages link with fewer mechanisms, that is, than the later ones do. By the time a child is fully in the Oedipal period, the full range of ego mechanisms is available, and any child's development will be completely unique to that child.

In the beginning, or near the beginning, of a child's life, oral greed or aggressiveness becomes apparent, and the mother's breast (or the milk she supplies) is the chief object. Oral greed and aggression are typically associated in the early childhood oral stage with the mechanism of projection. If this association is particularly strong, and a child regularly projects its greed and aggression onto others, who are experienced as aggressors, then the child may develop into an adult who always finds the environment hostile. (Melanie Klein would call this kind of projection typical of the "paranoid-schizoid" position all children pass through in the first six months of their lives, and she noted a degree of paranoia as characteristic of a person who never gets over the effects of this position.) To such adults, people seem unreliable, discriminatory, persecutory, bent on theft or swindle. But not all children project their oral aggression. Some repress it. Some build up the defenses called "reaction formations" against it, so that they are characterized by their unaggressiveness, their self-deprivation, lack of demandingness, meekness, asceticism. Others displace their oral aggressiveness onto types of food, drugs or cigarettes, kissing. And some sublimate the aggressiveness, seeking not food but—say—knowledge or success. They are hungry for learning, for books; they have an insatiable appetite for praise (4:132). The creativity that is derived from sublimated oral aggression is restless, voracious in use of materials (and possibly other people), and full of clamoring (to others or in fantasy) for appreciation.

Between the ages of one or one and a half and three and a half, children's anal-sadistic libidinal and aggressive urges are dealt with by three basic ego mechanisms: repression, reaction formation, and sublimation. When children are intolerantly handled and cleanliness is forced on them too early and too quickly, repression is the result. If repression is unsuccessful, the child resorts (unconsciously) to reaction-formations. He or she acts disgusted at all kinds of dirt, passionate about order, precise about time, possessions and money, and stubborn about instructions from others. Aggressions are held in check and attitudes of moral righteousness and sympathy for suffering people and animals develop. The obsessive or anal character emerges to exercise control over an assertive, messy, chaotic earlier little person, and a particular configuration of traits often appears: "People with obsessional characters are well known to displace the reaction formations against their hostile impulses and death wishes from human beings to material things, thereby becoming unable to discard anything, down to the most valueless, useless and superfluous matters" (4:306). But sublimation of the anal-sadistic erotic and aggressive urges, which is permitted by more tolerant handling, will produce instead a child who, for example, loves to play with sand, water, clay, paints, and the possibility of an adult whose creative media are extensions of these. Halfway between these possibilities are those creative players with their hands who also cannot discard anything, who keep a studio full of stuff—or keep acquiring studios for their constantly proliferating stuff.

The sexual curiosity so pronounced in most children during the phallic stage can combine with any number of ego mechanisms. It may lead, in Anna Freud's words, "with equal probability, to the perversion of scopophilia (when regressed to in later life), to pseudodebility (when severely repressed), to discreetness or indifference toward other people's affairs (when held down by reaction formations), to intellectual alertness and the attitude of the scientific investigator (when sublimated)" (4:133). Anna Freud left the last possibility unexplored in this statement, but we can turn for elaboration to Freud's remarks, in the Leonardo biography (11:79), about the "three distinct possible vicissitudes" open to children's phallic or sexual curiosity after it begins to be checked by internal and external repression in latency. The first possibility Freud sketches is inhibition, which covers the paths Anna Freud designated with "pseudodebility" (mental retardation without physical cause) and discreetness due to reaction-formations. Both the Freuds agreed with a statement Sigmund Freud jotted down late in his life: "The ultimate ground of all intellectual inhibitions and all inhibitions of work seems to be the inhibition of masturbation in childhood" (23:300).

The second two possibilities Freud noted produce two very different types of intellectual alertness. One, "compulsive brooding," seems to me to offer insight into the question Freud raised in *Civilization and Its Discontents* and "Libidinal Types" about the narcissist's pleasure in mental processes; the other, which Freud attributed to Leonardo, is sublimation strictly speaking. This is Freud's description of the three modes—inhibition, compulsive brooding, and the rarer form of sublimation proper:

> In the first of these, research shares the fate of sexuality; thenceforward curiosity remains inhibited and the free activity of intelligence may be limited for the whole of the subject's lifetime, especially as shortly after this the powerful religious inhibition of thought is brought into play by education. This is the type characterized by neurotic inhibition. . . . In a second type the intellectual development is sufficiently strong to resist the sexual repression which has hold of it. Sometime after the infantile sexual researches have come to an end, the intelligence, having grown stronger, recalls the old association and offers it help in evading sexual repression, and the suppressed sexual activities of research return from the unconscious in the form of compulsive brooding, naturally in a distorted and unfree form, but sufficiently powerful to sexualize thinking itself and to color intellectual operations with the pleasure and anxiety that belongs to sexual processes proper. Here investigation becomes a sexual activity, often the exclusive one, and the feeling that comes from settling things in one's mind and explaining them replaces sexual satisfaction; but the interminable character of the child's researches is also repeated in the fact that this brooding never ends and that the

intellectual feeling, so much desired, of having found a solution recedes more and more into the distance.

In virtue of a special disposition, the third type, which is the rarest and most perfect, escapes both inhibition of thought and neurotic compulsive thinking. It is true that here too sexual repression comes about, but it does not succeed in relegating a component instinct of sexual desire to the unconscious. Instead, the libido evades the fate of repression by being sublimated from the very beginning into curiosity and by becoming attached to the powerful instinct for research as a reinforcement. Here, too, the research becomes to some extent compulsive and a substitute for sexual activity; but owing to the complete difference in the underlying psychical process (sublimation instead of an irruption from the unconscious) the quality of neurosis is absent; there is no attachment to the original complexes of infantile sexual research, and the instinct can operate freely in the service of intellectual interest. Sexual repression, which has made the instinct so strong through the addition to it of sublimated libido, is still taken into account by the instinct, in that it avoids any concern with sexual themes (11:79–80).

In the nonpsychoanalytic literature on creativity, curiosity is often presented as one of the key elements—sometimes the key element—of creativity. But this is much too simple, because, as this last series of developmental paradigms indicates clearly, there is a type of curiosity specific to each libidinal stage. The person characterized by oral aggressivity will search out sources of nutrition—in the broadest sense of the word: search out things to use, people to draw from or attach to, audiences to be praised by. The curiosity is incorporative. The person characterized by anal sadism is task-oriented, wanting to solve problems, get things organized, make arrangements, and find all the best ways to do these things—for good or for ill, for hurting or for saving the world, depending upon the strength of his or her reaction-formations or the environmental moral standards. Organizational and strategic genius can be in the service, unfortunately, of anything; if kept away from the socio-political realm, as it is by those who put it to work on productive arts, it is safer. Sexual curiosity and its derivatives are mystery-solving, investigative, going behind the appearances of things (or the curtains drawn in front of things not for children) to the truth, transcending particulars to find general rules, exposing secrets to show what is really going on.

A SECOND ORIENTATION: CHARACTER PATHOLOGIES

The developmental indications given by symbols, regular associations of id and ego represented in behaviors or symptoms, and typical associations of libidinal stages and defenses (including sublimation) can be read together with another approach to characterology. In the psychoanalytic literature after Freud, there are many rich efforts to delineate specific character-types on a libidinal stage base, but with careful attention to developing object-relations and to ego and superego development. The emphasis in these portraits is usually on character pathology, but character pathology is viewed as an intensification or extreme of a normal character. Oral characters, for example, are associated with the pathological type "hysterical characters"; anal characters with the pathological type "obsessional characters" (sometimes called compulsive characters); and the urethral-phallic character with the pathological type "narcissistic characters." The last association is confusing on two separate counts. First, it is obviously designed for males, and takes females into account only insofar as they have a "masculinity complex"—it is, in Ernest Jones's term, phallocentric. Second, it implies that narcissism is a pathological state in and of itself, like hysteria or obsessional neurosis. But there is a degree of narcissism in everyone, and narcissism in an unhealthy degree characterizes a type of neurosis and a character disorder quite different from hysteria and obsessional neurosis. The latter two are known by psychoanalysts as "transference neuroses" because they involve an unconscious transference of love and aggression from one early love object to a later one and because such a transference is repeated in the analysand's relation to the analyst. A "narcissistic neurosis," on the other hand, was thought by Freud to preclude transferences, because narcissistic self-love and love of others were taken to be strictly opposite, exclusive. Psychoanalytic theory of narcissism has changed considerably since Freud's day, however, and no discussion of "narcissistic character" can ignore the revisions.

I am going to review briefly this psychoanalytic characterology literature, character-type by character-type and also historically, focusing particularly on what is relevant in it to study of creativity. Another grid of concepts will, then, fit to what has been built up: the relationships between libidinal types and character-ideal types that have been suggested will link to character-types and character pathologies. Something like this:

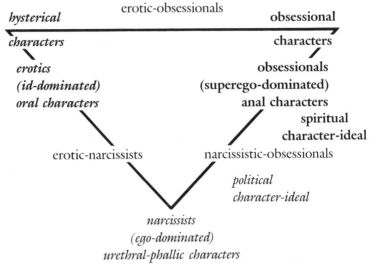

The first of Freud's colleagues to focus his attention on oral characters was Karl Abraham. Abraham suggested that the infant's oral period is subdivided into two phases, a preliminary one of passive sucking, and a second of more active biting, or of "oral cannibalism," comparable to the more active anal phase of "anal sadism." Different oral traits, Abraham argued, flow from the two phases. But it is not clear just how this transformation or sublimation of orality into oral traits comes about, or how these early events are related to the infant's evolution into a child with an ego, a sense of the world exterior to itself, defenses.

Abraham's work, particularly "The Influence of Oral Erotism on Character Formation" (1925), was published just as Freud was making his preliminary communications about "the structural theory" and as child analysts were adding their insights into "the pre-Oedipal period." The same historical moment is reflected in the other important early contribution on the topic, the English analyst Edward Glover's "Notes on Oral Character Formation" (1924). But Glover lived longer and came to understand clearly, as he said in a retrospective on his early work, that psychoanalytic characterology needed "radical revision" because its base, the correlation of one libidinal phase or subphase predominance to one character-type, was too simple, too divorced from any sense of ego mechanisms. The problem is immediately apparent in Glover's 1924 description of how a person of oral character would probably appear:

> One would expect to find, either in positive or negative form, the character-istics of omnipotence, ambivalence in object relations, sensitiveness in regard to "getting" and to the maternal function of the environment, quick emotional discharge, alteration of mood and rapid motor reactions [of dashing things to the ground, scratching, stamping when frustrated], to-gether with character traits associated with viewing, touching, smelling, etc.

The vagueness of this description, which contains so many elements that can be analyzed differently or attributed to other character-types, is dissipated somewhat when Glover turns to details, for example, when he says concretely what he means by the phrase "in positive or negative form." The omnipotence of people who were, as infants, orally gratified is a kind of excessive optimism and an expectation that a source of gratification is always going to be at hand—and expectation that does little to foster hard work. On the other hand, the omnipotence of the once dissatisfied is a kind of pessimism, often depressed and withdrawn, in which expectations are always being disappointed through someone else's fault. This is the oral aggressivity that Anna Freud presented as externalized through the mechanism of projection, and Glover notes that Freud himself once called the attitude "eternal suckling." Alternations between optimism and pessimism are common among oral characters, and can resemble manic-depression, which many analysts think also has oral stage roots: "As a matter of fact, those who study patients with strong oral interests cannot fail to be struck by the labile nature of their moods. They are sanguine and optimistic and moody and depressed in turn; if anything, an easy relapse into pessimistic depression is more often noticeable."

The relationships psychoanalysts have delineated between oral charac-ters and hysterical character disorders have depended upon how they construed the relationships between oral preoccupations and repression of genital sexuality. Sandor Ferenczi put in a nutshell the basic insight from Freud about hysterics by claiming that they "genitalize" everything, that is, they are fixated on the genital stage of development with its incestuous Oedipal loves. They both find those loves everywhere and have to work ceaselessly to repress them. Their bodies are their battle-grounds, the sites of their conflicts, and parts of their bodies or their entire postures and comportments are full of sexual tension, often—without intention or awareness—in sexually provocative or flirtatious modes. However, the hysterical character's genitalizing was noted before much attention was paid by psychoanalysts to the infantile era known as "pre-Oedipal," and the oral preoccupations of hysterics were, thus, interpreted as displacements of genital desires upward to the oral region (as Freud argued in the "Dora" case, published in 1905) or as products of unconscious equations of mouth and female genital. Eating disorders, so common among hysterics, were viewed as rejections of genital sexuality (and the possibility of pregnancy) in the medium, so to speak, of the mouth, which may be fantasized as the organ for becoming pregnant. On the basis of this view of the hysteric (and writing with a powerful tendency to idealize genital sexuality as the *sine qua non* of health), Freud's younger colleague Wilhelm Reich wrote in his 1933 book *Character Analysis:*

> The hysterical character has little tendency to sublimation and intellectual achievement and a much lesser tendency to reaction formations than other character types. This is also due to the fact that the libido is neither discharged in sexual gratification, which would reduce the hypersexuality, nor do the sexual energies become extensively anchored in character; rather, they are discharged in somatic innervations or in anxiety or in apprehensiveness. The mechanisms of hysteria are often used to prove the alleged antithesis of sexuality and social achievement. What is overlooked is the fact that the outspoken inability to sublimate is a result precisely of the sexual inhibition in the presence of genital libido, and the fact that only the establishment of the capacity for gratification liberates social interest and achievement.

Later work on hysteria and hysterical characters points to a more important, less derivative, role for orality. Significant fixation in the pre-Oedipal oral stage (or regular regression to it) is now more often interpreted as signaling a child's failure to separate from its mother, either because she is too available or because she is not available enough to the infant (as Glover noted in speaking of oral optimists and pessimists). Sexual behavior, then, is viewed as the medium through which oral needs are expressed. The hysteric does not so much repress his or her genital sexuality as refuse it in order to stay an infant, or use it to solicit love which, if forthcoming, the hysteric cannot accept on the genital level. Even if the relationship between orality and genitality in hysteria is reinterpreted in this way, however, Reich's remarks about how uncommon sublimation is among hysterical characters are certainly relevant: love-searching and not work is the hysterical character's main occupation and medium of gratification, as we noted before of the pure erotic libidinal type.

In the terms that I proposed before, oral characters do not formulate a character-ideal, unless they are of a mixed type, intermixed with obsessional or narcissistic elements. In the libidinal type Freud called erotic-obsessionals, for example, there are often oral character-features, and these are apparent in the swings of mood common to the type. (We will consider later the possibility that the psychotic extreme of the oral or hysterical character is the manic-depressive.) Not particular hysterical symptoms, but an entire way of life can be full of swings, which a mixture of obsessionality is meant to check. Such hysterical characters with an admixture of obsessionality tend to play at life, starting things and working compulsively but not finishing them, being very excited and organized and then falling into a lethargy, moving from one relationship to another, one project to another, as if at a smorgasbord, often needing strong others—lovers, teachers, partners, employers, directors, commanders—to stay in place or carry anything through. The work that hysterical characters do take up is sexually charged, and they behave toward it with the inhibitions characteristic of their mode of love. They are drawn toward work—like acting—that requires assuming a part, playing a role, but which is full of change, traffic, excitement. The emphasis that the somewhat obsessional hysteric puts on shaping herself or himself, even to the point of the anorexic's dangerous body-shaping through self-starvation or the muscle-man's rigid regimes, can merge into the self-shaping character-ideal of the erotic-obsessive libidinal type. This is Richard Ellmann in his recent biography of Oscar Wilde, for example, describing Wilde as he was trying to write his *Picture of Dorian Gray* (a literary character who is himself a male hysteric):

> There was a long brooding before *Dorian Gray* came into being. Wilde had been much concerned with images. He had painted self-portrait after self-portrait: at Trinity he experimented with a beard, then shaved it off; he let his hair grow long at Oxford and had it waved, then in Paris had it cut and curled Roman-style, then let it grow long again. His clothing also passed

through transformations: dandiacal in London, it became outré in America, elaborately decorous afterwards. No wonder he spoke often about poses and masks. "The first duty of life is to assume a pose," he said; "what the second duty is no one has yet found out."

The book that Wilde wrote gave him trouble for a reason that is connected to his love of display, of pose, of winning attention with his presence and his lovely voice, his oral instrument of seduction. "I am afraid," he said of the book, "it is rather like my own life—all conversation and no action. I can't describe action, my people sit in chairs and chatter."

In the psychoanalytic literature on the anal character, the most important early contributions came from Karl Abraham, again, and Ernest Jones. Jones's well-known essay "Anal Erotic Character Traits," was published in 1918, and it suffers from the same problem Glover had noted about his work on oral character—an unproblematized relation between libidinal phase dominance and character-traits. But the essay does contain a very significant refinement of the touchstone description of the anal character offered by Freud. Jones noted that interest in the process of defecation seems to give rise to a different set of character-traits than interest in the products of defecation. Obstinacy, for example, is characteristic of those who once put a great deal of emphasis on controlling their bowels, retaining and eliminating feces at their own pleasure or to provoke parental reactions. Orderliness relates more to a child's attitude toward his or her feces. The two types of anal traits, Jones was quick to add, are not clearly demarcated—parsimony seems to stem from both sources—and they may blend into one another—as orderliness can turn into obstinant orderliness.

Inveterate retainers of their bowels may be characterized later by their brooding procrastination and their tendency, at the last possible moment, to fling themselves into a pleasurable eruption of rapid work, during which they will suffer no distractions. People may lean so far to the one side or to the other of this pattern that they cannot overcome their procrastination or are "burned up" by their plunges into last-minute productivity. Very few people have a capacity like Samuel Johnson's for putting things off and then being able to lock themselves in a room and write twelve thousand words in a day. Few, also, consider that the most important thing for a young writer to learn is, as Johnson said, to compose as quickly as possible, for "it is so much more difficult to improve in speed than in accuracy."

Thoroughness and persistency are the bowel controller's intellectual characteristics, which may be admirably displayed in the quality of their work, but which may also make them pedantic, boorishly unable to tolerate others' views, to delegate responsibility, or to acknowledge that anyone other than themselves can do their task. Jones notes that tasks to which there is an "ought," a sense of duty, attached are particularly likely to be drawn into this type of anal character's typical pattern of procrastination followed by feverish work: moral tasks, organizing tasks like housework which involve "waste products" or money, obligatory letter writing. The feverish work must, in turn, be done perfectly, and intense attention is given to all matters of justice, fairness, correct distribution of time and money connected with the work, verbal precision or logic-chopping. Sometimes, as a commentator on Jones's work, Bertram Lewin, once observed, the feverish work has itself to be "clean," as in the kind of "clean thinking" that is undertaken by those who cannot bear the concrete, who must stay in realms of semantic dispute, statistical purity, and abstraction. They avoid messy life by putting epistemological and methodological problems to themselves (How do we know that we know? What is verifiability?) so that they cannot chance upon an emotion. Dissociation of ideas from affects is the typical intellectual mode. For such perfect and perfectly clean work to take place, everything must be perfect, just right, just so—the mood for work, the environment and atmosphere for living, the conditions of production. Injustices, like interruptions during periods of intense work, may provoke violent, sadistic reactions in this obsessive type, either of the constantly irritated sort or of the temper tantrum sort.

People who focus their unconscious attention on fecal products and their symbols—certain kinds of food, all kinds of waste products, secretions, dead bodies, refuse, money—either value these things as they did their feces in childhood, or operate from a reversal of valuation, substituting repulsion for pleasure. The two phases of concern for defecation that Jones noted, retention and explosive production, influence attention to products, which may manifest itself as refusal to give and desire to gather and hoard, or, on the other hand, extreme generosity, extravagance. It is the second manifestation that can be sublimated into love of smearing or moulding and playing with material things, and also love of imprinting a personality on things, making an impression, manipulating loved ones.

Jones does not suggest it, but it may be that the most creative of anal characters are those who relish both the process and the product of their work, and who, quite specifically, enjoy quick, bold discharge of work that is on issue nearly perfect or easily perfectable. Such types avoid the boorishness of a prolonged creation period after a period of retentive brooding. In this passage from *Broswell's Journal of a Tour to the Hebrides*, Dr. Johnson speaks of the "power" of quick production and the "judgment" in quick revision, which might, extrapolating from the previous quotation, also be called speed and accuracy. The discussion is about making one's *toilette:*

> BOSWELL: We have all observed how one man dresses himself slowly and another fast. JOHNSON: Yes, sir, it is wonderful how much time some people will consume in dressing: taking up a thing and looking at it, and laying it down, and taking it up again. Everyone should get in the habit of doing it quickly. I would say to a young divine, "Here is your text; let me see how soon you can make a sermon." Then I'd say, "Let me see how much better you can make it." Thus I should see both his powers and his judgment.

Jones summarized his catalogue of anal traits with a balance sheet very characteristic of his own conception of himself as a man of power and judgment:

> Some of the most valuable qualities are derived from this [anal-erotic] complex, as well as some of the most disadvantageous. To the former may be reckoned especially the individualism, the determination and persistence, the love of order and power of organization, the competency, reliability and thoroughness, the generosity, the bent toward the arts and good taste, the capacity for unusual tenderness, and the general ability to deal with concrete objects in the material world. To the latter belong the incapacity for happiness, the irritability and bad temper, the hypochondria, the miserliness, meanness and pettiness, the slow-mindedness and proneness to bore, the bent for dictating and tyrannising, and the obstinacy which, with other qualities, may make the person exceedingly unfitted for social relations.

This summary catalogue of Jones's also shows how difficult it is to distinguish contributions to character from the anal-erotic complex from

128

contributions flowing out of the phallic-urethral phase, particularly in the absence of an "ego psychology," a sense for defenses more complex and layered than just reaction-formation. The difficulty is clear in the way in which Jones matter-of-factly identified as an anal-erotic character Napoleon the brilliant strategist, a man as unable to delegate responsibility as he was to rest from his compulsive labors, while Wilhelm Reich, just as matter-of-factly, identified the same Napoleon as a phallic-narcissistic character, citing the general's astounding energy, ruthlessness, and vengeance toward women. Jones saw a Napoleon rather like Jones, and Reich saw one rather like Reich, but it is not just the subjectivity of the classifiers that created their disagreement. Jones himself indicated that many of the traits he had cited in connection with the two phases of anal-eroticism "are closely related to narcissistic self-love and overestimation of self-importance, a fact which indicates the importance of the contribution made by anal-eroticism to infantile narcissism." But he did not pursue this hint. And Reich construed the anal-eroticism of the phallic-narcissistic character entirely as something to be defended against, warded off.

The histories of psychoanalytic work on the phallic-urethral character and on narcissism are enormously complex, as I indicated before, and the histories are currently intertwined with a development called "self-psychology," which has pushed characterology in general and the phallic-urethral character in particular quite to the margins of its theorizing, off in the "old-fashioned" corner. Before this development, however, Wilhelm Reich's description in *Character Analysis* of "the phallic-narcissistic character" was the touchstone in psychoanalytic study of the type:

> Even in outward appearance, the phallic-narcissistic character differs from the compulsive and hysterical character. While the compulsive character is predominantly inhibited, self-controlled and depressive, and while the hysterical character is nervous, agile, apprehensive and labile, the typical phallic-narcissistic character is self-confident, often arrogant, elastic, vigorous and often impressive. The more neurotic the inner mechanism, the more obtrusive are these modes of behavior. . . .
>
> Such individuals usually anticipate any expected attack with an attack on their part. Their aggression is very often expressed not so much in what they say or do as in the manner in which they say or do things. . . . One of their most important traits is aggressive courage. . . . [although this is] also compensatory, having to ward off opposite strivings [and regression to passivity and anality]. . . . [This character's] achievement differs from

that of the compulsive character by a greater boldness and lesser attention to details. . . .

Typically, analysis reveals an identification of the total ego with the phallus, in women the fantasy of having a penis; also, a more or less open display of this ego. . . . The pride in the real or fantasied phallus goes hand in hand with strong phallic aggression. To the unconscious of a man of this type, the penis is not in the service of love, but is an instrument of aggression and vengeance. . . . The infantile history regularly reveals serious disappointments in the object of the other sex, disappointments which occurred precisely at the time when attempts were made to win the object through phallic exhibition. In men, one often finds that the mother was the stronger of the parents, or the father died early or was otherwise out of the picture.

The frustration of genital and exhibitionistic activity at the height of their development by the very person toward whom the genital interest is displayed results in identification with that person on the *genital* level. That is, the boy will give up and introject the female object and will turn to the father in an active (because phallic) homosexual role, while the mother is retained as an object with only narcissistic attitudes and impulses of sadistic revenge. . . . In phallic-narcissistic women, conversely, the leading motive is that of taking vengeance on the man, of castrating him during the [sexual] act or of making him impotent or of making him appear impotent. This is in no way at variance with the strong sexual attraction which these strongly erotic characters exert on the other sex. Neurotic polygamy, active creating of disappointments for the partner, and passive flight from the possibility of being left alone are very often found.

Narcissism, which in early psychoanalytic literature like Reich's *Character Analysis* was so tied to the phallic stage and phallic investment— what might be called love of the penis-as-ego—had a career of its own after Heinz Hartmann introduced the term *self* into the psychoanalytic lexicon. Freud had considered narcissism, which he defined as the sexual instincts taking the ego as object (13:88), as a normal, necessary stage on the way to object-love, a stage which is retained in object-love to some degree by everybody. It is an advance beyond autoerotism, in which the sexual instincts are invested in parts of the body, usually before the ego has fully developed. Narcissism is only pathological if it arises secondarily, as a person withdraws from love of objects, returns all love to the ego, which may (in men) be identified with the penis, and is often (in women) identified with the body as a whole (on which beauty care is lavished) or with the body fantasized as a penis. Amending

130

this description, Heinz Hartmann argued that it is a his or her "self-representation" rather than the ego that the narcissist loves or reverts to.

"Self" meant for Hartmann the whole person of an individual (body parts and body as well as psychic parts and psyche) and he used the term *self-representation* for the ego's endopsychic image of the bodily and psychic self. As people who love others love their object-representations, their images of the beloved, so people who love themselves love their self-representations. (In this theory, a narcissist might represent himself or herself as a phallus and love that representation, but this would only be one specialized form of narcissism, not the whole story as Reich had argued.)

Self-love (or self-representation-love) was, Hartmann argued, a much broader concept than the ego-love Freud had focused on, and Hartmann thought it was important to use the broader concept because ego-love does not entail withdrawal from the world, as self-love does. That is, without withdrawing from the world, a person can love his or her ego-functions—like thought, memory, imagination—and thus strengthen them in relation to the world and to other parts of the psyche. And all creative people do just that, Hartmann noted. They convert ego-love (and also aggressivity) into ego-strength by a complex process of neutralizing the energy, making it available to ego-functions. Hartmann does not cite Freud's description of the narcissistic-obsessional in "Libidinal Types," but he might well have. This mixed type, Freud had said, is "the variation which is most valuable from a cultural standpoint; for it adds to independence from the external world and a regard for the demands of conscience a capacity for vigorous action, and it strengthens the ego against the superego" (21:219).

Throughout the early history of psychoanalysis, there was a tendency to associate narcissism with creativity, and to associate creative narcissistic characters with the boldest products—if not the products most easily appreciated or most filled with *amor mundi* and love of other people. In the late 1970s, this tendency in psychoanalytic thought was reinforced, but in a novel way, by a Chicago-based emigré analyst named Heinz Kohut, who took off from Hartmann's work but proposed two separate lines of normal development involving narcissism. On the one hand, there is a line from autoerotism via narcissism to love of others or object-love—the line Freud had elaborated. On the other hand, Kohut said, there is a line leading from autoerotism via narcissism to higher forms and transformations of narcissism such as creativity, empathy, appreciation for the transience of worldly things, humor, wisdom. This line was Kohut's appropriation of Hartmann's "self" emphasis, for purposes that were far from Hartmann's.

As his work evolved, Kohut turned the distinction Freud had drawn between transference neuroses and narcissistic neuroses into a revisionary distinction between pathologies based on psychic conflict and understandable by Freud's theory of drives and objects, and pathologies of the self, which traditional Freudian psychoanalysis cannot comprehend. In their childhoods all people, Kohut claimed, have an exhibitionistic, "I am perfect" self-representation (he calls this "the grandiose self") and a representation of a parental figure who is also idealized as perfect and omnipotent. As the child grows and structures these images into itself, the self-representation becomes the basis for later self-esteem, and the parental image, built into the superego, becomes the basis for self-approval and approval for others. But normal development does not take place unless the child's parents, especially the mother, respond to its needs empathically, neither neglecting nor rejecting it nor exploiting it for their own narcissistic purposes. The mother must be a mirror for the child's sense of itself as valuable, and must not shatter its idealizing expectations. (Kohut distinguishes between female and male development only by stressing the importance of the ideal mother for the girl and the ideal father for the boy.) Frustrated for lack of either a mirror or an ideal or both, the person with a "narcissistic personality disorder" will pathologically retain the grandiose self-image and/or search constantly (and always futilely) for someone on whom to transfer the idealizing parental image.

The term *personality* is present, but "character" is noticeable by its absence in Kohut's work. He does not speak of phallic narcissism and he explicitly rejects the traditional Freudian description, for example, of "anal character" because it seems to him to miss the key ingredient of anality—the mother's attitude toward her child's interest in defecation and feces. In *The Restoration of the Self*, Kohut argued:

> The child . . . experiences the joyful, prideful parental attitude or the parent's lack of interest, not only as the acceptance or rejection of a drive, but also—this aspect of the interaction of parent and child is often the decisive one—as the acceptance or rejection of his tentatively established, yet still vulnerable creative-productive active self. If the mother rejects this self just

as it begins to assert itself as a center of creative-productive initiative . . . or if her inability to respond to the child's total self leads her to a fragmentation-producing preoccupation with his feces—to the detriment of the cohesion-establishing involvement with her feces-producing, learning, controlling, maturing total child—then the child's self will be depleted and he will abandon the attempt to obtain the joys of self-assertion and will, for reassurance, turn to the pleasures he can derive from the fragments of his body-self.

Within Kohut's scheme, creativity is entirely a matter of infusing talents and skills with the grandiose self-image and the idealized parental image. Psychoanalysis can help with this achievement. Thus Kohut's description from the same book (in the same unique and uniquely opaque language) of a successful case:

> We can say, then, that the psychoanalytic treatment of a case of narcissistic personality disorder has progressed to the point of its intrinsically determined termination [has brought about the cure of the disorder] when it has been able to establish one sector within the realm of the self through which an uninterrupted flow of the narcissistic strivings can proceed toward creative expression. . . . Such a sector includes always a central pattern of exhibitionism and grandiose ambitions, a set of firmly internalized ideals of perfection, and a correlated system of talents and skills, which mediate between exhibitionism, ambitions, and grandiosity, on the one hand, and the ideals of perfection, on the other.

Outside of the consulting room, in the general culture, the healers of fragmented selves—their own and others'—are the artists. Unlike the nineteenth-century artists, who anticipated psychoanalysis with their images of Oedipal conflict, of drives and object relations, the great twentieth-century modernists have been Kohutian self-psychologists *avant la lettre,* according to Kohut:

> But the emotional problems of modern man are shifting, and the great modern artists were the first to respond in depth to man's new emotional task. Just as it is the understimulated child, the insufficiently responded to child, the daughter deprived of an idealizable mother, the son deprived of an idealizable father, that has now become paradigmatic for man's central problem in our Western world, so it is the crumbling, decomposing, fragmenting, enfeebled self of this child and, later, the fragile, vulnerable, empty self of the adult that the great artists of the day describe—through tone

133

and word, on canvas and in stone—and that they try to heal. The musician of disordered sound, the poet of decomposed language, the painter and sculptor of the fragmented visual and tactile world: they all portray the break-up of the self and, through the reassemblage and rearrangement of the fragments, try to create new structures that possess wholeness, perfection, new meaning.

Kohut's notion of creativity, unlike Freud's, is not based on sublimation of libido. His artist is a man (he does not discuss women artists) who has been frustrated in his childhood—neglected or rejected or narcissistically used—and who searches for a way to heal himself and restore meaning to his life. He is a broken man making himself whole or searching for wholeness. Freud's narcissistic character, and Reich's version of the same, was a person who, as a creator, could successfully channel into products a strong self-love—making all work, then, either directly or indirectly triumphal autobiography. The type Freud had in mind was the type he called—speaking of himself—a conquistador.

SYNTHESIZING DEVELOPMENTALLY

I have been cataloging clues to character—recurrent symbols, patterns of behavior (or symptomology), and associations of libidinal developmental stages and types of defenses. Clues like these provide a way to "read" lives and works for the characters and character-ideals they manifest. Clues like these also, I think, argue with their multiplicity and their intricacy against reductionism; against, to take the example just cited, reducing all development to the adequacy or inadequacy of maternal mirroring and ideal-maintenance in the first few years of life. (I find Kohut's libidoless notion of narcissism quite inadequate, although the interplay he notes of "the grandiose self" and the "idealized parental image" is valuable, and I will return to it below in the context of a discussion of social conditions for character development.) Without looking for a single causal key to character development, I just want to use this survey of clues as a kind of psychoanalytic thesaurus for translating back and forth between different registers of character-discussion.

If we take this thesaurus of clues and return to the relationships between libidinal-types and character-types (reflected in character-ideals), possibilities for elaborating those relationships present themselves. In the next chapter, I am going to take up these possibilities through a series of biographical vignettes, but I want to make some quick general sketches here before turning to more extended studies.

The political character-ideal is projected, as noted, by a person whose libidinal-type is narcissistic (in Freud's sense) or phallic-narcissistic (in Reich's sense) or obsessional-narcissistic (leaning toward the narcissistic side). The ideal reflects such a person's ambitions (and urethral-phallic urges), and it promotes his or her self-confidence, sense of power, breadth of vision, search for historical place. The active or productive work such a person does is usually marked by a very direct competitiveness with peers and predecessors (often with predecessors rather than actual fathers, whose virtues can be appreciated while the predecessors receive criticism). Also characteristic is a certain *esprit de système*. The person takes pleasure not just in his or her mental processes, but in the range, coherence, and organizational strength of the concepts or visions or actions generated. The person's system has an evolutionary bent to it, and the evolution traced is presented as coming up to the present moment, in which the person lives and envisions. That is, the person imagines himself or herself as poised for a grand view, situated for truth, in the right place at the right time. The originality or innovation of the view, which is a source of great pride, is tied in the person's mind to the perspective. Thus Aristotle imagines his encyclopedic view as made possible by the advance toward perfect form made in philosophizing since the days of his predecessors—an advance comparable to the one in tragedy that made Sophocles' work possible. No later heir to Aristotle's evolutionary method ever took this proclivity further than Hegel, but Marx did make quite a deity of History. Less philosophically, Freud attributed his personal strength in the face of criticism and dissension in the ranks of his followers to the historical destiny of his science: "Men are strong so long as they represent a strong idea: they become powerless when they oppose it" (14:66).

Among people of this type, the kind of curiosity typical of the phallic stage is very prominent. They are keen to discover what is hidden, unknown to others. They love looking more than being looked at, and what they look for is the laws and generalizations they assume are lying behind what seem to the naked senses lawless or chaotic events. They look *into* things, in the way that children do when they are figuring out the mystery of pregnancy. And, in accord with the *esprit de système*, the more general the law they find, the better. Assessing themselves as they were in adolescence, people of this sort typically say something like what

Charles Darwin wrote in his *Autobiography* on the topic of his "zeal": "Looking back as well as I can at my character during my school life, the only qualities which at this period promised well for the future were that I had strong and diversified tastes, much zeal for whatever interested me, and a keen pleasure in understanding any complex subject or thing." He had a vivid memory of how a well-known geologist with whom he studied at Cambridge failed to take interest in a find, and thus failed where Darwin himself was later so successful: "But I was then utterly astonished at Sedgwick not being delighted at so wonderful a fact as a tropical shell being found near the surface in the middle of England. Nothing before had ever made me thoroughly realize, though I had read various scientific books, that science consists in grouping facts so that general laws or conclusions may be drawn from them."

People of this sort may also add something about their phallic aggressions that resembles Darwin's next self-observation: "In the later part of my school life I became passionately fond of shooting, and I do not believe that anyone could have shown more zeal for the most holy cause than I did for shooting birds." Similarly, Darwin, when noting his zeal for collecting beetles during his university years, did not emphasize the collections themselves (as a more pure "anal character" hoarder would), but the conquest, the hunt: "I will give proof of my zeal: one day, on tearing off some old bark, I saw two rare beetles and seized one in each hand; then I saw a third and a new kind, which I could not bear to lose, so that I popped the one which I held in my right hand into my mouth. Alas it ejected some intensely acrid fluid, which burnt my tongue so that I was forced to spit the beetle out, which was lost, as well as the third one." This story of failure was then followed by items of success: "No poet ever felt more delight at seeing his first poem published than I did at seeing in Stephen's *Illustrations of British Insects* the magic words, 'captured by C. Darwin, Esq.' " Darwin the bird and beetle hunter was a young man struggling for recognition from his esteemed but rather remote and preoccupied father—his mother died when he was eight— and in this project he had five siblings (four sisters and a charming older brother) to compete with. In the domain of symbols, he was a sibling hunter. The father, Robert Darwin, was a man whose recognition was also a mysterious thing, because he possessed what Charles Darwin considered extraordinary abilities as a judge of character. Robert Darwin could look inside or see through people to find their governing traits: "The most remarkable power which my father possessed was that of reading the characters, and even the thoughts of those whom he saw even for a short time. We had many instances of this power, some of which seemed almost supernatural." When he was young, Darwin was convinced that his father found him hopeless, lazy, mediocre, untalented. Without ever making a point of it, he proved his father's supernatural judgment quite wrong.

Among people with the artisanal or artisanal/sexual character-ideal, and the erotic-obsessional libidinal type, there is also a struggle with parental (particularly paternal) authorities, but it takes a different form. Actively, as a self-fabricator, such a person rejects the father or supplants him and takes his place; passively, in the maternal mode of the sexual ideal, the person submits to the father. The person projecting both ideals is ambivalent; he or she suffers what the literary critic Harold Bloom called "the anxiety of influence," part rebellion against the past, part desire for continuation and inheritance. When such a person defends against passivity (what Anna Freud called "warding off passive trends"), complaints proliferate about maltreatment and discrimination from parental figures and their surrogates. (These complaints differ from those of people who project oral aggressivity onto others, for they do not stress how the hostile others are going to eat them up or steal from them; the enemies are imagined as attacking, trying to enter them, take over their spaces, or deprive them of having a room of their own.) When the person defends against activity, he or she leans—so to speak—in the direction of obsessionality and practices obsessional rituals, like Oscar Wilde's rituals of impersonation. The erotic-obsessional combinatory type, in other words, is a passive-active combinatory type. People of this sort feel their bisexuality—it is close to consciousness—and they often either acknowledge their "desire to be both sexes" (in Kubie's phrase) or subscribe to some kind of ideal androgyny or androgynous utopia. Thus, for example, Virginia Woolf in a well-known passage from *A Room of One's Own*:

> And I went on amateurishly to sketch a plan of the soul so that in each of us two powers preside, one male, one female; and in each man's brain, the man predominates over the woman, and in the woman's brain the woman predominates over the man. The normal and comfortable state of being is that when the two live in harmony together, spiritually co-operating. If one is a man, still the woman part of the brain must have effect; and a woman must have intercourse with the man in her. Coleridge perhaps

meant this when he said that a great mind is androgynous. It is when this fusion takes places that the mind is fully fertilized and uses all its faculties. Perhaps a mind that is purely masculine cannot create, any more than a mind that is purely feminine.

Woolf suggested that Kiplingesque self-assertive virility—a man defending himself against any femininity in his mind—is as deadly to literature as self-assertive femininity. The ideal is a consummated mental marriage, the two sexes in oneself joined to produce the child that is the work.

The erotic-obsessional or artisanal/sexual dimensions of the libidinal-type and the character-ideal are reflected in two further desires typical of people of this sort. On the one hand, they desire beauty and formal order or perfection, and they are exquisitely sensitive to the elements of their craft or to strategy and anticipatory planning. The impulse is to restore a lost whole or regain a paradise lost, often a paradise of mother-child communion or symbiosis. On the other hand, they are very anxious about their productivity and always wonder if they have done enough, worked hard enough, made a powerful enough mark on their genre, their time, history. Among men, the productivity desire reflects fear of castration or mutilation; among women, more often anxiety about having been denied phallic power or about not having been born beautiful. Imperfection is ugliness and ugliness is lack, inferiority. The appearances of things are of tremendous importance, and these people are often exhibitionistic either in person or in the medium of their works and actions. Exhibition is to bring reassurance of wholeness, intactness, beauty, perfection of form, so that exhibition also meets with and serves the desire for perfect form. The "compulsive brooding" that Freud described in his Leonardo essay is as common to this type as it is to the political type: thoughts, works, deeds, become sexualized, and, often, must be exhibited to be enjoyed. Often people of this type, like Nietzsche, sing the glories of productive solitude, which is sexually safe, but lament that no one knows them, no one understands them, no one sees their point.

Projectors of the third type of character-ideal, which I have been calling the spiritual character-ideal, whose libidinal-type is obsessional or narcissistic-obsessional, are much closer to the "anal character" (and also to the pathological obsessional character) than either of the other two types. Among them, concern with parental (and especially paternal) influence upon their achievements is not marked. They may accept such influence as beneficence or resign themselves fatalistically to being tainted by parental inheritance. In general, their attitude to the past does not conform to the usual images of time as a river that flows toward them from a beginning or a set of steps mounting upward to the step upon which they stand. As often, they imagine themselves facing the past—it enters into them as the future—or standing above time in a mystical *nunc stans*. Along with the precision about clock time that is typical of the "anal character" runs a kind of timelessness that may be expressed as feelings of great sympathy or connection to figures of other eras, other cultures. (Doctrines of reincarnation stress that a soul can take on many physical forms while remaining the same through all time.) Their identifications are either equally strong with mothers and fathers or predominantly maternal, and in either case much less ambivalent than the split-up identifications of the artisanal/sexual type. They are nurturers, or, if they identify with a mother whose mothering was experienced as unsatisfactory, they are hypochondriacal, dissatisfied with the care given them by their environment (and sometimes inclined to try to cure themselves by being nurturing to others). Identified with their mothers, they may be quite passive and adoring toward their fathers (and this, too, contributes to their lack of anxiety of influence). Identified with their fathers, they will imagine their essential self—the self they see revealed in their character-ideal—as masculine (even if they are female).

Because people of this sort very often repress a great deal of their aggressivity, developing what Anna Freud called "undue interest in the misfortunes of others," they have extra energy from this instinctual source to devote to nurturing and to somewhat hypochondriacal self-nurturing. On a grand scale, they become humanitarians, dedicating their lives or works to abstractions like "the welfare of humankind" or to egalitarian visions in which all people are worthy or—more to the point—no people are special. Accordingly, their works are very seldom in material media. They are not the children who sublimated their anal passions into play with sand, clay, paint; they are the children who did not, and who—at a later point—converted their reaction-formation of asceticism into creativity in the media of clean words or spiritual deeds (which may, however, bring them in a spiritualized way into the dirty realms of other people's sickness, poverty, menial labor). But they may also, as I will note later in more detail, have to undergo a crisis of dirtiness and catharsis, a descent into material hell, in order to come forth pure and creative.

People with spiritual character-ideals assert themselves for the rights of the oppressed, dedicate themselves to relief of suffering, and idealize purity, incorruptness, moral goodness. Truth and power, the ideals of the political type, and beauty and productivity, the ideals of the artisanal/sexual type, will often strike the spiritual type as potentially dangerous boundaries between people. Battles over truth, they think, degenerate into mere battles; beauty, which is felt to be in the eye of the beholder, just traps beholders in their subjectivities or their particular esthetic ideas or tastes. Only as absolutes or attributes of the Absolute do Truth and Beauty inspire the spiritual type. They take pleasure in feeling their own mental processes drawn toward the Absolute, or in saying humbly that the Absolute is beyond human grasp and should not be an object of striving at all. The spiritual type relishes the paradoxes that express such feelings. Thus, Simone Weil in the *First and Last Notebooks:*

> One of the most exquisite pleasures of human love—to serve the loved one without his knowing it—is only possible, as regards the love of God, through atheism.

Or, in his fashion, Marcel Proust in the second volume of *Guermantes Way:*

> An artist does not need to express his thought directly for his work to reflect the quality of that thought. It has even been said that the greatest praise of God lies in the negation of the atheist, who considers creation sufficiently perfect to dispense with a creator.

Chapter Seven

Six Characters In Three Types

BIOGRAPHIES AS SOURCES

Biographies of the creative vary considerably in the extent and manner of their attention to their subject's ways of working. Sometimes they are very satisfying descriptively, but without analysis; sometimes they are very analytic—as "psychobiographies"—but lack rich descriptive texture. The shortcomings of the literature on creativity that I noted in my introduction have equivalents in the field of biography writing. Some biographers take up "the creative process," some explore motivations and developmental histories, some focus on social conditions, some on what the subject actually made (poetics) or did, but a comprehensive life–study is hard to find and reductionism in the direction of one approach or another is very common, particularly when either biographical fashions or the documentary materials available in a given case are weighted in one direction.

When I take up a biography to test my notions about creative characters—about character-types and character-ideal types, about theories, of creativity and creative practices—I often find that I receive only glimpses from it, bits and pieces of the kind of material I am looking for. I use the biography, then, as a guide to the documents that will be more richly useful to me (usually to the subject's autobiographical writings) or to work produced in the subject's late adolescent years (and usually not available to the public in the subject's lifetime). The more the biography quotes the subject, lets the subject speak in his or her own words or works, the more useful it is to me—and, to my tastes, the better the biography is.

The biographical sketches I am going to make in this chapter are drawn from different kinds of biographies, they focus on people working in different fields and literary forms, living in different historical periods. Sometimes I follow the outlines provided by one biography, sometimes I use more than one, and sometimes I use biographies as indexes to the subject's own work. In each case, I will indicate why the biographical literature I use is or is not helpful to study of character-ideals. This chapter constitutes a critical approach to biography writing from a particular point of view.

As each of my six biographical subjects is introduced along with a segment of biographical literature about them, questions will arise about the influence of social and historical milieus on these characters, about the importance of their genders, the particularities of their types of work, but these will get a separate hearing in Chapter 9. For the moment, I only want to illustrate the three character-ideal types and take a step further the exploration conducted over the last two chapters into developmental correlates of character-ideal types. I will start with two examples of the spiritual character-ideal type (this time, two male examples, while before we met four females), move to the artisanal/sexual type (with a male and a female example, while before the British esthetes we met were all males), and then to the political type (continuing the Charles Darwin story started in the last chapter, and introducing Emily Dickinson as the first female example of the type).

THE VANITY OF HUMAN WISHES: THE SPIRITUAL CHARACTER-IDEAL

W. Jackson Bate's *Samuel Johnson* is a frustrating book, at once very rich and very superficial. Bate emphasized again and again that he had no desire to protect his subject from scrutiny or to obscure the fact that Johnson had suffered through at least two long episodes of mental illness and many depressed periods. Johnson was the father of modern biography writing, and his biographer set out to follow the advice Johnson gave about the uses of biography:

> If nothing but the bright side of characters should be shewn, we should sit down in despondency, and think it utterly impossible to imitate them in *anything*. The sacred writers (he observed) related the vicious as well as the

virtuous actions of men, which had this moral effect, that it kept mankind from despair.

But Bate did not, on the other hand, really explore Johnson's illness, even though he used somewhat Freudian terminology and spoke vaguely of obsessions and compulsions. The biography is completely overshadowed by Bate's reverence and sense of Johnson's greatness: "Samuel Johnson has fascinated more people than any other writer except Shakespeare," goes the opening line of Chapter 1. What this means is that extensive acquaintance with Johnson's life and work is presumed—no literate reader could possibly be uninformed—and the biographer's job is to shape that acquaintance into admiration. Every trouble or tribulation in Johnson's life is viewed as something he magnificently endured or overcame, thereby establishing himself as a model for mankind. Bate is so impressed by Johnson's character that he takes it for the quintessence of humanity. This seems to be a case of the biographer and the subject being so characterologically similar (though on different levels of creativity) that the biographer cannot see the subject's key conflicts.

From the start, there were troubles aplenty for Johnson to endure and overcome. After a difficult and dangerous labor, he was born "almost dead" to his forty-year-old mother—her first child. To protect her strength, the baby was given to a wet-nurse who turned out to be tubercular, so that he contracted scrofula, a lymph gland infection that spread to his eyes and ears, leaving both his sight and his hearing impaired and his face scarred. An incision that was made in his arm to drain the infection was then kept open until he was nearly six. The character-trait that Bate sees arising from these awful events is what he calls "self-demand, a feeling of complete personal responsibility," or "self-management," a need to be in control, and he notes how Johnson began, as a child, to "push through and deny his physical infirmities."

The child was intellectually precocious, and mortified that his father took great pride in—as he said—"exhibiting" him. One of his friends recalled:

> That (said he to me one day) is the great misery of late marriages, the unhappy produce of them becomes the plaything of dotage: an old man's child (continued he) leads much such a life, I think, as a little boy's dog,

teized with awkward fondness, and forced, perhaps, to sit up and beg . . .
to divert a company, who at last go away complaining of their disagreeable
entertainment.

Johnson expected to be a disappointment, and he knew that he was
valued for his intellectual precocity, his wit, not his appearance. But
Bate does not stop to consider how confusing it is to a child to have his
own exhibitionism confounded by a parent's exhibitionism, which
makes him feel that showing off is wrong, embarrassing, and—worst of
all—useless as a means to gain love and attention.

Bate tells the story of Samuel Johnson's adolescence through the
medium of a contrast: his subject's two chief role models are set over
against his elderly father, who was melancholy, well-meaning but finan-
cially inept. "Without the combined influences of Cornelius Ford and
Gilbert Walmesley, it is very doubtful that Johnson would have been at
all what he was by the age of nineteen." The two patrons were worldly
men, experienced in "life and manners," cultivated and refined but not
innocent of pleasures ("each had a somewhat rakish past"). Gilbert
Walmesley was older than Ford, more argumentative—he was a lawyer—and a fierce political partisan. The "competitive side" of Johnson,
of a boy who worked to overcome his physical handicaps and his poverty, warmed to Walmesley. (Bate does not consider how verbal quarrel-
ing may be related to earlier forms of aggression or exhibitionism). But
this identification with the argumentative lawyer came into conflict with
the conciliatory side that warmed to Cornelius Ford:

> Cornelius disliked argument and dispute, realizing how little they can
> achieve in all matters human, fluid, speculative, or imaginative—matters
> that make up the bulk of what interests or engages the passions of mankind,
> and where interpretation, opinion, early influence, and emotional bias—as
> contrasted with clearly demonstrable certainty—are inevitably involved.
> Johnson took this to heart, was to find the truth of it exemplified throughout
> his life, and whatever his own practice, was to write about the treacheries
> and futility of argument with as much insight as any writer on human
> nature has ever shown.

In these passages, so characteristically laced with the biographer's
desire to speak in universals about "mankind" and to make Johnson into
an epitome of this mankind, Bate sounds a theme of internal division
which he develops in many ways as the biography unfolds. With the

intellectual patronage of the two role models and a small legacy from his mother's side of the family, Johnson went to Oxford, where he hoped to make an impression and find a financial patron. He did make an intellectual impression, but he did not find a patron, and had to face leaving only a year after he arrived. At this time, he began to record in his diary that he was conducting a battle against a powerful enemy. Bate takes the beginning of the record for the beginning of the battle with the enemy, whom Johnson imaged as female and named "Sloth," that is, the one of the seven deadly sins that encompasses all spiritual inactivity or laziness in pursuit of virtue. Again and again, he tried to get rid of his seductive enemy: "I bid farewell to sloth, being resolved henceforth not to listen to her syren strains."

Like many of his contemporaries, Johnson believed that sloth or indolence is the root of all evil and the direct cause of madness. "He was beginning to develop his lifelong conviction—against which another part of him was forever afterward to protest—that indolence is an open invitation to mental distress and even disintegration, and that to pull ourselves together, through the focus of attention and the discipline of work, is within our own power." When he returned to his home from Oxford, defeated and deeply depressed, plagued by "embarrassing tics and other compulsive mannerisms," Johnson fought more and more strenuously in the pages of his diary. On April 21, 1764: "My purpose is from this time (1) To reject or expel sensual images and idle thought. To provide some useful amusement for leisure time. (2) To avoid idleness. To rise early. . . . Deliver me from the distresses of vain terrour . . . . Against loose thoughts and idleness." He was fighting to release himself from the part of himself he thought was diseased, and his period of depression and preoccupation lasted about two years.

Johnson wrote, at the age of twenty, a poem in couplets called "The Young Author." This poem, which announces the themes that appeared again in the mature writer's *The Vanity of Human Wishes*, shows Johnson instructing himself to "defend himself by turning not against others but against himself, as he instinctively begins to bludgeon his own intense hopes before life itself should leave him broken or stranded." His failure at Oxford led him to resolve not to be caught unawares. Horace's maxim *praemonitum, praemunitum* ("forewarned is forearmed") became his own and he worked to be able to survey situations in advance, to take every possibility into account. Very specifically, the young author, who is "panting for a name," must learn that audiences are fickle and untrustworthy, that giving up hope of transitory fame for hope of "endless fame" is just making inevitable disappointment all the greater. When he gets a taste of how audiences really are, when he hears the jeers and hisses, the young author will be, Johnson says, "glad to be hid, and proud to be forgot." Ambition and activity and exhibition—all of them counters to sloth or indolence—became just as forbidden as sloth, which implies that they were not opposites in Johnson's mind. Both ambition and indolence had to be stripped away.

Because it was never completely or lastingly successful, the stripping process went on relentlessly, as Bate relates:

> "The great business of his life," Johnson told Reynolds, "was to escape from himself; this disposition he considered as the disease of his mind." The part of himself from which he needed to escape was the remorseless pressure of "superego" demand, of constant self-criticism, and all the unconscious ruses of insistent self-punishment. Arthur Murphy appears to have sensed something of this when he said that there was a "danger" for Johnson in indolence; for his "spirits, not employed abroad, turned with inward hostility against himself. His reflections on his own life and conduct were always severe; and, wishing to be immaculate, he destroyed his own peace by unnecessary scruples."

Bate does not inquire into the content of the sensual images and idle thoughts with which Johnson was preoccupied, he simply notes the censorship of Johnson's superego, the heavy weight of the "scruples" he directed against his enemy forces. He assumes Johnson tried to rid himself of his solution (the strong superego) not of his problem (the frightening desires). Bate also presents the "scruples" (Johnson's code word for obsessional ceremonials) as all the same sort of thing, while they look much more like two different sorts of thing: compulsive physical actions or mannerisms, particularly his habits of pacing back and forth, taking all-day hikes, touching every post he walked by, and what he called "gesticulation in company"; and the intellectualized defenses typical of the "anal character" such as counting rituals, minute measuring of time and effort, obsession with numbers, arithmetic. That is, these look like defenses against masturbation or phallic exhibitionism—or against the hands that do the devil's work—and against anal-sadism, aggression more specifically directed against a child's trainer, usually the mother. In Bate's biography, the reader can infer (but without much help) that the twenty-year-old Johnson had as yet no sexual experience and apparently no infatuations, but there is no comment on the fact that masturbation was considered a direct route to mental illness in Johnson's youth—as still in Freud's. Freud was the first to study beating fantasies—fantasies in which a young man is beaten by an older one for his sins and allowed, thus, to enjoy a moment of masturbation in peace, having paid the punishment price in advance. The mode of satisfaction is masochistic.

For my present purposes, though, the important thing to note about Johnson is that his modality for self-cure was extirpation: he wanted to rid himself of all in himself that was impure, inessential, distracting. His character-ideal was of the self-stripping spiritual type. And it was not until late in his life that Johnson realized how easy it is for a person bent on purification to go too far. He said that one of the chief tasks of biography writing was to learn how people went about making themselves miserable: "not how he lost the favor of his prince, but how he became discontented with himself." The "scruples" with which he sought to control his indolence became, themselves, something he needed to conquer. In his diary for Easter 1766, he wrote: "I prayed in the collect for . . . deliverance from scruples. . . . O God hear me. I am now trying to conquer them."

The young man who struggled against his own aggression by counting ceremonials and by criticizing argumentativeness as an intellectual pacificist, and who struggled against his "indolence" with explosive, feverish work routines (to use Ernest Jones's adjectives for the anal character who broods and hoards and then works indefatigably), was ideally suited to be an assiduous compiler of the first modern English dictionary. His ideal was the kind of encyclopedic erudition he thought typical of Renaissance savants—he was a knowledge collector. On rare occasions, the aggression burst forth, as when Johnson was accused of being lazy by one of his employers, a coarse and ignorant man, and responded by knocking the man to the floor with a huge seventeenth-century Greek Bible. Lazy and indolent was exactly what he was not, Johnson felt compelled to insist on imagery that could as well be showing bowels swelling as penises growing erect:

> Repeatedly Johnson clung to the conviction (it is also one of the themes of his moral writing) that employment and activity beget activity; that the momentum of effort, if once under way in any direction, is more easily transferred than summoned out of nothing. . . . [He wrote about] the

147

insidious power of habit, pictured as pigmies that smoothe one's path up the "mountain of existence," valuable and docile when in the service of Reason and Religion, treacherous when allied with Passion and Appetite, and capable of swelling to giant size as one fights against them.

Johnson imagined a Reason which could extirpate its enemies, strip them away. He had a version of the ideal I noted above as "clean thinking," sometimes known among psychoanalysts as "the computer ideal," a conception people have of themselves as a mind without a body, an intellect without feelings. As Anna Freud remarks: "Such attitudes are defensive, not in the sense of warding off or immobilizing a particular instinctual trend, but more generally in the sense of trying to do away with sources of danger altogether. When they are successful, the need for further defense activity is eliminated at the expense of a character or behavior change, and no obsessional neurosis proper is organized" (5:259).

What seems to have been organized in Johnsons's case was not an obsessional neurosis, but a very pronounced and thoroughgoing obsessional character. The narcissistic component in this character is clearest in Johnson's household. He collected around himself and his work a "squad of ragamuffins and waifs" whom he supported and promoted in the way that is typical of people who do unto others as they would like to have had done unto themselves, usually by their mothers (playing, in Kohut's terms, the role of idealized parent). His wife, who was a new widow twenty years his senior when he met her three years after his Oxford breakdown, won his gratitude because she overlooked his physical appearance and his strange mannerisms; and he treated her, in turn, with great generosity as she lost her looks, turned away from him sexually, and declined into indolence in the form of alcoholism and ill health. The maternal figure joined the retinue of those who needed maternal care. Johnson's anger went into scathing remarks—spoken and written—about how ill suited for marriage human beings are: "Marriages would in general be as happy, and often more so, if they were all made by the Lord Chancellor, upon a due consideration of characters and circumstances, without the parties having any choice in the matter." After his wife's death, Johnson did not indulge himself in a second try at matrimony, which, he said, could only be a "triumph of hope over experience." That is, he stripped himself of his wish for female company, in the manner prescribed by *The Vanity of Human Wishes*.

Johnson's poem, which has had such appeal to people of similar spiritual character-ideals, like T. S. Eliot, could very well have supplied the title for the whole of Gustave Flaubert's life and work. When he was the same age Johnson had been during his post-Oxford breakdown, Flaubert failed his law examinations at the University of Paris and came home to Rouen suffering from the mysterious hallucinations and attacks—some biographers have suggested they were epileptic seizures, some say hysterical convulsions—which convinced him that he should extirpate all his own vain human wishes. " 'Since what I fear is passion and movement,' he wrote, 'I think that if happiness can be found it must be in stagnation: ponds have no storms.' "

As he slowly recovered from his attacks, helped by restrictions on his huge consumption of tobacco, coffee, alcohol, and food, Flaubert worked on a first novel, under the title *L'Education sentimentale*, a title which he later used again for quite a different novel, one of his masterpieces. His late-adolescent book features two young friends from the provinces whose paths diverge. Henri, a successful student, goes to the city, wins for himself another man's wife—a woman rather like one who had compelled Flaubert's attention and haunted him—and establishes himself for a socially brilliant but essentially banal bourgeois life. Henri was an experiment with the road not taken, and Flaubert conjectured through him that this road, initially so alluring, would have led eventually to the life Flaubert feared most: entombment in bourgeois marital triviality and an office job (which claustrophobic job he assigned to the hero of a play written shortly before his death, *Le Sex faible*). Jules stays in the country, fails at winning the affections of an actress, but is able to make himself into an artist by purging himself of all his false romantic opinions and acquired subjectivistic ideas. One might say that Henri went off to the Oedipal drama of love for a woman who belongs to another and is ultimately inaccessible, while Jules stayed behind to renounce the Oedipal drama for asceticism. An English biographer, Philip Spencer, writing his *Flaubert* in the early 1950s, describes this process of self-purgation that Jules—and Flaubert himself—went through:

> The study of human nature, however, which belongs to the domain of art, is not only a matter of observation and intelligence; it demands a hardening of oneself—a hardening that Flaubert practised in the analysis of his own malady; and Jules realizes that he can no longer dismiss part of his experience

as ugly, but that he must seek in it the beauty and harmony which it certainly possesses. Criticism, therefore, whether of nature or of art, becomes more objective: it is not enough to record one's personal reaction to a poem or a landscape. And creative writing becomes objective at the same time, spurning lyrical effusions and striving for a style that is increasingly subtle and strong and for a vision of the world that is sufficiently true. Indeed Jules is so convinced of the parallel development of vision and style that he rejects the heretical distinction between form and content, maintaining that once an idea has been adequately conceived, the right expression is thereby found. . . .

No one more than he was aware of the fickleness and unreliability of the human mind; his own faculties often seemed on the verge of dissolution; but that same mind, however feeble, was the vessel of a beauty he was only beginning to perceive; and his theory of art triumphantly declared the intensity, the "otherness' of that experience, and afforded him a kind of religion in which the existence of an absolute beauty displaced the existence of God.

Flaubert's retreat from Paris to his family's home, and from direct engagement with the world into intense esthetic spectatorship and objective analysis, a religion of beauty, coincided with two terrible losses. His father, the physician who had treated him in his illness, and his beloved sister Caroline, both died. His retreat was reinforced: " 'Remain always as you are,' he told [his friend] Chevalier, 'Don't get married, have no children, indulge in as few affections as possible, allow the least hold to the enemy.' "

Flaubert made his retreat, hoping to transform himself into a pond without storms, when he was twenty, but he had wanted little to do with the world since his childhood—or, he said, making a legend of himself, since his birth. "I came into the world bored," said Flaubert, "it is the disease that eats me up." "It is strange," he wrote to a friend in 1846, when he was twenty-five, "how I was born with little faith in happiness. When I was very young, I had a complete presentiment of life. It was a nauseous smell of cooking escaping from a vent. You don't need to eat it to know it will make you sick." Although he was sociable enough to organize a little theater and produce plays as a boy, Flaubert was very solitary and spent hours daydreaming and reading. "According to his mother he used to sit for hours at a time with his finger in his mouth like a simpleton; if he was reading he became so absorbed that he sometimes overbalanced on to the floor."

All of these details give the impression of a boy who was fighting against any instinctual upheaval, damping himself down—resorting to boredom, which signals enormous effort given over to unconscious battle with instincts. His description of life as something nauseating is both oral—it relates to cooking, eating—and anal—smells escape a vent. In school, Spencer relates, Flaubert was a devotee of a puppet theater where "The Temptation of Saint Anthony" was performed. He identified with the hermit, and with the hermit's fight against his demons: "Messieurs les démons, laissez-moi donc! Messieurs les démons, laissez-moi donc!"

As a student in the local *collège*, Flaubert was a dedicated romantic, devoted not to hermits—though he was swept away by Goethe's *Faust*—but to literary rebels, to Byron, Hugo, Chateaubriand, and to the then fashionable, noble, often condescending, always antibourgeois, despair. It was then that he fell in love with a woman eleven years his senior, married and the mother of an infant girl. He became more morose than usual, was frequently in a state Spencer describes as "lassitude" or "depression," and put on a great amount of weight, obscuring his handsomeness and ruining his strength. But he did, nonetheless, go to Paris for a year at the university, where he could visit, as well, Mme. Schlesinger, his love. The attacks that began at the end of this year (late in 1843), which resulted in his "conversion" to a life without incident or involvement and to the religion of art, are presented by Spencer with a flat paraphrase of a very vivid Flaubert letter:

> He felt taut and overstrained as though his sensibility was screwed up to an abnormal degree; through closed doors he could sometimes hear the softest whisper. Then, when an attack ensued, a million ideas and images exploded in his mind in the space of a second, like a vast fireworks display, with a rending pain as if body and soul were being torn apart. Several times he thought he was dead; but although he could not speak, he was convinced that throughout the attack he never lost consciousness. His soul, he said, was turned inward on itself, like a hedgehog tortured with its own prickles.

Spencer debates whether the attacks might have been epileptic, or whether they were *grande hystérie*, and then astonishingly concludes that, no matter what the diagnosis, the illness "affords no clue to his life and work." Not a page later, he remarks that Flaubert responded to the "disorders of his imagination by studying them deliberately and scientifically; sometimes, indeed, he induced states akin to his nervous attacks and endured their pain in order to examine them."

The limitations of Spencer's biography are palpable in these passages. He does not reject psychological inquiry, he simply cannot practice it. Quite the opposite is the case with Jean-Paul Sartre's massive three-volume *L'Idiot de la famille* (1971–72), which is an intricate mapping of Flaubert's Oedipal drama and a careful examination of how that drama, clearly manifest in the hysterical attacks of 1844, influenced every one of Flaubert's works. Sartre writes as a detective, organizing almost every paragraph in his text around a series of questions and a list of possible answers from which the reader, following the writer, is able eventually to choose the correct one. Sartre's answers are the background, then, for a recent volume of "psychocritical" essays on Flaubert, and specifically on Flaubert's late text "The Legend of Saint Julian the Hospitaler." The collection's title, *Saint/Oedipus*, captures in a stroke the retreat into asceticism that was the outcome of Flaubert's Oedipus complex and its revival in his late adolescence.

But for these psychoanalytical studies, the Oedipus complex has no developmental antecedents. The destiny of little boys unfolds without an oral stage or an anal stage; it is phallic and genital exclusively. And the complex interplay of fixation and regression that is typical of the formation of an obsessional character or the emergence of an obsessional neurosis is not taken into account. Freud often noted—and child analysis since has borne out his insight—that behind an obsessional neurosis there lies a hysteria. In Flaubert's case, the hysterical attacks on a grand scale in adolescence are well documented, while whatever childhood antecedents existed are not. The obsessional features of Flaubert's life as he recuperated, worked to control his appetites, and dedicated himself to his religion of art are obvious in Spencer's descriptions, if not to Spencer. While he worked on *Madame Bovary*, Flaubert described his indefatigable labors as at once control of language and control of his appetitive (masturbatory) hands, a common "anal character" configuration: "Since style was invented, I don't think anyone has taken as much trouble as I. . . . As I write this book, I am like a man playing the piano with lumps of lead on each finger."

The most elaborate of Freud's studies of events and symptoms leading to an obsessional neurosis is "The Wolf Man" (as the text called "From the History of an Infantile Neurosis," 1918, is known). This young Russian aristocrat, who had witnessed as an infant a "primal scene" of intercourse between his parents, developed hysterical symptoms beginning at age two with an eating disorder; exhibitionism, urethral-erotism at two and a half; castration anxiety after a seduction by his sister at three; regression to anal-erotism and sadistic treatment of animals under the impact of castration fear; beating fantasies at age three and a half; phobias after a terrifying dream of wolves at age four; and obsessional religious ceremonials from four and a half to ten. The obsessional rituals allowed him a more or less normal latency marked only by intellectual inhibitions and disinterest in social situations, but he had a breakdown at eighteen under the influence of a gonorrheal infection and the castration anxiety aroused by it. The "developmental line" (to use Anna Freud's designation) from hysteria through beating fantasies to phobias to obsessional symptoms is typical of people who emerge in adulthood with an obsessional neurosis or character. Anal-sadism, developing as a regressive response to castration anxiety in males or penis envy in females, and becoming masochistic in the medium of beating fantasies, is also typical, but almost never documented in biographies for the simple reason—I think—that most nonpsychoanalyst biographers are completely unfamiliar with Freud's and Anna Freud's work on beating fantasies as composites of images of anal-sadism and of control over masturbation or masturbating hands. Flaubert's juvenilia are replete with masochistic beating fantasies that indicate a history of regression to the anal phase insofar as they end with scenes in which the protagonist is buried alive, stuck in mire, covered with muck. One, dating from the year of his unrequited love for Mme. Schlesinger, 1836, and called "Rage et impuissance," for example, ends with a man buried alive, who dies uttering blasphemies and eating the flesh of his own arm. A 1837 story called "Le Rêve d'enfer" is about a young alchemist who tells Satan that when he was innocent and pure he lived in bliss, but then he returned to a life of boredom: "Then everything turned black before my eyes . . . my life became a long death-agony, and the earth a tomb wherein they buried men alive." The same idea is part of the contemporaneous "Mémoires d'un fou": "To have dreamed of heaven and to fall into the mire!" In a June 24, 1837, letter to his friend Ernst, Flaubert turned the whole bourgeois civilization he hated into a Rabelaisian compendium of saccharine food, anal displeasure, entombment, and sadistic death: "Oh! this fine civilization! this stupid lump that has invented railways, prisons, rectal-pumps, cream tarts, royalty and the guillotine."

Flaubert himself understood very well that he was projecting upon

153

society and even upon the cosmos his image of what he wished to escape, strip away—the filthy anal-sadistic and masturbatory desires. Sometimes he worked to strip them away, sometimes he sank into a despair over them, as he reported quite clearly in a text called *Novembre*, written in 1841 or 1842, two years before his breakdown. This text shows his character-ideal in formation, and also shows how he could not live up to it, follow its instructions to abandon his desires. His desires are imaged as a deity who overpowers him, as Samuel Johnson's desires were deified as Indolence.

> . . . I was only a mummy embalmed in my own sorrow, the fatality which had bent me from my childhood spread out for me over the whole world . . . It became an atrocious deity, which I worshipped as the Hindus adore the ruling colossus that passes over their bodies; I took pleasure in my gloom, stopped trying to throw it off, I even enjoyed it with the despairing joy of a sick man who scratches his wound and laughs when his nails drip with blood. . . .

Only after the breakdown and his retreat from the world could Flaubert manage a regime, solidify an obsessional character, to obey himself. In this, he was more successful than Samuel Johnson, who put such a strain on his obsessional defenses by marrying the maternal Tetty.

One of the most interesting facets of the psychic technique that Flaubert developed, his spiritual discipline, is that it required of him that he strip himself of unwanted desires in a specific manner: he put them in a literary character who was himself—"Madame Bovary, c'est moi," as he famously admitted—and then sent the character to his or her ruin or death. The artisanal/sexual character-ideal type commonly splits a self-image in two, usually along sexual lines, projecting a male self and a female self (as we shall see in the examples just below). But the purpose of this projection is reunion, marriage, an androgynous whole in which both male and female join in a creation or a procreation. Flaubert imagined a self—like the character Henri in the first version of *L'Education sentimentale*—and then purged himself of that self. He was like Proust stripping away his constraining, asphyxiating surfaces to let the ascetic, desireless *le moi profond* breathe, live. Like a Stoic sage or a Christian mystic, Flaubert experienced a dark night of the soul before he could emerge purified. In his late work "The Legend of Saint Julian the Hospitaler," he presents his purification graphically: his worst self is a leper, filthy, covered in flowing sores, with only a hole where his nose (his penis?) had been eaten away, his breath coming out of his mouth "thick like a fog and foul." The leper demands that Saint Julian strip himself naked, lie on top of him, merge with him: "Julian stretched himself out on top, mouth against mouth, chest against chest." Immediately, the leper is purified, and Julian ascends blissfully to heaven, "face to face with our Lord Jesus."

WE TWO: THE ARTISANAL/SEXUAL CHARACTER-IDEAL

The *Bildungsroman*, the novel of growing up and replacing innocence with knowledge, or at least cultivation, frequently takes the form of a journey. A youth goes from the country to the city, from one culture or country to another and back home again, from a place of some kind of rags to one of some kind of riches. Americans often go abroad, English leave their island for something larger and wilder. For creative people who project the artistic form of character-ideal, the journey can coalesce with a story of self-formation or self-procreation or both. Among writers whose character-ideal has a sexual dimension, it is often apparent in a first novel, the first project of late adolescence, and it takes the form of what might be called a complementary romance. A young person finds an other-half who has everything the young person needs. Together they are a perfect whole in which feminine and masculine are balanced; they are like the semispheres described by Aristophanes in Plato's *Symposium*, which wander about until they find the other-half from which they were once separated by divine wrath. In the perfect sphere, sexual desire is controlled, given a characteristic form, and spiritual progeny result.

This story comes in as many varieties as there are erotic-obsessional or passive-active libidinal combinatory types and varieties of ego and superego development related to them. Biographers who are particularly sensitive to the recurrent structures in literary works are particularly adept at catching the late-adolescent storyline as it grows clear and settles. I will look at two psychologically rich biographies, one of a male writer and one of a female, that also extend the "perfection of the life or of the work" theme we noted earlier among the British turn-of-the-century esthetes.

Leon Edel's massive biography of Henry James provides a vivid

155

account of how a character-ideal of the artisanal/sexual type can be projected as a historically oriented social vision. As a young man who had traveled abroad a great deal—probably too much—while his family fulfilled the educational prescriptions of the restless Henry James, Sr., the novelist hit upon what might be called his "Americans made in Europe" theme. Like his Russian friend Turgenev, James had what he called "a poet's quarrel" with his native land, and his various versions of this quarrel were made up of projections of an inner quarrel of the "reason versus the passions" sort. Europe typically played the role of civilization and wisdom in contrast to American wild ignorance and strident parochialism; but Europe could also play passionate cruelty and corruption in contrast to American innocence and over-reasoning Puritanism. In a more general sense, what James called "the march of history" could also play the role of passion, change and motion: "I regard the march of history very much as a man placed astride of a locomotive, without knowledge or help, would regard the progress of that vehicle. To stick on, somehow, and even enjoy the scenery as we pass, is the sum of my aspiration." The rider was not able to direct the locomotive in any way, but he could command it as a vantage point for his spectatorship.

In his first full-scale novel, finished when he was a very adolescent and chaste thirty-two years old, James presented his title character Roderick Hudson as a romantic artist, an inspired genius, reckless and adventuresome. Hudson's patron, the stuffy and heavy-handed Roland Mallet, guides him around Rome and tries to oversee a process of tempering reform, only to be thwarted by Christina Light, a half-American, half-European beauty, moody and ruthless, with whom Hudson falls in disastrous love. Edel describes the "doubling" of James's two leading male characters and the complex—ultimately untenable—balance of the American and European characteristics they represent:

> Rowland's observation of Roderick is that "the poor fellow is incomplete." This is true; and it is Rowland who, in a sense, completes him. He possesses the cool measuring mind, the dispassionate heart, which Roderick needs—but also rejects. It is as if James has abstracted the incandescence of his genius and placed beside it his decorous, cautious, restrained self, or his mother's warnings beside his own desires. Rowland Mallet is thus the watchdog of his own spirit. He literally is a watcher, for we see the greater part of the story through his eyes. But he is also Roderick's other self. James

seems to be answering the unanswerable question: how can the artist, the painter of life, the recorder, the observer, stand on the outside of things and write about them, and throw himself at the same time into the act of living? How become involved in life—and remain uninvolved? It was as if a wall of glass stood between Henry James and his desires. The glass at least permitted him to look at life.

James was sufficiently a Rowland to realize that he could never be a Roderick. Instead of acting out his passions he could invest his characters with them. In this novel the *feeling* self had to die. It was too great a threat to the rational self.

Edel's description shows a character-ideal projected but unattained—currently unattainable. Variations in the ideal mark adjustments, and James eventually came to a more satisfactory configuration: Roderick became female. The American figure in the novel becomes, more and more frequently, a lady whose portrait was framed by, and set in contrast to, European males. Only once did a more radical reconfiguration take place, and that was, Edel notes, late in the novelist's life. After a humiliatingly unsuccessful search for money and glory in the theater, James was depressed, full of questions about whether his life had been an arid, passionless affair. He took into his own orbit several figures of passion—energetic, witty, artistic young men, including a handsome Roderick Hudson–like sculptor—toward whom he could be older and wiser and somewhat maternal, and he put into the orbit of his fiction "a remarkable sequence dealing with female children, juveniles and adolescents," almost as though he were doing his own childhood and adolescence over again, differently, and in female form. "Unconscious self-therapy," Edel calls these novels as he notes James's frequent evocations of his healing Muse, his beneficent activity of writing. At the age of fifty-seven, at the turn of the century, the novelist saw himself at the edge of a new career: he changed his appearance, shaving off the beard he had worn since the Civil War, and he returned to what Edel calls "the 'international' subject by which he had first established his fame" for the plot of *The Ambassadors*.

Henry James's career is one of tremendously fruitful adjusting of the character-ideal: the dualistic structure of it stays the same, but the roles of the shaper and the shaped, the maker and the made, change with new needs and new self-knowledge. By contrast, in Virginia Woolf's career, the character-ideal as reflected in literary works stays constant, structurally and in terms of the roles, from the adolescent first novel forward.

But when Virginia Woolf felt herself far away from the character-ideal, she despaired and slipped back into the psychic state that had preceded the formation of the ideal.

Phyllis Rose's study of Virginia Woolf, *A Woman of Letters*, which sets out to rescue Woolf from "biographical emphasis on her illness and suicide by showing the extent to which she took her life into her own hands," gives one of the clearest descriptions in the voluminous Woolf biographical literature of the character-ideal. Because she emphasizes Virginia Woolf's struggle—not her defeat—without, in the process, "normalizing a unique and complicated person," Rose can use Woolf's own structuring of her experience, her personal mythology, her metaphoric systems, to illuminate her creativity. The biographical assumption is "that life is as much a work of fiction—of guiding narrative structures—as novels and poems, and that the task of literary biography is to explore this fiction."

In my terms, the "guiding narrative structures" in a person's life are configurations of a character-ideal. But they also provide clues about how the person may have been unable to live up to the ideal—that is, clues to the nature of a person's illness or suicide. In the service of her rescue operation, Rose hardly mentions Virginia Woolf's nervous breakdown in 1895, after her mother's death; her second nervous breakdown and first attempt at suicide (by jumping out of a window) in 1904, after her father's death; her second suicide attempt in the fall of 1913 (with sleeping pills), after she had married and published her first novel; and the long period of disturbance, up to 1916, that followed. On the other hand, Rose offers a very suggestive interpretation of the depression that followed *To the Lighthouse*, and this interpretation does bear directly on Woolf's character-ideal as it becomes apparent in her earlier writings, particularly *The Voyage Out*. This first novel is the novel of Virginia Woolf's late adolescence, and it shows her character-ideal emerging.

Virginia Woolf's youth was shaped by traumatic experiences. She was sexually abused when she was six and again at twenty, first by one and then by the other of her step-brothers. Her mother Julia Stephen died when Virginia Woolf was thirteen, and her substitute mother, her oldest stepsister Stella, two years later. As he mourned his wife, Woolf's father Leslie Stephen sold their gay summer house in St. Ives and plunged his entire household into a year-round and years-long gloom in London. Like many children who have been traumatized, Virginia Woolf tended to view her world through the contrasts it presented and to dichotomize metaphysically on the basis of the contrasts. Her contrasts extended temporally (before and after), geographically (here and there), morally (good and bad, proper and improper), and in terms of groups (the talented and the beautiful, the commonsensical and the pretentious, the well-educated and the ill- or over-educated, etc., and, most importantly, the feminine and the masculine). Like most traumatized children, she was also uncertain about where she herself fitted into the scheme of bifurcations—with the overvalued or the despised, the sources of love or the sources of aggression.

Woolf noted the sexual episodes in her diaries and memoirs, but only found in them configurations of a frigidity that she said she had been born with, a "congenital asexuality," as Rose calls it. Her understanding of what her mother's death meant was more graphic. In her own assessment, Virginia Woolf was "unhealthily" obsessed with her lost mother, whose presence and collaboration she sought—and saw and heard—throughout her days. She noted in her diary, however, that she was released from the obsession when she was forty-four and had finished writing *To the Lighthouse*, a novel in which the character Mrs. Ramsay embodies the chief quality shared by her mother and her stepsister Stella and her older sister Vanessa—intuitive sympathy, attention to people. "Virginia uses metaphors of weaving and connection in describing her. She supported the fabric of their lives." After finishing *To the Lighthouse*, Virginia Woolf recorded: "I suppose I did for myself what psychoanalysts do for their patients. I expressed some very long felt and deeply felt emotion. And in expressing it I explained it and then laid it to rest."

In her work, Virginia Woolf is herself a sustainer of the fabric, a weaver, a reconciler of the very dichotomies with which she operates so pervasively, a blurrer of boundaries. Rose comments:

> Virginia connects her deepest impulse as a writer with this attempt to see the intruding, destructive, assertive elements of life as part of a whole. Constructing such "wholes" would be her equivalent of sexual activity. . . . Woolf's art, too, softens the harsh angularities of fact by placing them in a context of affective perception. Even a puddle of water must be seen in connection to something else, placed in a context, or it becomes unbearable. Rigid boundaries between perceived and perceiver, rigid boundaries between one part of reality and another are abhorrent to her. *The Waves*, her most ambitious novel, seeks to portray six individuals as aspects of one being; seeking continuity is her hallmark as a writer.

159

What this sensitive description does not show, however, is how the construction of wholes took place—on what constructing principles. The elimination of boundaries is the result, not the mechanism. The mechanism was, like most of the key mechanisms of literary creativity, an achievement of adolescence. Virginia Woolf's dichotomizing thinking gave way to a kind of thinking in which an opposition is posed and then one side is shaped and given its meaning by the other. The thinking is clearest and most extensively developed in Virginia Woolf's reflections on femininity and masculinity.

In her late adolescence, after her father died and she and her siblings moved from their Kensington house of mournings to one on Bloomsbury Square, Virginia Woolf began to associate with her brother Thoby's Cambridge University friends and also to concentrate her attention on her own writing. The young men from Cambridge, many of them homosexual, most of them dedicated to an image of themselves as an elite of pure intellects, were "pale, preoccupied, & silent," as Virginia Woolf noted contemptuously. She had envied them their educational opportunity, but she came to view them as corrupted by it, while she, at home, was in a sanctuary of common sense and lack of pretense. Rose presents the change in Virginia Woolf's view as a change in storyline:

> If before this the autobiographical "plot" had been the myth of liberation, the story of the immured maiden freed at last from bourgeois captivity, now the elements recombine and take shape as a concern with two ways of knowing which are at war. At its least biased, the dualistic myth presents masculine and feminine traits as very different but both valuable; at its most biased, it opposes masculine sterility to feminine creativity. In formulating this myth, largely in reaction to the masculine exclusivity of her brother's friends, Virginia began to create a more positive and distinctive sense of herself.

The novel in which the change of storyline was both recorded and reworked is *The Voyage Out*, which Virginia Woolf labored over for a period of seven years, from 1905 to 1912, the year she married Leonard Woolf. The novel went through ten drafts. In the course of the seven-year gestation, the central character Rachel Vinrace, a motherless young woman of startling ignorance in all matters sexual, traveling with an older woman companion, underwent a transformation more revealing than the one undergone by Rachel Vinrace in the final version of the novel. The earlier drafts present a Rachel who is Virginia Woolf in a mode of nearly direct autobiography: she is obsessed by the memory of her mother; she is ignorant of sex; but she has read widely, can assert herself, argue self-confidently—she is vicariously experienced, bookishly sophisticated. In the final version, only the bare fact of her mother's death is mentioned, and Rachel Vinrace is deprived of all her strength and self-confidence. She becomes a young woman whose vulnerability is palpable, not hidden, and whose innocence is so complete that the plot can very easily take the form of a *Bildungsroman* in which she has everything to learn on a trip to South America.

In the earlier drafts there was little change in Rachel over the course of her voyage out, while in the final version the change takes place in two stages. The first is conducted by the older companion, the maternal Helen Ambrose, who helps Rachel interpret a kiss she has been given— against her will and to her terror—by an older married man. In all versions of the novel, Rachel's disgust is clear, even after the facts of life have been explained to her, but in the later version, Helen protects her and helps her get over her fear. In the second stage, her education comes at the hands of two young Cambridge types. St. John Hirst, modeled on Lytton Strachey, is ugly, sadistically intelligent, misogynous, and he shakes what little self-esteem Rachel possesses, makes her feel powerless and stupid. Rachel fantasizes a retreat in which she has a female entourage at her service: "She would be a Persian princess far from civilization, riding her horse upon the mountains alone, and making her women sing to her in the evening, far from all this, from the strife of men and women."

Hirst's traveling companion, Terence Hewet, who has no Bloomsbury model, is, in Rose's description:

> sensitive, perceptive, down-to-earth, and eminently sane; and, as opposed to Hirst, he likes women, though he approaches them with something of the spirit of scientific curiosity with which Darwin approached beetles. He is going to be a novelist and he wants to write a novel about silence, about the things people don't say, an aspiration which has frequently been taken as identical to Woolf's own. There is "something of a woman about him."

This character, as Rose notes, grew over the various drafts of *The Voyage Out*. While she made Rachel Vinrace more unsophisticated and vulnerable, Woolf added passages "which serve to bring Terence out

161

more strongly and to present him as concerned and positive about Rachel's experience." He came to possess what Rachel lost over the various drafts—her self-confidence. So Rose rightly speculates that the two young people, who become engaged to each other, are "split projections of Virginia Woolf." This is not a story of female creativity and masculine sterility dichotomized; it is a story of perfectly complementary halves of an androgynous being.

The young lovers resemble in many details two characters in a wittily autobiographical novel Virginia Woolf wrote fifteen years later, *Orlando*. The title character, Orlando, spends the first half of the three hundred years of his fantastical lifespan as a man; then he becomes, miraculously and under mysterious circumstances, a woman. The female Orlando is happy enough in the eighteenth century to be single and footloose in London, changing sex as easily and as often as she changes her clothes. But in the nineteenth century she falls under the grim shadow of Victorian morality and feels that she must marry and reproduce. The men she knows in her literary life are St. John Hirsts of genius, pompous modern Cambridge men *avant la lettre*. But she is saved from their company by the appearance of a gentle, sensitive, feminine man who likes to ride, to hunt, to adventure. She is also saved from the inconvenience of sex by an immaculate conception that leads eventually to the immaculate birth of a son who then disappears from the novel without a trace. The love felt by Orlando and her husband-to-be when they meet in a forest is instantaneous, and no strife between men and women disturbs it. Certainly no lovemaking disturbs it, as none is needed to produce "their" child. Even their little periods of questioning serve only to reveal their kindred spirits, to keep them from an identity-destroying Victorian coupling:

> "Are you positive you aren't a man?" he would ask anxiously, and she would echo,
> "Can it be possible you're not a woman?" and then they must put it to the proof without more ado. For each was so surprised at the quickness of the other's sympathy, and it was to each such a revelation that a woman could be as tolerant and free-spoken as a man, and a man as strange and subtle as a woman, that they had to put the matter to the proof at once.
> And so they would go on talking.

In this period of marital and reproductive happiness, Orlando is finally able to complete a poem she has been working on for most of her three-hundred-year existence. The poem is born as magically as the son, because language is reproductive: "they would go on talking" is putting sex to the proof.

In my terms, Virginia Woolf had the idea, the ideal, that she could fabricate herself, remake herself, as a double being, a woman-man. She did not—in the Platonic manner—set out to keep unruly sexual appetites in check; rather, she kept her mysterious, needy, hungry femininity under masculine check, as it were underneath masculine clothing. She could protect her feminine inner world, the harem she and her mother inhabited, by this kind of intrapsychic marriage or synthesis of her feminine and masculine sides. Self-fabrication, as Rose noted, kept all dualities from parting, kept everything part of a whole, without intrusions or losses. The procreational dimension of this ideal is presented in *Orlando*: a son and a poem are born of the perfectly matched self-partnership.

Orlando was written in an exuberant mood, as a celebration of Virginia Woolf's love for the exuberant and affectionate Vita Sackville-West, and it was not followed by one of the depressions that frequently came when Woolf completed a book. Indeed, *Orlando* (1928) seems to have been an anti-depressent or a termination for the especially severe, suicidal period after *To the Lighthouse* (1927), the book that Woolf had initially viewed optimistically as a self-therapy, a reconciliation with her lost mother, or with the loss of her mother.

Rose suggests that the main character in the novel, Mrs. Ramsay, was a portrait of Virginia Woolf's mother as an artist, a hostess who could make a day or a dinner party into a work of art. Mrs. Ramsay, then, could be more like Virginia Woolf, and like the character who represents Virginia Woolf in the novel, Lily Briscoe, a painter who desperately, almost pathetically wants Mrs. Ramsay's love and approval. In the person of Lily, Virginia Woolf could feel absolved and forgiven for not being a Mrs. Ramsay, a wife and mother. (She could also survive Mrs. Ramsay, whose art was not of the immortal sort to which Virginia Woolf aspired, and which took her angrily beyond her mother, showed her mother's limitations.) But, Rose argues, the result of loving Mrs. Ramsay so strongly (death wishes and all) was that Virginia Woolf allowed herself—through Lily, through the novel—to become passive and dependent, wrapped in her mother's and Mrs. Ramsay's emotional artistry. In general, Rose concludes:

Virginia Woolf had to pay an enormous psychic price for the privilege of writing. She was proud of the number of works she managed to write, and well she might have been, for every book was wrested from an enemy within, the angel in the house she never completely succeeded in killing. Perhaps because the mother she loved so perfectly embodied the Victorian ideal of womanhood, perhaps because no other ideal of womanhood was available, some part of Woolf judged herself by the standard she tried consciously to reject. The martyr of stereotypes she was trying to destroy, she nevertheless succeeded in illuminating in her fiction—preeminently in *To the Lighthouse*—the tensions and fears that can afflict a creative woman.

Rose's interpretation of the daughter's need of her mother and fear of that need is very compelling, as is her suggestion that Virginia Woolf was split between the social role her mother had played and the role of the artist, perfection of the life (in her mother's terms) or of the work. But it seems important to me that *To the Lighthouse* contains no female character who either embodies the feminine-masculine balanced ideal or finds a complementary masculine other-half. There is not even an odd and precarious couple like the one Woolf had recently made in *Mrs. Dalloway*: the very social, somewhat frivolous Clarissa Dalloway and the very solitary, deep, haunted, and suicidal Septimus Smith. I read the absence of a couple in *To the Lighthouse* as a signal that Virginia Woolf was out of her carefully achieved intrapsychic balance or complementarity. Lily Briscoe may be absolved and forgiven in the novel for her singleness and her singularity, but she has no masculine dimension with which to surround her love of Mrs. Ramsay or to attract Mrs. Ramsay; she is no Orlando.

MIND AND COSMOS: THE POLITICAL CHARACTER-IDEAL

In his *Autobiography*, Charles Darwin declared simply and directly that "the voyage of the Beagle has been by far the most important event in my life and determined my whole career." It struck him as marvelous that the chance to go on the ship as a naturalist had almost eluded him twice, once because his father had disapproved of the plan and once because the ship captain, a believer in Lavatar's physiognomic character-ology, had judged Darwin's nose a poor augury for his success. His uncle had rescued him from Robert Darwin's judgment, and Fitz-Roy, the captain, had not let his characterology deprive him of a cabin-mate. Darwin's *Autobiography* is a record of his joy:

> I have always felt that I owe to the voyage the first real training or education of my mind. I was led to attend closely to several branches of natural history, and thus my powers of observation were improved, though they were already fairly developed.

Darwin's biographers have had great difficulty in taking him at his word and putting his interest in his own mental processes—his narcissistic pleasure, to use Freud's terms—at the center of his story. They present him as naive and unintrospective, even while they cite him writing very clearly to his fiancée: "During the five years of my voyage (& indeed I may add the two last) which from the active manner in which they have been passed may be said to be the commencement of my real life, the whole pleasure was derived from what passed in my mind." Peter Brent's *Charles Darwin* is psychologically astute about Darwin's character, and Howard Gruber's huge *Darwin on Man* treats Darwin's scientific creativity in enormous detail, but these two books together barely touch the significance Darwin himself gave to his formative experience—his improvement—on the Beagle.

Among the branches of natural history he pursued while he was traveling, Darwin felt that geology was the most important to him, because "reasoning here comes into play." Reasoning, he thought in the Aristotelian manner, draws order out of chaos:

> On first examining a new district nothing can appear more hopeless than the chaos of the rocks; but by recording the stratification and nature of the rocks and fossils at many points, always reasoning and predicting what will be found elsewhere, light soon begins to dawn on the district, and the structure of the whole becomes more or less intelligible.

At the time of his trip, he had written about the emotional or affective meaning of being a recipient of chaotic impressions, of the exquisite superfluity of the world:

> The delight one experiences . . . bewilders the mind; if the eye attempts to follow the flight of a gaudy butterfly, it is arrested by some strange tree or fruit; if watching an insect one forgets it in the strange flower it is crawling over. . . . The mind is a chaos of delight. . . . To a person fond of Natural

165

History, such a day as this brings with it pleasure more acute than he may ever experience.

Darwin described in his *Autobiography* the source of order—good work habits, particularly the habit of disciplined mental concentration:

> . . . the habit of energetic industry and concentrated attention to whatever I was engaged in, which I then acquired. Everything about which I thought or read was made to bear directly on what I had seen and was likely to see; and this habit of mind was continued during the five years of the voyage. I feel sure that it was this training which enabled me to do whatever I have done in science.

Further, when he reflected back on his experience, Darwin felt that during the five years of his voyage and his self-regulation, he had recapitulated the course of evolution. Both he and all of nature were, he thought, self-regulating mechanisms. The human species would progress as he had while he gradually gave up the great passion of his youth, which was for shooting birds, and replaced it with scientific work, particularly with "making out the geological structure of a country."

> I discovered, though unconsciously and insensibly, that the pleasure of observing and reasoning was a much higher one than that of skill and sport. The primeval instincts of the barbarian slowly yielded to the acquired tastes of the civilized man. That my mind became developed through my pursuits during the voyage, is rendered probable by a remark made by my father, who was the most acute observer whom I ever saw, of a sceptical disposition, and far from being a believer in phrenology; for on first seeing me after the voyage, he turned round to my sisters and exclaimed, "Why the shape of his head is quite altered."

Very literally, Darwin concluded that his brain had been altered by his intense, revolutionary period of work. Very Freudianly, he spoke in the terms that later underpinned the theory of sublimation or redirection of libido to higher and finer pursuits.

What Darwin had learned to do was assert control over his own mental processes, converting the habit of industry into methods of discovery. He viewed his mind as a scene in which different types of thought both complement and compete with each other. For example, he distinguished "castles in the air" (fantasies) from scientific and logical

166

"trains of thought" and described the ideal relationship between the two in his telegraphic Notebook-M prose:

> Therefore (independent of improving powers of invention) such castles in the air are highly advantageous, before real train of inventive thoughts are brought into play, & then perhaps the sooner the castles in the air are banished the better.

The fantasies should, then, be kept out of mind, even at the price of "severe disappointment," says Darwin, recalling his father's "positive statement that insanity is only cured by forgetfulness." Those who are able to forget or banish "desultory thought" are those capable of "keeping one idea before your mind steadily, & not merely thinking intently," who are capable of the "excessive labor of inventive thought."

People who believe that their castles in the air or their dreams are real are insane—and such a condition would come about, in Darwin's view, if castles in the air or dreams dominated the mind's scene too much and became habitual. In general, Darwin believed that we are creatures of "double consciousness." One self is made up of all things we do unconsciously, without thinking or in a state of forgetfulness, the other is our conscious "ordinary state of mind." An insane person experiences the first consciousness as if it were "a second & unreasonable man" housed within and in control. A person, on the other hand, who has self-control and can even change his habits, improve himself, must be able to grasp his history and his heredity: "If one could remember all one's father's actions, as one does those in second childhood, or when drunk, they would not be more different, & yet they would make one's father & self one person." Darwin understood himself as his father's product—"I am Darwin & take after my Father in heraldic principle"—and as someone who had the ability to both use and surpass his heritage through the exercise of his conscious reason. This was Darwin's character-ideal. And in terms of libidinal types, it was a perfect balance of obsessionality given over to observation (which Darwin said was his father's great gift) or collecting, and narcissism given over to theorizing, enjoying the mental process of ordering all the collections, soaring beyond observation, seeing natural history as a version of his own history.

After he returned to England and married Emma Wedgwood, who was, he assured her, capable of bringing about further improvement in him—keeping him on the evolutionary track by socializing him—Darwin finished the first of the ten volumes and many short special studies that grew out of his Beagle industriousness. But he did not publish the theory of evolution he was developing in his private notebooks and sketch manuscripts. In these notebooks he focused on two areas: general evolution, and human evolution, particularly human psychology, about which he never did publish a separate work. In his private writings, particularly two notebooks labeled M and N, he often extrapolates from the domain of human (especially his own) psychology to the natural world, while his later publications consistently reason toward human beings from the physical environment and the histories of other living beings. Only in private did Darwin use himself as a model for nature.

Almost twenty years passed between the end of the Beagle voyage and Darwin's first effort at the book that was finally converted into *Origin of Species* (1859) under pressure of Alfred Russell Wallace's concurrent work on evolutionary theory. Twelve more years passed before he published *Descent of Man* (1871), but neither of these two works, the most influential in Darwin's huge corpus, include the range of work on human psychology represented in the M and N notebooks. Darwin's biographers have variously explained his slow and indirect pace toward making public his theory of evolution and his reticence (particularly noted by Gruber) about situating human beings, and particularly human mental capacities, in his evolutionary scheme. They note that he hated polemics and had no desire to do battle against the reigning Natural Theology of his day. He was also not eager to be a martyr for his materialism or to stir up trouble within his family, where evolutionary views were well represented but not in the form he offered and where some, like his wife, were very uncomfortable with atheism. In his M notebook, Darwin considered how he might present his views on human psychology: "To avoid stating how far I believe in materialism, say only that emotions, instincts, degrees of talent, which are hereditary are so because brain of child resembles parent stock."

This much materialism was in praise of parental stock, but what Darwin was really after was a theory allowing for improvement on parental stock, for continual improvement of the human species. Insofar as this theory was sweepingly ambitious and based on his own psychological experience during the Beagle voyage, Darwin held it back; insofar as it was modest and a cautiously reasoned contribution to science, he published it. His secrecy feels like the secrecy of a boy whose masturbation fantasies are ambitious, conquistadorial. But Darwin did not have Freud's confidence in the universalizability of his self-analysis, the confidence that his dreams could be the key to something generally human. In Freud's terms, it would be most unusual for a man whose mother had died when he was eight to have his masculine ambitions without great inner checking, because Freud put such stock—from his own experience—in the mother's love surviving and sustaining beyond the period of its repression, the Oedipal period.

Darwin went to great trouble in his notebooks to convince himself that a theory allowing for human improvement was much more humble and unarrogant than any theory claiming that God had created an immutable man with nothing to strive for. But his evolutionary view was also the one that most comfortably accommodated the tensions in Darwin's character between enormous ambition and great self-effacement; between quickness of hypothesizing ("the mind is at first irresistibly hurried into the belief . . .") and self-criticism; between self-centeredness and a fabled sweetness of manner as a reaction-formation against egotism. He was a man who chastized himself continually to keep his aspirations under control; to keep himself from too quick a jumping to theoretical conclusions and too much competition with and surpassing of his father and his peers; to let himself evolve as species do, slowly. The nature of the debilitating illness that overtook Darwin in his later years has never been clearly determined, but it is clear that in the years after the Beagle voyage he harmed his health with overwork, and overwork to the point of collapse can also be a form of self-punishment for excess of ambition or "zeal" (to use the word that recurs repeatedly in the *Autobiography*).

Peter Brent sensed how important Darwin's self-critical streak was, but he could only imagine it as a matter of critical voices in Darwin's youthful surroundings somehow and to some degree internalized:

> On some matters at least, and at certain levels, Darwin appears all his life to have stood as though outside himself. From that quasi-external stance, he looked back at himself with a surly, critical gleam in his eye. Was he at those times his father? Was he the elder brother Erasmus . . . ? It is hard now to be certain—there had also been at times, after all, a certain stridency in the voices of the sisterhood. Whatever the reason, he seems always to have been ready to play this older person, and to take his part—that of the accuser, the unanswerable critic—against the suspect "I," the working,

active self whose efforts were never, despite all the successes through the years, enough to placate that watchful, interior hostility.

To the question, Why would Darwin identify with the critical voices? Brent offers no answer. But the self-criticism makes psychological sense if it served not to placate his father and family but to check his desire, which would have been hurtful to them if they had known of it, to surpass them all, leave them all behind in evolutionary terms. Darwin's father and others had certainly pointed up Darwin's lack of youthful ambition, but it seems very likely that Darwin's idleness was tremendous ambition awaiting a focus, an opportunity, a mode that Darwin could call legitimate, a type of gambling quite different from the gambling he had done as a young man "to a most disgusting degree." When the opportunity came on the Beagle, his youth and everyone in it became the hereditary past, steppingstones. "My father's mind was not scientific, and he did not try to generalize his knowledge under general laws, yet he formed a theory for almost everything which occurred." His older brother Erasmus had a remarkably clear mind and wide interests, but he was physically weak and "he failed in energy." The sisters had "strongly marked characters" and were affectionate, he said, but he owed nothing to them intellectually. Darwin felt his own superiority, and to his own children he was determined to present an improved hereditary foundation:

> My wish to improve my temper, what does it arise from but organization, that organization may have been affected by circumstances & education & by the choice which at that time organization gave me to will—Verily that faults of the fathers, corporeal & bodily, are visited upon the children.

A man with his view of the importance of inherited "organization" would, Darwin concluded, "be most humble, he would strive [to do good,] to improve his organization for his children's sake & for the effect of his example on others."

The link between his science and his self-improvement campaign is obvious in a notebook of observations Darwin started keeping in 1840, "A Biographical Sketch of an Infant." He set out to record the experiment of which he was literally the father, concentrating on observable expression of emotion, the realm where a child's relations with its parents are most influential. In 1877, after a delay of thirty-seven years, Darwin published his observations of his son, who by that time had a son of his own—so that Darwin could observe (but not comment on) an experiment over two generations.

Ability to improve was, Darwin had decided before he became a father, the mark of civilization. As he wrote on October 2, 1838, in a journal he later set aside under the title "Old and Useless Notes":

> The difference between civilized man & savage, is that the former is endeav-ouring to change that part of moral sense which experience (education is the experience of others) shows does not tend to greatest good. . . . The change of our moral sense is strictly analogous to change of instinct amongst animals.

What allows humans to change themselves is that they have "reasoning powers in excess, instead of definite instincts—this is a replacement in mental machinery, so analogous to what we see in bodily, that it does not stagger me." The improvements that individual human beings ac-quire can be transmitted or translated from the realm of habit into the realm of structure, as Darwin insisted in an unpublished 1844 manuscript:

> These facts lead to the conviction, justly wonderful as it is, that almost infinitely numerous shades of disposition, of tastes, of peculiar movements, and even of individual actions, can be modified or acquired by one individ-ual and transmitted to its offspring. One is forced to admit that mental phenomena (no doubt through their intimate connection with the brain) can be inherited, like infinitely numerous and fine differences of corporeal structure.

Darwin's biographers have not given much attention to how self-confirming and wonderful for all human beings the prospect of evolution seemed to Darwin. But his projection of his personal evolution during the five-year Beagle voyage into the goal for human evolution is very apparent in his notebooks and perhaps clearest in a long passage in the Notebook-M on happiness:

> Definition of happiness the number of pleasant ideas passing through mind in given time—intensity to degree of [happy] pleasure of such thoughts. . . . Those thoughts are most pleasant, when conscience tells our mind good has been done . . . pleasure of intellect affection excited, pleasure

of imagination. . . . A wise man will try to obtain this happiness, though he sees some [intellectual] good men, from insanity etc. unhappy—perhaps not so much as they appear & perhaps partly their fault—whether this rule of happiness agrees with that of New Testament another question. . . . If we obey literally New Testament future life is almost sole object.

Darwin did not set his eye on happiness in the Christian afterlife; on the contrary, he spoke quite freely about the possibility that men might, in this life, in the course of evolution, become angels. "Men make angels." He could imagine this, he said in his *Autobiography*. "Believing as I do that man in the distant future will be a far more perfect creature than he is now."

Emily Dickinson, too, focused her intense and passionate aspiration on perfectibility, and she agreed with Darwin that perfection would be a mind filled with pleasure-giving thoughts. They both enjoyed their abilities to read in their own minds the course of nature: "The Outer—from the Inner/Derives its Magnitude," as Emily Dickinson said (in poem #451 of the Johnson edition, which will be cited below). They were both creatively narcissistic in the sense Freud had noted in *Civilization and Its Discontents*, that is, they sought their main satisfactions in their internal mental processes. Her image of satisfaction was of an autonomous mental kingdom, evolved to be so embracing that it could embrace the universe—as Dickinson's forebearers had imagined that God's mind did—and could compass the universe with a natural historical sweep that even Darwin would have found audacious:

The Brain—is wider than the Sky—
For—put them side by side—
The one the other will contain
With ease—and You—beside

The Brain is deeper than the sea—
For—hold them—Blue to Blue—
The one the other will absorb—
As Sponges—Buckets—do

The Brain is just the weight of God—
For—Heft them—Pound for Pound—
And they will differ—if they do—
As Syllable for Sound—

(#632)

Her own mind, Emily Dickinson often wrote, was torn, divided, haunted, embattled: "The Battle fought between the Soul / And No Man—is the One / Of all the Battles prevalent— / By far the Greater One—" (#594). But her goal—her character-ideal, in my terms—was a mind triumphant over its civil wars and become like a harmonious domain ruled over by a thought-rich and benevolent king. A fantasy about this kingship appears first in her adolescent letters and then in her poems from beginning to end, and she makes it always clear than only her own fear or inner battle keeps her from the fantasy's fulfillment.

> We never know how high we are
> Till we are asked to rise
> And then if we are true to plan
> Our statures touch the skies—
>
> The Heroism we recite
> Would be a normal thing
> Did not ourselves the Cubits warp
> For fear to be a King—
>
> (#1176)

Emily Dickinson's fantasy took different forms, but all the forms have in common that they presuppose withdrawal from society, self-enclosure. Sometimes she spoke from the point of view of the king, at other times as a subject in the king's realm, bowing before him, being blessed by his presence, or, as in the poem below, written in 1859 when she was twenty-nine, waiting to tell him her story:

> Mute thy Coronation—
> Meek my Vive le roi,
> Fold a tiny courtier
> In thine Ermine, Sir,
> There to rest revering
> Till the pageant by,
> I can mummur broken,
> Master, It was I—
>
> (#151)

This brief poem presents the king's coronation as a secret and the humble subject's confession in vaguely poignant terms. In other poems, like the one from early 1862, the last stanza of which is cited below, the listening and speaking imagery is bolder and also more complicated, as it mingles with imagery of marriage, dowry exchange. The thought is somewhat obscure, but it seems that Dickinson is rejecting the role of a poet who speaks to others, who publishes, because she wants to be both the regal or divine hurler of poetic lightning bolts and the still, reverential (indeed, "impotent") listener.

> Nor would I be a Poet—
> It's finer—own the Ear—
> Enamored—impotent—content—
> The License to revere,
> A privilege so awful
> What would the Dower be,
> Had I the Art to stun myself
> With Bolts of Melody!
>
> (#505)

Whether she identified herself with the king or with his subject, Emily Dickinson always stressed the king's power, which she construed sometimes in military and sometimes in sexual terms. When she was thirty-nine, she told one of her correspondents her first feeling about the Lord's Prayer as it appears in Matthew 6 ("For thine is the kingdom, and the power and the glory . . ."): "When a little Girl, I remember hearing that remarkable passage and preferring the 'Power,' not knowing at the time that 'Kingdom' and 'Glory' were included." But the king whom Dickinson imagined as the organizer of her life and mind was by no means the Lord of the Christians. That Christian Lord, on the contrary, she viewed as a disorganizing force in the cosmos, source of pain and death, a Being who maliciously taunted people—though He may have been, in his extracosmic and unknown domain, a Good Lord. She makes it quite clear that she had addressed prayers once to this Christian Lord: "Of course—I prayed— / And did God care?" (#376). When she was not heard, she distanced herself: "But I, grown shrewder—scan the Skies / With a suspicious Air— / As Children—swindled for the first / All Swindlers—be—infer" (#476). On earth, in this life, where the Christian Lord appears as the destroyer, her unamed king—in an almost gnostic or Zoroastrian way—played the role of the good and creative ruler. She, who defied her family and her community by refusing throughout her life to join the Church, explicitly contrasted her own condition of being ruled to those of Rebecca, the wife selected for Isaac, and an anonymous Persian (perhaps Zoroastrian?) convert:

> He touched me, so I live to know
> That such a day, permitted so,
> I groped upon his breast—
> It was a boundless place to me
> And silenced, as the awful sea
> Puts minor streams to rest.
>
> And now, I'm different than before,
> As if I breathed superior air—
> Or brushed a Royal Gown—
> My feet, too, that had wandered so—
> My Gipsy face—transfigured now—
> To tenderer Renown—
>
> Into this Port, if I might come,
> Rebecca, to Jerusalem,
> Would not so ravished turn—
> Nor Persian, baffled at her shrine
> Lift such a Crucifixal sign
> To her imperial Sun.
>
> (#506)

The identity of the "he" in this poem is unstated, and it is not clear whether he was—as I think—a person assimilated into an already existing mental role or a person pure and simple. Emily Dickinson's many biographers have produced a great variety of theories about which man she addressed in three surviving letter drafts as "Master," which man is invoked in the most intense period (1858–1864) of her love poems, which man played the role for her of the King. The question is not decidable on the extant evidence. But what seems most important is that Emily Dickinson always set her beloved or beloveds into the same image-system. In 1878, when her poetic output was quite diminished, she confessed her love for a recently widowed older man with a quite royal name, Judge Otis Phillips Lord, whom she had known since the 1850s, in terms that are precisely the same as those she had used in her poetry of the late 1850s: "Our Life together was long forgiveness on your part toward me. The trespass of my rustic Love upon your realms of Ermine, only a Sovereign could forgive—I never knelt to other." It is as though she was quoting her "Mute Thy Coronation . . ." (1859) and reimagining herself tucked like a tiny courtier in the royal ermine.

It was in 1858 that Emily Dickinson wrote the first of the three letter drafts to "Master," and also that she began to write poetry in earnest, beginning to display the ambition for her work which is so palpable in later poems. She produced a remarkable body of work in 1861, a year during which she was treated for a problem with her eyes that terrorized her, and then a truly astonishing stream of poems in 1862, the year when she also assembled and recopied many of her earlier poems, arranging a large portion of her oeuvre into a series of small sewn chapbooks. Her attention to her poems seems to have risen as the mysterious lover disappeared after a misunderstanding or an obstacle to their love became insurmountable. This short poem (in which the "Court" could allude to the court where Judge Lord presided in his hometown of Salem) is contemporaneous with one of the surviving letter drafts, from 1861:

The Court is far away—
No Umpire—have I—
My Sovereign is offended—
To gain his grace—I'd die!

I'll seek his royal feet—
I'll say—Remember—King—
Thou shalt—thyself—one day—a Child
Implore a *larger*—thing—

That Empire—is of Czars—
As small—they say—as I—
Grant *me*—that day—the royalty—
To *intercede*—for *Thee*—

(#235)

The story that other poems of this time tell is that the lover asked a less large thing—her sexual love—and she refused, arguing that she had given him her spirit and also implying that she feared her acquiescence would lead to rejection: ". . . a Maid / Always a Flower would be . . ." (#869). His departure then felt to her like a betrayal, which she likened to Peter's betrayal of Jesus (#203). By 1864, she seems to have turned back into herself quite firmly and become, again, her own royal hunter with his hound:

This consciousness that is aware
Of Neighbors and the Sun
Will be the one aware of Death
And that itself alone

Is traversing the interval
Experience between
And most profound experiment
Appointed unto Men—

How adequate unto itself
Its properties shall be
Itself unto itself and none
Shall make discovery.

Adventure most unto itself
The Soul condemned to be—
Attended by a single Hound
Its own identity.

(#822)

There was very little room in Emily Dickinson's world for secrecy; if she wanted "none to make discovery," she had to keep her secrets in her own mind. The "Sun" (presumably the royal, masterly Sun) and "the Neighbors" could not have missed one another, for she lived with her parents and her younger sister Lavinia, while her brother Austin and his wife Sue, Emily Dickinson's most passionately loved female friend, lived next door. But all "the Neighbors and the Sun" were close to each other in the further sense that Emily Dickinson seems to have experienced herself as made up of all her loved ones. She wrote to and about them all in similar terms, feeling herself merged or fused with them, as she once (in 1864) very graphically said of Sue: "Where my Hands are cut, Her fingers will be found inside." They were all in her like members of an audience for whom she performed poetically: they fired her imagination, heard her, admired her, beautified her, showed her herself, ruled over her desires. Their interchangeability—and her bisexuality—is most dramatically illustrated by a love letter in the form of a poem (#494) which exists in two manuscript versions, one addressed throughout to "Him" and one to "Her."

Dickinson had a habit, dating at least from her adolescence, of staying as apart as their proximity permitted from these loved ones in order to love them all the more and all the more intensely. "The Soul selects her own society / Then—shuts the Door . . ." (#303). She preferred poetry messages and letters to conversations, she kept her own company—to the point of reclusiveness in her later years. When she was twenty-one, she explained herself to her brother Austin: "If you talk to no one, you are amassing thoughts which will be bright and golden for those you left at home—*we* meet our friends, and a constant interchange wastes *tho't* and feeling and we are then obliged to *repair* and *renew*—there isn't the brimful feeling which one gets *away*." When she met with friends, she was "we" because she had her family inside her, where she could share her store of thoughts with them if she did not waste them on the others. The same idea is repeated in a letter the next year to Sue that equates the "brimful feeling" with a "kingly feeling" and finds it proof against insanity: "I have the old *kingly feeling* even more than before, for I know not even the *cracker man* will invade this solitude." Emily Dickinson felt that she preserved herself when she refused herself in every way but mentally to those she loved—to experience her love for them mentally all the more. The Poet, she wrote in 1862, is so full as to be invulnerable to theft: ". . . Of portion—so unconscious— / The Robbing—could not harm— / Himself—to Him—a Fortune— / Exterior—to Time—" (#448).

Emily Dickinson's stoical cultivation of self-sufficiency—of self-rule intended to produce internal richness—has seemed to some of her biographers an indication of ego strength and readiness to sacrifice sociability to art, while to others an early history of deprivation, particularly maternal deprivation, is signaled. Cynthia Griffin Wolff's feminist biography *Emily Dickinson* approvingly notes Adrienne Rich's assessment: "Genius knows itself. . . . Dickinson chose her seclusion, knowing she was an exception and knowing what she needed. . . . Given her vocation, she was neither eccentric nor quaint." At the other end of the evaluative spectrum, John Cody, a psychiatrist, offered this summary in his psychobiography of the poet, *After Great Pain*:

> That her intellectual and esthetic gifts were fiercely unsubservient must not, however, be allowed to obscure the fact that in practical life she exhibited helplessness, vulnerability, and *infantile* dependence. Studying her behavior and her explicitly expressed attitude, one is led to conclude that all her life there smoldered in Emily Dickinson's soul the muffled but voracious clamoring of the abandoned child. Although she herself was apparently never more than dimly aware that her compulsive self-entomb-

ment in the safe family mansion and her feeling that her mother had left her emotionally unsheltered were in any way related, it is certainly plausible that the life style and sense of loss and hunger are opposite faces of the one monolithic bereavement.

To Cody, Emily Dickinson was a person who suffered from multiple phobias, including agoraphobia, who responded to the marriage of her beloved brother to her beloved friend with not only a compensatory outburst of poetry but a seven-year psychotic episode, whose "Master" was sheerly fantasy (*pseudologia fantastica*), whose eye trouble was psychosomatic, and whose last years were lived out in a clinical depression. His Emily Dickinson has so many symptoms and such a plethora of different neurotic and psychotic pathologies that she is a virtual encyclopedia of mental illness.

Cynthia Wolff, like Phyllis Rose in her study of Virginia Woolf, explicitly rejects approaches that turn female subjects into patients, while advocating intricately careful attention to what the subject has to say for herself about herself, in her poems and letters, in recurring images and themes. The poems are not considered as records of symptomatology, registrations of the onset, development and remission of illness; they are literary productions, embedded in a literary history and a social context. Cody, on the other hand, sets out to refute all the biographers who have denied or muted the extent of Emily Dickinson's madness. His idea is that there is a direct proportion between the intensity of her illness, between 1857 and 1864, and her poetic production, in terms of both quantity and quality.

I think that this biographical controversy has its root in the particular nature of Dickinson's type of creativity. All the Dickinson biographers have been vexed by the fact that the key episodes in her life cannot be explored directly; they must first be constructed from oblique clues further complicated by the censorship of her family and editors, who deleted and destroyed letters and poems. The surviving written estate refers to her life only in poetic codes very difficult if not impossible to interpret. Wolff, who is an accomplished literary critic, is very accustomed to the imagery Dickinson drew upon for her coded, riddled poetry. Its sources in biblical and English and American literary traditions are familiar to Wolff, and the historical context normalizes the imagery for her. Cody is a psychiatric literalist. When he reads "I felt a Cleaving in my Mind— / As if my Brain had split— / I tried to match it—Seam by Seam— / But could not make them fit," he feels himself in the presence of a psychotic "thought disorder." He reads this image with those key to two other poems and jumps to his diagnosis: "The foregoing references—the snarl in the brain, the broken plank in reason, the cleavage in the mind—appear to be sufficient justification in themselves for concluding that the crisis in Emily Dickinson's life was a psychosis."

What is missed, it seems to me, from both of these angles is the imperative in Emily Dickinson's poetry. The self-command that goes: never be merely specific; every detail, every image must be a microcosm; looked at rightly, as if under a microscope, it should yield a cosmos. The right reader, to read rightly, would have a mind, a sensibility, an "ear" just like the poet's own. This is the ultimate requirement of the narcissistic creator. Or, as Emily Dickinson put her criterion:

> Good to hide, and hear 'em hunt!
> Better, to be found,
> If one cares to, that is,
> The Fox fits the Hound—
>
> Good to know, and not to tell,
> Best, to know and tell,
> Can one find the rare Ear
> Not too dull—
>
> (#842)

Chapter Eight

Art and Mental Illness and Theories of Creativity

ART AND NEUROSIS

In a 1945 essay entitled "Art and Neurosis," Lionel Trilling pointed out that in the course of the nineteenth century the idea that the exercise of artistic imagination is a kind of insanity grew more and more entrenched. Not the old notion, propounded (as we noted in Chapter 1) by Plato, that the poet is a god-possessed person, *en-theos* or enthusiastic, but rather a quasi-scientific, quasi-clinical equation of genius and insanity developed after the period we call Romantic. Essayists like Trilling, who viewed himself in a line extending from Charles Lamb ("On the Sanity of True Genius") through George Bernard Shaw, have ever since objected to efforts like that of the Italian psychiatrist Cesare Lombroso. Over a period of thirty years, culminating in 1894 with the sixth edition of *L'Uomo di genio*, Lombroso collected evidence of neurological diseases, neuroses, and psychoses among Western Europe's political and cultural leaders.

In this "art and neurosis" battle, a theory without a list was not considered well armed, so Havelock Ellis's examination of 1,030 lives from the *Dictionary of National Biography* was required to refute Lombroso's equation of genius and insanity on level statistical ground. "The association between genius and insanity is not . . . without significance," Ellis argued, "but in the face of the fact that its occurrence is only demonstrated in five percent of cases, we must put out of court any theory as to genius being a form of insanity."

As Ellis's metaphor indicates, much in this dispute depends on the

181

rules of its game, the parameters of its playing court. Definitions of genius and definitions of insanity determine the results of any inquiry about the relation of the two phenomena. Methods of defining are just as crucial. A place in the *Dictionary of National Biography* does not constitute a definition of genius, and diagnoses made retrospectively in the medium of a written record, a biography, brief or long, composed in most cases by a biographer with no more knowledge of mental illness than possessed by his subject or by contemporary observers of the subject, are even less reliable than diagnoses made in hospitals or consulting rooms with the subject to hand.

Both "genius" (or "art" in the general sense, or just plain "creativity") and "insanity" are terms that can embrace large populational ranges. Everyone, it could be argued, has genius in the two original senses of that word—the theological and the hereditary. "Genius" was used by the Romans to designate a tutelary spirit or protective agent, like the Arabic *jinni*; and speakers of languages derived from or influenced by Latin used "genius" to indicate a person's innate particular, rather than extraordinary, gifts. Everyone, furthermore, it could be argued on Freudian grounds, has a degree of insanity, if that word refers only to the neuroses and is not extended to the psychoses. At the wide ends of the ranges of "genius" and "insanity," there is congruence, and everyone has a bit of both. At the narrower ends of the ranges of the two words, where "genius" refers to rare, extraordinary abilities and achievements, and "insanity" refers to the psychoses, there may be some overlap, as Ellis noted, but the overlap is much, much rarer than either genius or insanity. Neither the congruence of the two broad categories in everyone nor the overlap of the two narrower ones in a rare few says anything at all, however, about the *relationship* between genius and insanity in any individual who qualifies for both categories.

Discussions of this topic may, by contrast, say a great deal about the relationship between political attitudes toward insanity and political attitudes toward art (where "art" indicates creativity in any sphere). People who value conformity or homogeneity in their populations, or even want all people to be equally mediocre, equate unusual creativity and insanity in a censorious spirit. The popular classification of homosexuality as a kind of insanity is very useful in such a political attitude toward homosexual creators. Conversely, those who want to excuse the behavior of an exceptionally creative person may argue that the occupational hazard to the person's mental health merits special dispensations. And those who want to protect a creative person from socio-politically motivated psychiatric classifications, like those which label insane any women who put creative work before all else in their lives, have both to detach "art and neurosis" and to redefine the terms.

I will return to the topic of creativity and socio-political attitudes in the next chapter, but here I want only to note that there is an obvious and reductionistic tendency, both among those who in some way equate genius and insanity or art and neurosis, and among those who are at pains to make distinctions. The common tendency is to blur all grada-tions among types both of genius and of insanity, art and neurosis. Differences in both types of creativity and types of neurotic symptoms, so apparent in the biographical vignettes of Samuel Johnson, Gustave Flaubert, Henry James, Virginia Woolf, Charles Darwin, and Emily Dickinson offered in the last chapter, are obscured completely in most *tout ou rien* discussions of "art and neurosis."

In this chapter, I want to try to enter into and explore a nexus of character-ideal types, types of creativity and psychopathological types. As I noted in Chapter 5, psychoanalysts have suggested various relations between character-types and types of pathology, but this area of their theorizing, it seems to me, is very fragmented. The fragmentation has arisen because the theory of character is so multidimensional and unsys-tematic and because, although the psychoanalytic theory of the neuroses is relatively untroubled territory, bedlam breaks out over the psychoses, both in terms of basic mental processes and in terms of causality.

Integrating a discussion of character-types and pathological types by means of a discussion of types of creativity, can, I think, cast some light on how and when and to what extent creativity is a sign that psychopathology has been prevented or cured or contained by being woven into a character-structure. In Chapters 1 and 2, I laid the founda-tion of the whole inquiry of this book by noting three ways in which creativity has traditionally been presented in images, and by suggesting how these three ways have been viewed as functions of character. For examples of these three modalities, I turned to three pairs of ancient and modern thinkers—Plato/Nietzsche, Aristotle/Freud, Zeno the Stoic/ Proust. Here, I will refer back to these figures and their theories, but concentrate on the modern scientific literature, particularly from within psychoanalysis. And I will also concentrate on images of mental (and thus characterological) failure. In each of the scientific theories I will take up below, a relationship—at least one—between creativity and psychopathology has been stated or implied, but, I will argue, the relationship has also been offered as the one crucial to all creativity, and to all creativity considered as one kind of process. It seems to me that each of these theories claims too much: a single psychic key to the mysteries of creativity, and thus to the mystery of how creativity is related to psychopathology.

CHARACTER-TYPES IN SELF-PORTRAITS OF THE ARTIST

In statements that creative people make about their creative processes, the differences between character-ideal types come through very clearly, but not always very boldly. Differences are subtly clear, not starkly. Consider, for example, a statement by a writer I have noted before as of the spiritual character-ideal type juxtaposed with one from a slightly older contemporary of his who is of the artisanal/sexual type.

> The progress of an artist is a continual self-sacrifice, a continual extinction of personality.

> The personality of the artist . . . finally refines itself out of existence, impersonalizes itself, so to speak.

At first glance, T. S. Eliot in "Tradition and the Individual Talent" sounds like James Joyce in Chapter 5 of *Portrait of the Artist as a Young Man*. But extinction is not refinement into a new form, as sacrificing is not fabrication. The goal, impersonality, means something different in the two cases.

Eliot's images of sacrifice and self-purification are different in turn from, say, those of A. E. Housman, for whom poems themselves were the self he stripped away, purged. Eliot's casting off of the veils of *maya* and his Christian asceticism are spiritualized versions of Housman's earthy process, still close to the body and to excretion. In "The Name and Nature of Poetry," Houseman presents his experience of poetry in its "first stage," the inspired stage before actual execution and revision, as a bubbling up from the "pit of the stomach."

> . . . If I were obliged, not to define poetry, but to name the class of things to which it belongs, I should call it a secretion; whether a natural secretion, like turpentine in the fir, or a morbid secretion, like the pearl in the oyster. I think that my own case, though I may not deal with the material so

cleverly as the oyster does, is the latter; because I have seldom written poetry unless I was rather out of health, and the experience, though pleasurable, was generally agitating and exhausting.

Eliot's and Housman's emptying-out processes, described in their two spiritual character-ideal modes, sound like exactly the opposite of the filling-up, expanding, empowering process of the narcissistic-obsessional person with a political character-ideal. Even though such a person may also feel a great need to get the work out of his or her system, the need is not so much for unburdening the self of some kind of distraction or excrement as it is for keeping the self's boundaries intact, making a mirror in which to see the self reflected or a brainchild in which to feel immortality. In the passage below, celebration of creative power alternates with fear that the channeling of that power will not prove strong enough. This writer is contemplating, in repetitive prose that itself threatens to go out of control, the similarity between his mind and his work:

> As I began to realize the true nature of the task I had set for myself, the image of the river began to haunt my mind. I actually felt that I had a great river thrusting for release inside of me and that I had to find a channel into which its flood-like power could pour. . . . Meanwhile, my creative power was functioning at the highest intensity it had ever known. . . . For one thing, my whole sensory and creative equipment, my powers of feeling and reflection—even the sense of hearing, and above all my powers of memory, had reached the greatest degree of sharpness that they had ever known. . . . At the end of a day of savage labor, my mind was still blazing with its effort. . . . I was unable to sleep, unable to subdue the tumult of these creative energies. . . . I wrote too much again. I not only wrote what was essential, but time and time again my enthusiasm for a good scene, one of those enchanting vistas which can open up to a man in the full flow of his creation, would overpower me, and I would write thousands of words upon a scene which contributed nothing of vital importance to a book whose greatest need already was ruthless condensation.

The prolix Thomas Wolfe wrote, of course, not an essay, but a whole book on the writing of his novel, and it is *The Story of a Novel* from which these sentences come. His title has something of the same awed and frightened distance—he says "a" novel, not "my" novel—that is apparent when he speaks of "creative powers" as though they had an existence of their own. He is different in this respect (as in others) from a purer narcissist like Henry Miller, whose "Reflections on Writing," from a volume self-aggrandizingly entitled *Wisdom of the Heart*, contains Miller's admission that he would like to write a whole book "on one small passage selected at random from my work," because a whole book would be necessary to tell everything of importance about that one passage's "inception, its genesis, its metamorphosis, its accouchement, of the time which elapsed between the birth of the idea and its recording," etc., etc. Such an educational book would be in line with Miller's image of himself as a benefactor of mankind who has traveled in his life the whole human evolutionary road. He tells how he began as a writer by imitating great writers of the past, his idols, how he failed miserably, and then began again:

> Immediately I heard my own voice I was enchanted: the fact that it was a separate, distinct, unique voice sustained me. . . . My huge failure was like the recapitulation of the experience of the race: I had to grow foul with knowledge, realize the futility of everything, smash everything, grow desperate, then humble, then sponge myself off the slate as it were, in order to recover my authenticity. . . . I find that there is plenty of room in the world for everybody—great interspatial depths, great ego universes, great islands of repair, for whoever attains to individuality. . . . This condition of sublime indifference is a logical development of the egocentric life. . . . The real problem is not one of getting on with one's neighbor or of contributing to the development of one's country, but of discovering one's destiny, of making a life in accord with the deep-centered rhythm of the cosmos. . . . Whatever there be of progress in life comes not through adaptation but through daring, through obeying the blind urge. . . . By daring one arrives at the mysterious X position of the artist, and it is this anchorage which no one can describe in words but yet subsists and exudes from every line that is written.

There is here an anal level—a period of being foul and needing to be wiped away, of being castrated—defended against or rejected by an intense display of phallic exhibitionism. Miller is a Wilhelm Reich "narcissistic character" who has found his channel. He claims that his ultimate goal is not creating artworks but creating himself. "All art, I firmly believe, will one day disappear. But the artist will remain and life itself will become not 'an art,' but art, i.e., will definitely and for all time usurp the field." Meanwhile, he says, he does not care what readers or critics make of what he writes: "I drop my fruit like a ripe tree. . . . I am not establishing values: I defecate and nourish. There is nothing more to it." The aggression in all of this is, obviously, palpable, but it is fascinating to note that the aggression Miller ascribes to his work—oral and anal—is so distinct in his mind from that ascribed to the self that is going to grow up and "usurp the field" once belonging only to older men's artworks. His vision is like that of Freud's renegade disciple Otto Rank, who, after he had given up being a son of Freud, constructed a rather Hegelian history of mankind and of art in which the highest attainment would be overcoming of art. As Rank said in *Art and Artist*:

> For artistic creation has, in the course of its development, changed from a means for the furtherance of the culture of the community into a means for the construction of personality. But the more successful this is, the greater is the urge of this personality away from art toward life.

Sometimes the metaphors for such a view refer to fabrication (the self as a work of art), but much more typically they present the "construction of personality" as a merger of self and cosmos, as what Rank terms an ability "to accept the psychical ego as part of the universe" and what Miller had called "making a life in accord with the deep-center rhythms of the cosmos."

Just as differences are clear, but not always starkly so, between the descriptions and images of creativity typical of people with the various character-ideals, so too are the differences or subtypes within the types clear but not easy to separate. Subtypes overlap and very complexly relate to developmental paradigms. This is particularly the case with differences along the continuum between relative normalcy, neurosis, and psychosis. It is typical, for example, of the narcissistic-obsessional creators I sketched in some biographical detail in earlier chapters— Freud, Darwin, Dickinson—and those just noted briefly here in the medium of their writings on writing, that they think evolutionarily and view themselves as recapitulations of an evolutionary process. Complete truth is the goal of the process. But the goal has quite different effects for the different creators. Freud saw civilization advancing, but at huge cost to instinctual life—a tragic dilemma; Darwin saw the future as more unadulterated happiness, lack of conflict in angelic (purely intellectual, almost disembodied) existence; Dickinson, more isolated and unhappy than either of the others, exalted in the prospect of mental conquest

("The Brain—is wider than the Sky"), but as often catalogued her fears as told her victory. Miller's vision of the evolutionary future is purely ecstatic, and this kind of rigid vision, I think his own images make clear, entails tremendous hostility toward the "lower" forms of life and work. The line between his vision and classic "delusions of grandeur" seems to be very thin.

But such a judgment raises the complex question of how creative productions should—assuming the possibility—be read with the producer's mental health in question. John Cody's "diagnosis" of Emily Dickinson provides a very instructive example of how this question of biographical method can go unposed. He put his attention to the literal content of Emily Dickinson's letters and poems, and proceeded to interpret that content, and only that content, as symptomatology. The poems were to be examined, he said, "solely as psychological documents," not as poems, not metaphorically, and also not in relation to any notion of mental process or of mental structure. As I noted before, Cody pondered these lines:

> I felt a Cleaving in my Mind—
> As if my Brain had split—
> I tried to match it—Seam by Seam—
> But could not make them fit.

And he interpreted: thought disorder, psychotic break. That is, he assumed that Dickinson was talking about being split as a psychiatrist might. This seems to me setting off on the wrong foot—the psychiatric one—and ending up with an enormous exaggeration and misunderstanding. Two questions (at least) that should have been asked did not get asked: What did the poems as poems mean to Emily Dickinson, and how did she imagine to herself her own mind—this mind that now has a cleft in it?

The second stanza of Dickinson's poem goes:

> The thought behind, I strove to join
> Unto the thought before—
> But Sequence ravelled out of Sound
> Like Balls—upon a Floor.

There is an analogy implied here between how her thoughts have been knitted together over time and how a poem, with its sequences of sound, has been patterned. Both systems can be unknitted, unraveled, back into their yarn balls, like a kind of devolution—but that is not happening in her poem, to her poem. She stresses in another poem (#997, from 1865), that "organized decays" (an excellent phrase for devolution) rather than quick breakages are what people in mental pain experience:

> Ruin is formal—Devil's work
> Consecutive and slow—
> Fail in an instant, no man did
> Slipping—is Crashe's law.

This poem has three stanzas, and it repeats the same thought three times, as "I felt a Cleaving in my Mind" repeats its similar thought twice in two stanzas. The repetition seems to me characteristic of the Dickinson poems that do not so much literally record a process as prevent one, by something like ritual incantation. The process prevented is precisely breakage of the sort she invoked in letters. She wrote to her friend Samuel Bowles after her brother's marriage: "In such a porcelain life, one likes to be sure that all is well, lest one stumble upon one's hopes in a pile of broken crockery." She felt herself to be breakable in a breakable world; or more precisely, she felt that the world with which she identified herself was breakable because she could not organize it as she wished, according to her hopes. But her reply, in the medium of poetry, was to try to channel her fear, to translate it into a slowed down, more formal fear of "organized decay" which could be captured in and countered with organized poems. "After great pain, a formal feeling comes—" (#341) ends with this stanza:

> This is the Hour of Lead—
> Remembered, if outlived,
> As freezing persons, recollect the Snow—
> First—Chill—then Stupor—then the letting go—

The "letting go" feels like a death until you remember it is a survivor's phrase. She wrote as a survivor. But sometimes she went further and made the "letting go" into a full journey of discovery. She imagined herself breaking out of the confines of her own mind and its fears; she wrote in and through a fantasy of expansion and power, even if power attained through pain. This poem, for example, narrates such a journey:

I felt a Funeral, in my Brain,
And Mourners to and fro
Kept treading—treading—till it seemed
That Sense was breaking through—

And when they all were seated,
A Service, like a Drum—
Kept beating—beating—till I thought
My Mind was going numb—

And then I heard them lift a Box
And creak across my Soul
With those same Boots of Lead, again,
Then Space—began to toll,

As all the Heavens were a Bell,
And Being but an Ear,
And I, and Silence, some strange Race
Wrecked, solitary, here—

And then a Plank in Reason, broke,
And I dropped down, and down—
And hit a World, at every plunge,
And finished knowing—then—

The poem tells how she broke out of her brain, where she felt numbed, leaden with melancholy and mourning: to experience sense and space, to give up the silence she felt abandoned into; to travel down through the floor of her mind, the floor made of reason's planks, and into the worlds of sense, sensation; to finish her quest for knowing in worlds where sound is everywhere, the great poem which being is but an ear. The consequence of the journey is left open—the final "then" is nonclosure.

John Cody, literally interpreting a break in reason's plank as a break in reason, and literally interpreting a fall as a fall into madness, into something worse than the funeral condition with which the poem opens, cites this poem as evidence of Dickinson's psychosis. The interpretation I have offered, which gives a positive meaning to "finished knowing," a phrase just as ambiguous as the earlier "letting go" if looked at in isolation, runs counter to Cody's because it reflects my inability to believe that a psychotic could write as Emily Dickinson did, that her oeuvre of intricately crafted poems, so carefully systematized and arranged, could have been produced by someone with what Cody calls a "thought disorder" *as a literal record of that disorder.* On the other hand, that Emily Dickinson's character was of the narcissistic-obsessional sort and that she was very vulnerable to feelings of extreme isolation and confusion about the boundaries of her ego seems to me quite a plausible contention. The interesting question is what saved her from her enclosed (technically speaking: schizoid) psychic disposition—and I think the answer is: writing poetry.

FROM THE POLITICAL CHARACTER-IDEAL THROUGH SCHIZOPHRENIA

Anyone who has spent any time at all with a seriously neurotic or psychotic person would conclude from observation that no matter how gifted such a person is, he or she cannot, in the grip of the illness, be creative in any sustained or publically communicable way—though flashes of creativity may escape the illness and similarities with works by more sane people may be apparent in such flashes. Insanity, in this sense, looks like it should be understandable as a condition that destroys or blocks creativity, renders it nonoperational. If a person of genius (in the narrower sense of that word) is or goes insane, that person's creativity is extinguished or can only operate between episodes of insanity (if the insanity is episodic or of variable intensity).

This way of speaking about genius and insanity is, to use Freud's term, "economic." And, to use a term from contemporary economics, it presupposes that psychic energy is a kind of "zero-sum game" in which energy given to insanity is taken away from genius, and vice versa. As he worked with this presupposition, Lionel Trilling quite appropriately quoted Freud's *Introductory Lectures* on the topic of how neurotic symptoms should be viewed as

> activities which are detrimental, or at least useless, to life as a whole; the person concerned frequently complains of them as obnoxious to him or they involve suffering and distress for him. The principal injury they inflict lies in the expense of energy they entail, and, besides this, the energy needed to combat them. Where the symptoms are extensively developed, these two kinds of effort may exact such a price that a person suffers a very serious impoverishment in available mental energy which consequently disables him for all the important tasks of life. This result depends principally upon

191

the amount of energy taken up in this way; therefore you will see that 'illness' is essentially a practical conception. But if you look at the matter from a theoretical point of view and ignore this question of degree, you can very well see that we are all ill, i.e., neurotic; for the conditions required for symptom-formation are demonstrable also in normal persons.

Freud's assumption was that psychic processes and energy can manifest themselves in many ways: in all our productions, our works, and deeds, but also in all of our daily actions and behaviors, in our fantasies and daydreams, in all of our nightly sleep behaviors and dreams, in neurotic symptoms large and small, from the elaborate rituals of an obsessional neurosis to the one-word-for-another slips called parapraxes. These different facets of life, made up of the same ingredients and the same basic mechanisms, can also substitute for one another—though some substitutions are useful to life and some make life hardly worth living.

When a neurotic symptom is formed, a mental complex (a pleasure aim, its associated object, plus the libidinal energy with which the aim is charged, plus the "primary-process" unconscious thinking that knits aim, object, and energy) has been kept from entering into consciousness by a countervailing energy force commanded by the ego or superego. The symptom is, as Freud put it, "A substitute for what did not happen at that point" (15:292). To stay with the same example: a symptom substituting for the entry of the aim (sexual gratification) into consciousness where it could be acknowledged, named, and pursued with all the resources of conscious planning and "secondary process" rational thinking. Instead of pursuing his mother, a boy pursues something or someone else with whatever of his energy has not been repressed along with the image of his original beloved. His turn away from the aim of sexual gratification and the original beloved object may lead him into destructive and debilitating behavior—a pattern, for example, of loving only in dangerous circumstances, where a rival is near, or loving only unavailable women. But if the aim he substitutes for his first love is, as Freud vaguely said, "higher," or if he converts his frustration into activity in the world (12:32), he may, for example, pursue Mother Nature as a biologist, putting all his lover's ingenuity into his research. The difference, that is, between neurotic symptom formation and sublimation is a difference not of energy source or type but of aim.

Sublimation does not, as is commonly said by people who find Freud's view offensive or mistaken, preclude love or sexual pursuit. It does not take all of a person's libido, only a portion of that which has been attached to a forbidden aim and object (while another portion may remain attached to the forbidden aim and object, but in a condition of repression). The amount of libido attached to the forbidden aim and object may be considerable, but need not be. A boy could, for example, sublimate a portion of his mother-love but little or none of his father-love, which did not command repression from the ego during his Oedipal years. Such a boy as an adult might enjoy homosexual loves, perhaps identifying himself with his mother, or simply pursue his sublimation(s) in the company of male partners with whom he is erotically bound.

In Freud's view, a person who is capable only of repressing forbidden desires will be neurotic, while a person who is capable of sublimation has an alternative, as does a person who is "perverse," that is, who acts on forbidden desires, more or less directly. (Freud often pointed out how commonly homosexuals are creative, if social animosity does not destroy them: "perversity" and sublimation in cultural pursuits have in common that they are alternatives to repression, and thus to neurosis.) Sublimation is also an alternative to the tendency within the psychic economy that Freud postulated in his later instinctual theory, that is, the tendency of the system to seek peace, quiescence—the tendency that Freud called "the death instinct." The death instinct can be aimed toward or fastened onto representations of objects in the form of sadism or aggression, but these can also be sublimated or directed toward "higher" aims. The biologist who pursues "Mother Nature" can also, in his pursuit, outdo his father, by achieving more than his father did and perhaps also by formulating a theory in which fathers are outdone. (It is, of course, much easier to formulate self-serving theories in psychology than in biology or any other science in which the scientist's psychology is not commonly assumed to be determining or influencing the outcome. In the "hard" sciences, the theorizing activity usually contains more of the overcoming than does the theoretical result itself; thus there is great struggle over whose method is the most "hard" and strict.)

Creativity is, in Freud's theory, avoidance of neurosis, or of some part of a neurosis, but it is also avoidance more generally of pain. Freud characteristically (that is, as a matter of his character) did not think of pleasure as the absence of pain. Such a conception of pleasure is much more characteristic of people whose stoicism is bound up with a spiritual character-ideal. Freud, rather, considered pleasure a barrier against pain.

This conception underpins the passage from *Civilization and Its Discontents* that I cited in Chapter 2 to show Freud's view about the psychic function of intellectual work and sublimation generally: sublimation creates a barrier, but "no impenetrable armor against the arrows of fortune, and it habitually fails when the source of suffering is a person's own body" (21:80). (Freud was in his thirteenth year of battling cancer of the jaw when he wrote this assessment.)

Creativity and sublimation, in addition to providing an alternative to neurosis and repression and a barrier against pain, also give a way for people to tell the story of their desires rather than acting on them. They make possible projections not just of the id's "primary-process" thinking but of the ego's "endopsychic perceptions." To elaborate the example I have been constructing: there is a link between artistic creation and parricide, both in the sense that artists (Freud argued) surpass their fathers in the medium of their artistic achievements and in the sense that they sublimate in their achievements their hostility toward their fathers. The Oedipus complex of the artist (who is always male in Freud's discussions) is played out both through and in the work—and that is, also, the basis for the appreciation won by great works of art from all who share the Oedipal experience of the artist. Psychoanalysis applied to art and art-reception is, thus, an exposure of the Oedipal themes, and its main methodological-emotional problem is the art critic's own reluctance or joy or ambivalence at exposing the artist's motivations. The critic (and the critic's reader) also perpetrates a kind of parricide or deflation of the artist's hero status. Symbolic parricide, or sublimated Oedipal hostility toward the father, is civilization's great achievement— it is the decisive advance beyond the founding act of parricide Freud postulated in *Totem and Taboo*.

These various functions of creativity and sublimation are all consistent with Freud's characteristic systematic-evolutionary way of thinking, which emphasizes increasing structuration. He worked with an image of psychic energies floating free, fastening onto aims and objects, and then changing location or being rechanneled, in a closed system or field which evolves over time by internal reconfigurations, slowly developing topographical regions or structures. Maturity is structuration. Borders appear, alter, expand—but there are always borders. And this image is, it seems to me, an image generated by a narcissistic-obsessional character. It is also most suitable to such a character, although it reaches out to embrace all human types, aspiring to universality.

The narcissistic creative character, who, as Freud himself so clearly noted, takes the greater part of his or her satisfaction from mental activity, feels mentally rich in thoughts and energy (and fears mental poverty or diminishment). Such characters have had some version of the experience that Emily Dickinson captured in the poem "It was given me by the Gods—" (#454) about a gift (presumably, her poetic gift) that she received as a little girl. This is the last quatrain:

> Rich! 'Twas myself—was rich—
> To take the name of Gold—
> And Gold to own—in solid Bars—
> The Difference—made me Bold—

Frequently, the enrichment experience is felt as a compensation for some preceding state of impoverishment or of being unloved or inadequately loved, or some state of being injured—narcissistically wounded, in Freud's term. But, at any rate, the image of the mind as a well-stocked storehouse or a self-sufficient system is the narcissistic character's "endopsychic perception." Sublimation or some similar idea of intra-systemic channeling and reorganization is, then, the process that allows for growth: boundaries change and expand, but are not dissolved.

The narcissistic creative character is very likely—to continue this description in another way—to veer away from any feeling state or experience that spells dissolution of boundaries. In *Civilization and Its Discontents*, Freud responded to his friend Romain Rolland's remarks about a boundless "oceanic feeling" with an effort at comprehension and a declaration of failure: "I cannot discover this 'oceanic' feeling in myself." His remoteness is obvious in his description:

> This, [Rolland] says, consists in a peculiar feeling, which he himself is never without, which he finds confirmed by many others, and which he may suppose is present in millions of people. It is a feeling he would like to call a sensation of "eternity," a feeling of something unlimited, unbounded— as it were, "oceanic." This feeling, he adds, is a purely subjective fact, not an article of faith. . . . One may, he thinks, rightly call oneself religious on the ground of this oceanic feeling alone, even if one rejects every belief and every illusion (21:64).

Considering Rolland's feeling, Freud was as puzzled as Aristotle would have been trying to comprehend the Stoics' pantheistic, holistic feeling of cosmic *tonos*. He could only grasp the feeling's "ideational content," which he presented as "a feeling of an indissoluble bond, of being one with the external world as a whole." But one can hardly imagine a content more distasteful to a character-type such as Freud's than fusion of self and world—the opposite of structuration.

This distaste is also, it seems to me, what made it so difficult for Freud to appreciate the longing, so palpable in people of the artisanal/sexual character-ideal, for perfect union, dyadic fusion, boundless love, recreations of pre-Oedipal bliss at the mother's breast. Freud could note clinically that a person who "falls in love" feels for a time that there is no boundary between self and loved one; and he could present this condition analytically as "a state suggestive of a neurotic compulsion, which is thus traceable to an impoverishment of the ego as regards libido in favor of the love-object" (14:88). In other words, the person in love directs all his (Freud thought of such love as a male *spécialité*) libido to the love-object and away from himself. But this is an "economic" description without an affect, without any emotional tone.

It is important to note that Freud, even when he was on foreign psychic territory like "the oceanic feeling," had enormous curiosity about how the natives of those territories feel and think. He was tied to the world as strongly as it is possible to be while fending off any fusion. In this, he was quite far from the schizoid thinking typical of people who are narcissistic to a greater and even pathological extreme. Such people, as Robert Waelder pointed out very clearly in a paper "On Psychoses" (1924), have no interest in observation. Waelder described T., a talented mathematician who loved to theorize:

> He likes to see every theory fitted as soon as possible into a systematic structure. His aim is to deduce all his conclusions from a few clearly defined postulates which are independent of one another. He endeavors always to get down to elementary concepts which cannot be dissected further and to build up his theory from a synthesis of such concepts. He willingly abandons the interpretation of phenomena which are too complex for such a synthesis. . . . The reason, and the only reason, why T. escaped the psychosis which his disposition would otherwise have produced was that his choice of profession [mathematics] and the path taken by his sublimations did bind a great part of his narcissistic libido in a manner perfectly in accord with reality. . . . To use a happy phrase of T. himself, [his sublimations] constitute a *channel* ready for the reception of the volume of libido which, in psychotic dispositions of this sort, is perpetually flowing back to the ego.

Doing mathematics gave T. what writing her linguistic puzzles, her exquisite cryptograms, gave Emily Dickinson—a channel.

What I am suggesting is that there is a continuum along which narcissistic and narcissistic-obsessional types range: it runs from relatively more connection to the world to relatively less connection to the world, that is, from normalcy to psychosis. Further, people of this type offer the theories of creativity most illuminating for this type—theories which have wider applicability, beyond the type, in proportion to how connected the theorists are to other people, the world. There is a particular lack of inhibition among people of this type about mental phenomena that other people, more worldly, more dependent on love and good opinion coming from the world, do not have. Waelder's patient T., for example, offered Waelder restricted illustration of the characteristic that made Freud able to formulate his theory of the Oedipus complex:

> Once, when I was giving [T.] some theoretical explanation of psychoanalysis and the nature of psychosis, I told him of a demented patient who demanded as a matter of course that his mother should have intercourse with him. I pointed out that the man's narcissism prevented his acknowledging the incest barrier, whereupon T. objected that he, too, never could understand the incest barrier and above all had never even felt it. . . . The adaptation to reality which governed his conduct would accordingly seem to be simply due to recognition of its outward necessity and not to the compelling effect of inner experience, so that even the moral content of his ideal was determined by narcissistic impulses, the will to live and fulfill himself. For this reason he could think forbidden thoughts without any resistance or sense of guilt.

Freud, much less purely narcissistic than T., had to struggle with his resistance and guilt, but he had an ability to think forbidden thoughts that impressed most of his contemporaries and many people since as horrible. Freud's ability to generalize or universalize those thoughts—to see the Oedipus complex universally—has seemed to many just as horrible. And along the same line of outrageousness there is the moment in Freud's case study of the psychotic Dr. Schreber (his only extended study of a psychotic) in which Freud notices that the delusional system Dr. Schreber constructed looks remarkably like an "endopsychic perception" of the very flow of narcissistic libido Freud had posited in *his own* theory of narcissism: "It remains for the future to decide whether there is more delusion in my theory than I should like to admit, or whether there is more truth in Schreber's delusion than other people are as yet prepared to believe" (12:79).

It is this independence from other people's love and good opinions, this capacity to think forbidden thoughts and attribute them to everybody, that qualifies immensely creative narcissistic types in "economic" psychic terms to be what the historian of science Thomas Kuhn called "paradigm shifters." They can see the problems in existing systems, and they can create systematically. The narcissistic creative character also has the parricidal or parenticidal impulse against predecessors that is particularly salient in people with artisanal/sexual character-ideals, and may have as well the past-transcending impulse of the spiritual character-ideal type. But the narcissistic creator's independence, it seems to me, is what undergirds his or her originality for system-building.

Creative people of the narcissistic type who are or become extreme enough in their type to be psychotic can be reached therapeutically not by traditional psychoanalysis, which requires the transference reactions which such people do not have, but by using their system-building theoretical capacities. A therapist can enter into the mental world they have made and help them understand it, decode it, while arousing their interest in what lies outside of this world, what it does not compass. A version of the same procedure can be applied physically to the most extreme, institutionalized chronic schizophrenics. It has often been noted that chronic schizophrenics, so remote and inaccessible, go into remission when they are in pain or physically ill. They then pay attention to their increased body sensations, which leads to an increase in their ability to distinguish their bodies, or their body-egos, from the surrounding world. Using Freudian terms, Thomas Freeman and his collaborators remark that, in general, it is

> a disturbance of the development and maintenance of adequate ego boundaries which, on the basis of clinical observation, we have come to regard as the central feature of the schizophrenic disease process. . . . 'Ego feeling,' or the ability to differentiate the self from the environment . . . is damaged in chronic schizophrenia, thus leading to the patient experiencing internal and external sensations as a continuum.

Robert Waelder cited a statement by the playwright August Strindberg that tracks his journey back from such a psychotic condition and shows clearly the role investment of libido in intellectual work played in his reattachment to the world:

My ego began as it were to coagulate and to solidify around an inner core, where all I had ever experienced and accumulated was digested and absorbed as mental food. Meanwhile it became my habit to reproduce in literary form all that I saw and heard in the house, in the street or outside in the world of nature. Thus I related all my observations to my work of the moment, and in so doing I felt my power grow, and my solitary studies proved more valuable than those which I had pursued outside in social intercourse with my fellow creatures.

This seems to me a return to a condition that Emily Dickinson sustained all her writing life, through her writing:

> To hear an Oriole sing
> May be a common thing—
> Or only a divine.
>
> It is not of the Bird
> Who sings the same, unheard,
> As unto Crowd—
>
> The Fashion of the Ear
> Attireth that it hear
> In Dun, or fair—
>
> So whether it be Rune,
> Or whether it be none
> Is of within.
>
> The "Tune is in the Tree—"
> The Skeptic—showeth me—
> "No Sir! In Thee!"

FROM THE ARTISANAL/SEXUAL CHARACTER-IDEAL TO MELANCHOLIA

Certain features of Freud's theory of creativity, his successors noticed, were difficult to reconcile with what some artists have to say about themselves, about their way of working and about their work. Among the most respectful questioners was Freud's younger colleague Ernst Kris, originally an art historian. Kris did not publish a systematic statement of his theory of creativity, as his preference was for detailed studies, on specific types of art (caricature, comedy, tragedy), art produced by psychotics, creative processes, and biographical patterns in portraits of artists. But in these studies, collected in *Psychoanalytic Explorations in Art* (1952), a few recurrent theoretical themes are obvious, and these had great influence on Kris's contemporaries and successors.

Most importantly, Kris noticed that Freud's emphasis on psychic structuration as the crucial manner of growth and sign of maturity could not explain how artists gain or regain their access to the id and its "primary process" thinking. Approaching this problem, Kris stressed that the artist's repressions are more flexible than other people's. Artistic inspiration involves a temporary "regression in the service of the ego" (that is, an ego-controlled regression). The inspirational process is passive, and then it is followed by an active, synthetic elaboration, the work of the secondary processes such as intellection. Historically, Kris argued, art has developed from a form of magical action into a form of communication, and this implies a greater and greater role for the secondary process elaboration. Finally, Kris stressed that sublimation (channeling of energies through change of aim, as Freud defined it) is not the same as binding of energies or neutralizing of energies—that is, actual changes in the energies themselves, not just of goals. Creative people, Kris argued, have at their disposal a large reservoir of sexual and aggressive instinctual drives that have been "neutralized." And, he later suggested in an article called "Neutralization and Sublimation" (1955), they may also be endowed from birth with a great reservoir of energy that is "of noninstinctual origin." (This mysterious phrase he did not explain.)

In these general themes of Kris's work, it seems to me, an image dominates: the ego of the creative person has the capacity to shape and mold the energy of the id and the primary processes of the id. The ego draws close to the id in controlled regression or keeps its distance; it sublimates sexual and aggressive energy, or it works with energy that has been neutralized. That is, the ego is an artisan in relation to the materials of the id.

This image was the one with which Kris's colleague in New York, Phyllis Greenacre, focused a series of questions that spurred her to an extremely important contribution to creativity theory—an approach quite different from Freud's, and particularly appropriate to one of the creative character-types that Freud was not: the type with an artisanal/sexual character-ideal.

In a number of biographical studies of English literary figures and in a sequence of theoretical essays, written in the late 1950s and early

1960s and then collected in a volume called *Emotional Growth*, Greenacre pursued her main questions: What exceptional materials-of-self (biological endowments, for example) does the creative ego work with? What are its shaping processes? What relationships obtain between the work the ego does on its own materials and the creative product? She began by defining Ernst Kris's energy "of non-instinctual origin," that is, by positing in the gifted an "early sensory oversensitivity together with . . . greater reactivity to rhythm and gestalt relationships of form" that "bring the infant into a wider range of awareness of his own body and the surroundings as well." In answer to the question about ego processes in creativity, Greenacre suggested that an exceptionally endowed child begins at the end of its first year to handle its vibrant sensory experience by creating "collective alternates." This term designated objects in proximity to the primary sensed and loved objects that excite the infant. Onto the proximate objects, the infant extends its involvement, its reactions. A gifted child does not focus its attention on its mother's breast, for example, but extends attention to all kinds of objects that the child senses are related to the breast, by smell, shape, texture. The child's ego modality is sense-based synthesis or collecting—a fine foundation (though Greenacre does not remark upon this) for a future lyric poet or, in general, metaphor-maker. Eventually, the child extends its reach out to a fantasy of a collective audience or recipient of the relationships it had with its first loved ones. The artist has a "love affair with the world," and gives to an imagined collective audience in this world "love gifts."

"The artistic product has rather universally the character of a love gift, to be brought as near perfection as possible and to be presented with pride and misgiving." Artistic people, Greenacre suggests, never solve or dissolve their Oedipal bonds, they simply bypass them in favor of the larger, more powerful collective bond. One consequence is that in their lives as in their works a "family romance" of idealized parental and sibling figures often plays a central role.

Greenacre emphasizes one feature of this relationship between exceptionally strong sensory experiences and those ego processes that create "collective alternates" from the start, that is, which have an incipient creativity to them. A gifted child's tendency to create "collective alternates" has an effect, in turn, on its ego development. And what this means it that a gifted child, growing up, may develop a split in its own self-representation. There is a vivid loving-the-world self, then there is an other (or others).

It is evident in studying the lives of markedly creative people that such splits in self-representation, going over into even a split in the sense of identity, do occur and relatively frequently—sometimes developing along parallel lines and sometimes alternating, one emerging from the cover of the other. The division into the two or more selves may be experienced in childhood with some distress and with the wish to deny the creative self in favor of the social stereotype, which exerts so much constricting pressure during the school years. The creative self is felt to be freakish, abnormal, and to be fought. Under many circumstances, this struggle continues into adult life, when the more conventional self may be more or less guardian or enemy of the creative self.

One form that this interior split can take, Greenacre noted, is obvious in biographies of imposters: the creative self is given an identity and acted out in another domain than the ordinary self, which may even deny the existence of its twin.

One of Greenacre's most brilliant elaborations of her themes concerned the imposter-identity of the artist and its relationship to two other psychic phenomena: transitional objects and fetishes. The English child psychoanalyst D. W. Winnicott wrote an article in 1953 that has been influential on many theorists of creativity—and on Winnicott's own later ideas about how people make a "cultural space" for themselves. He suggested that infants leave their initial enmeshment with their mothers, when they make no distinction between "me" and the mother, by means of a "transitional object." They have a piece of blanket, a stuffed bear, a ribbon, which has the familiar feel and smell of their nursing and nursery, and they carry this with them as they explore the wider world that is not-them, that is other. It protects them like a talisman, offers solace against the frustrations of the world, carries on their infant fantasies of omnipotence, and provides a target for both anger and tenderness. The transitional object, the child's first sustained creative product, Greenacre suggested, has magical qualities, as does a fetish, which is adopted by a badly isolated and disturbed child at just about the time in latency when the transitional object has outlived its function for a normal child and has been discarded or set on a shelf. A child's fetish carries on some of the transitional object's nourishing functions, and also defends the child against castration anxiety. The fetishes of adolescents and adults, then, are concentrated on the specific task of supplying a representation of a phallus that allays his (and much less frequently her) castration anxiety and fear of the female genitals.

The fetish is a product of a "need for reparation because of the persistence of an illusion of defect in the body" and has something of the quality of a delusion. But people who do not establish a fetish, although they do have some of the anxieties it allays, may find another solution, more like an adult version of their original security-producing transitional object—a work of art.

The connections Greenacre drew between the transitional object and the fetish were designed, like the connections she drew between the creative child's split self-representation and the imposter's assumed identity, to cast the normal ingredients of creativity into bold relief by means of pathology. Her point was to shift the burden of explanation for creativity away from the ego-id relation of sublimation, which she took to be only one ingredient, and onto intra-ego processes, particularly splitting. In this she was following not only Ernst Kris, but an essay Freud left unfinished at the time of his death, "The Splitting of the Ego in the Process of Defense" (1938).

In this essay, Freud had described an alternative to repression that was different from sublimation. A little boy whose sexual pleasure is masturbation becomes anxious under a double shadow: his masturbation is forbidden with a castration threat, and he discovers contemporaneously that females do not have a penis. He both acknowledges the threats and sidesteps them. The method for his detour is to create a fetish that represents the phallus a female has—that is, he denies that she is penis-less and that he himself might become like her as a punishment for masturbation. So, having eliminated the image of castration, he no longer needs to give up masturbation. Freud says of this way of dealing with reality (23:277) that it "almost deserves to be called artful," implying just the idea that Greenacre later formulated—that ego-splitting is a condition of artfulness.

In Greenacre's view, ego-splitting was the condition of all artfulness, all types of creativity. But it seems to me that she brilliantly isolated the conditions of only a certain kind of creativity—the kind typical of people of erotic-obsessional libidinal type who project an artisanal/sexual character-ideal. These are creators whom I have characterized before as imagining themselves (more or less unconsciously) as two people, one of whom either shapes and molds or impregnates the other. They are consciously bisexual or androgynous; very caught up in their pre-Oedipal two-character-maintaining dramas and their Oedipal third-character-eliminating dramas and family romances; tied to the praise and appreciation that must flow nourishingly from their real or imaginary audiences; concentrated on the perfection and beauty of their products, which they feel as connected to their bodily perfection and beauty, and about which they have anxieties like those typical of hysterical characters and hypochondriacs. Such creators tend, also, to accept a disjunction between their creative selves (and their periods of intense creativity) and their ordinary selves; they say with an exclusive "or," that Yeats's "perfection of the life or of the work" is their law.

Although I think that Greenacre's portrait of the creative person fits only one type particularly well, I also think that her investigation of the physiological conditions of creativity in exceptional sensory alertness and her notion about "collective alternates" have much wider application. Creation of collective alternates may be a more satisfactory concept than "projection" for trying to explore the origin of the tendency, present in people of all creative types, to "swell up to the macrocosm" (as Nietzsche said) or to feel "always the inmost becomes the outmost" (as Emerson said). The formation of a character-ideal in adolescence could, then, be viewed as a continuation of a process of collective alternate creation started in childhood: the character-ideal is a collective alternate to a person's endopsychic perceptions, a composite of them.

Further, it seems to me that Greenacre's reflections on ego-splitting and the impostor character have a wider application than she gave them. She noted that in the creators she investigated a complex relationship had come to exist between the ordinary self and the creative self—a relationship of guardianship or hostility, or some mixture of the two. She suggested, in passing, that such splitting may have something in common with the psychopathological condition known as multiple personality: "One suspects, however, that some "hysterical" amnesias and dual or multiple personalities are conditions related to imposturous characters." Greenacre never followed out her intuition, but her emphasis on ego-splitting implies very strongly that the creative character she presented lies on a continuum with the pathologies of splitting—that is, with the very severe form of multiple personality, but, more generally, depression and manic-depression.

What these pathologies have in common is that they involve encapsulation in the mind of traumatic or extremely frustrating experiences (combined with images of the objects associated with or responsible for those experiences) and then construction of a pattern of reactions to the encapsulated complex—a "self," or a part of the ego. At its most extreme, the process results in many "personalities" in the mind with whole lives of their own—each unknown to the others—that are acted out in imposturing ways. This extreme process, almost always signaling a childhood filled with severe abuse or molestation, quite inaccessible to the adult's consciousness, is a horrifying intensification of experiences common to everyone. An infant frustrated, say, when its mother's breast is unavailable trains a stream of rage on its mental representation of the beloved, desired breast (the "good" breast as "incorporated"); but this rage, conflicting as it does with the infant's love and desire, is unacceptable; so the rage is split off, kept internalized, and kept focused on the mental representation transformed (sometimes called "the bad breast"). The rage not taken out on the mother's breast is converted into self-punishing behavior. Splitting, in general, is a way to still conflict by separating the love and the hate sides of the ambivalent feelings that are inevitable when an infant's fusion with its mothering figure comes to an end and the separation is both enjoyed and ferociously resented. Although it may intensify in later childhood or adolescence, splitting has the oral features—"incorporation" of the object is a kind of greedy eating—of its originating period. The melancholic is a person disappointed in love beyond the level of disappointment in love familiar to everyone.

Freud himself was the first to associate splitting with melancholia or depression. But at the beginning of his unfinished late essay on ego-splitting and fetishism, Freud wondered whether the essay's ideas had a precedent in his work. "I find myself for a moment in the interesting position of not knowing whether what I have to say should be regarded as something long familiar and obvious or something entirely new and puzzling" (23:275). The puzzlement, it seems to me, stemmed from Freud's leaving unstated in the essay his own earlier theory about splitting, which he had presented in his major statement on depression, "Mourning and Melancholia" (1917). In that paper, he had offered the following description of the melancholic, who has in common with a mourner the loss of a love object—although the melancholic usually does not know he or she is bereft, while the mourner certainly does:

> The patient represents his ego to us as worthless, incapable of any achievement and morally despicable; he reproaches himself, vilifies himself and expects to be cast out and punished. . . . He is not of the opinion that a change has taken place in him, but extends his criticism back over the

past; he declares he has never been any better. This picture of a delusion of (mainly moral) inferiority is completed by sleeplessness and refusal to take nourishment, and—what is psychologically very remarkable—by an overcoming of the instinct which compels every living thing to cling to life (14:246).

The melancholic has a split ego. Hatred of another, of a loved one, has been attached to a representation of the object, internalized, and expressed as self-hatred, self-reproach. The person who wants to end his or her life also wants to kill the hated object or objects.

After he formulated the structural theory in the early 1920s, Freud referred to the chastizing part of the ego, the conscience, as the superego. And this idea that the depressive person's psyche is a scene for ego and superego conflict rather than intra-ego conflict may be what made Freud think his later discussion of intra-ego splitting was novel. But the difference between the two conflicts seems to me to be only one of emphasis and developmental stage, as the superego is made up, in Freud's understanding, of objects that have been incorporated and then identified with. What begins as a civil war or war of secession in the ego may progress or blend over into a war between nations in which the superego nation rests its moral supremacy on inherited tradition, internalized parental authority.

Creative characters who operate psychically in the mode Kris and especially Greenacre described seem to me to save themselves from extreme forms of melancholia by working on the "bad" part of themselves, which is conceived as a chaotic, appetitive material part—to use Plato's characterizing terms. This "bad" part may be—to use Greenacre's terms—either the ordinary self or the creative self, whichever one is experienced as the locus of a deep love covered by a thick layer of rage and aggression. They seek to heal the bad part, restore it, let it be acted out by a character in a work of art, keep it from tearing them in two; or they seek to unite with it sexually to produce a good and beautiful spiritual artistic child. In the works of such creators, pairs seeking union are featured: lovers seeking romantic union; siblings, particularly twins, trying to be complementary rather than hostile to each other; Doppelgangers and "secret sharers" (of the sort the very depressive Joseph Conrad wrote about) being discovered; Dr. Jekylls and Mr. Hydes being collapsed into each other or controlled in a magical way. Journeys are made into the heart of darkness to find the "other," or into family pasts to find the mysterious missing relative, or to hot, wild countries from grim, rainy ones (or vice versa) to find paradise. Creators of this sort often have two kinds of work that function in the same unifying way. They are writers and painters (like Goethe), or graphic artists and scientists (like Leonardo). D. H. Lawrence spoke characteristically of his other art in "Making Pictures," presenting painting as light in contrast to the darkness of his writing:

> Art is a form of supremely delicate awareness and atonement—meaning at-one-ness, the state of being one with the object. But is the great atonement in delight?—for I can never look on art save as a form of delight. . . . I believe many people have, in their consciousness, living images that would give them the greatest joy to bring out.

Creative characters with artisanal-sexual character-ideals are also given, in their lives, to trying to find a complementary partner, a perfect and beautiful match. A friend who is everything they are not—as Ford Maddox Ford was supposed to be for Joseph Conrad; or a friend who can help control their uncontrollable, uncraftable self, forming an alliance with the crafting self in them; or a partner (of the same sex or the opposite) who can be an androgynous complement, either in the sense that the partner is androgynous (as Orlando's husband was) or that the partner is the missing half of the creative one's sexuality (as Aristophanes, in Plato's *Symposium*, imagined all true lovers to be).

Each character-ideal type seeks its own type of partner or friend, as a glance at the partners sought by people with a political character-ideal shows clearly. Emily Dickinson said of her friend and sister-in-law Sue Gilbert: "You are my universe." The friend is supposed to be a universe, as the creative one is, and also like the creative one. As Aristotle said, the friend is another self, an *alter ego*. Picasso's friend Apollinaire could compass the painter's work in prose, interpret him, give him a literary voice; the painter Braque could collaborate with him, to the point that during their collaborative period neither signed his paintings, leaving it to others to tell them apart. Freud expected his alter egos to think as he did, to see the world as he did, to participate in his vision and let him participate in theirs, united in a single cause. Fliess disappointed him, Jung disappointed him—perhaps it is no exaggeration to say that the only partner who fulfilled the requirements was his daughter Anna.

FROM THE SPIRITUAL CHARACTER-IDEAL
TO PARANOIA

The political character-ideal and the artisanal/sexual character-ideal creators tend to use their creative work medicinally: to prevent rupture with the world, in the first case, and to cure internal splits that might spell depression, in the second case. Their creative work stands between them and pathology, as an alternative, a means to character organization or a means to prevent disorganization. Or, to put the matter another way, as a character defense.

The defensive function of creativity is stressed by Anthony Storr in his *The Dynamics of Creation*, which is a collation and elaboration in his own terms of ideas formulated by Carl Jung, Melanie Klein, and others of the English "object relations" school of psychoanalysis. Storr begins by accepting Klein's claim that each and every human being passes through two psychotic "positions" as an infant. In the first, the "paranoid-schizoid position," infants incorporate images of "part-objects" (good and bad breasts, penises) and react to their internal images with violent love and hate; in the second, "depressive position," they are able to relate to and incorporate images of whole persons, and they react to these as well as make reparations to their whole mother for the assaults they made earlier upon her frustrating breast. In Storr's understanding, the two periods have predominating influences later in two different creative characters, which are the two that Carl Jung had described as introverted (concerned with their own thought processes) and extra-verted (attached to the world):

> Not only is schizoid apathy different in quality from depression . . . but the two states of mind tend to occur in persons of very different temperament and character structure. In Kleinian terminology, the people who are threatened by a sense of futility and meaninglessness are those who have not progressed beyond the very early stage of emotional development called by Melanie Klein the "paranoid-schizoid" position. Broadly speaking, these are introverted or frankly schizoid characters. The people who suffer from misery and hopelessness have, again according to Melanie Klein, progressed a little further in their emotional development, but are also arrested at an early stage; that of the so-called "depressive" position. Both of these early stages would come under the heading of "oral phase" in Freudian terminol-ogy; the former being concerned with supposed primitive emotions accom-

panying the act of sucking and incorporation; whereas the latter is concerned with biting as well as sucking, in other words, with the discovery and disposal of aggressive feelings toward the very person who is also providing food and love.

In Storr's view, people use their creative capacities defensively, to protect themselves against whichever type of "position" predominates in them. The schizoid creator is characterized by inability to come close to people, pulled away as he (Storr analyzes only male schizoids) is by feelings of both inferiority and intellectual superiority. Both feelings will be apparent in the person's work. Inner reality is secured in its specialness by being valued over external reality; unpredictability is challenged by productivity; and meaninglessness and futility are banished in the order and control of a work. On the other hand, people who remain in the depressive position are not distant from people so much as they are dependent on them and their opinions. "Rejection and disapproval are matters of life and death; for unless supplies of approval are forthcoming from outside, they relapse into a state of depression in which self-esteem sinks so low, and rage becomes so uncontrollable, that suicide becomes a real possibility." For this type, creative work can provide recognition, praise, applause, and thus buttress self-esteem. Work also gives an outlet for rage, particularly against unloving or unsatisfactory parental figures, which may take the form of rebelliousness against artistic or scientific predecessors. The depressive's defense against depression may also be manic—a prodigious, grandiose, frantic amount of effort may be needed to win the fame, riches, love, reputation that are need to stave off despair and rage.

Much of what Storr attributes to schizoid types is very similar to what I have attributed to narcissistic-obsessional people with political character-ideals, as much of what he attributes to depressive types (for whom Virginia Woolf briefly serves him as an example) is similar to what I have attributed to erotic-obsessionals with artisanal/sexual character-ideals. Both of Storr's types are arrested in the oral phase, however, and anal and phallic elements that are so important in Freud's scheme of libidinal types are quite secondary when they are mentioned at all. The Oedipus complex is also secondary—as all rage against parental figures is compassed by depressive rage against the mother (from which rage against the father would presumably be derived). The reintegrations and reorganizations of character that take place in adolescence are also simply derivative. Further, in the domain of pathology, "schizoid" and "paranoid" seem to be completely interchangeable terms. Indeed, all forms of pathology are derived from one. This was so for Klein because she held that the paranoid state that is hyphenated to "schizoid" is the genetic predecessor of all forms of depression: "The depressive state is based on the paranoid state and genetically derived from it," Klein declared. This makes it impossible to ask why people develop different forms of psychopathology.

Anthony Storr does not really pursue Melanie Klein's psychopathology past the elementary distinction between two positions on which it rests. But his scheme is restricted by the dualistic Kleinian basis on which it is set. This becomes obvious in Storr's book when he splices in a chapter, which has no theoretical connection with the distinction between schizoid and depressive creators, to deal with "Creativity and the Obsessional Character." Obsessionality is neither schizoid nor depressive, but Storr has to include it because he carefully observed that many creative people are obsessional, or have to fight mightily against extremes of obsessionality. This problem of obsessionality's disappearance from the theoretical scene, it seems to me, holds a clue to the nature of obsessional creativity.

Dualistic characterologies are the sort favored precisely by people of the obsessional-narcissistic, anal character, spiritual character-ideal sort. The two types of characters posited in such schemes represent two forms of temptation that the positor of the scheme feels must be avoided. Both types, viewed as extremes, cover over or obscure the truly pure inner core of human beings, which the person with a spiritual character-ideal wishes to find in himself or herself.

Characteristically, someone who develops a dualistic characterology does so by pointing to the insufficiencies of two exemplars. This was Carl Jung's procedure when he first set out the scheme that he eventually elaborated, with profuse detail, with hundreds of examples, in *Psychological Types* (1920). He came to his thesis in 1913, as he was distinguishing his views from those of Freud, and as he was systematizing his theories of psychopathology. In an essay called "A Contribution to the Study of Psychological Types," Jung started out by presenting the differences between hysterics, whose libido Jung describes as "extraverted," and schizophrenics, who are withdrawn and "introverted." The distinction sounds like proto-Klein:

As Binet has pointed out so aptly, a neurosis simply emphasizes and throws into excessive relief the characteristic traits of a personality. It has long been known that the so-called hysterical character is not simply the product of the manifest neurosis, but pre-dated it to a certain extent. And Hoch has shown the same thing by his researches into the histories of schizophrenic patients; he speaks of a "shut-in" personality which was present before the on-set of the illness. If this is so, we may certainly expect to find the two types outside the sphere of pathology. There are moreover numerous witnesses in literature to the existence of the two types of mentality. Without pretending to exhaust the subject, I will give a few striking examples.

The first example he invoked was William James's *Pragmatism*, with its delightful descriptions of the two kinds of philosophers, "tough-minded," fact-oriented materialists and "tender-minded" spiritualists ("intellectualistic, idealistic, optimistic, religious, free-willist, monistic, dogmatical"). These types are, in Jung's terms, extraverts focused on the world and things in the world, and introverts focused on their own minds. Freud, Jung went on to argue, was an excellent example of a "tough-minded" empiricist who tried to reduce everything to its simple ingredients and its historical antecedents. Alfred Adler, who broke away from Freud's circle before Jung himself did, tender-mindedly imagined people relatively independent of their pasts, guided by their life-plans and "guiding fictions" and asserting their power to attain their wishes. Jung viewed himself as the man who could bridge the two types with a psychology of types.

As his work proceeded, Jung multiplied his types by claiming that introverts and extraverts can have either introverted or extraverted forms of four mental functions (thinking, feeling, sensation, and intuition). This means there are not two character-types but eight. And then, after this typically obsessional multiplication of grids and distinctions, Jung gave up the whole business of characterology, claiming that it is superficial, that it deals only with consciousness and not with the unconscious. Toward the unconscious, the domain of truth, he turned, after a period of great mental confusion, hesitation and fear, and took a plunge.

But then, I hit upon this stream of lava, and the heat of its fires reshaped my life. . . . The years when I was pursuing my inner images were the most important in my life—in them everything essential was decided. It all began then; the later details are only supplements and clarifications of the material that burst forth from the unconscious, and at first swamped me. It was the *prima materia* for a lifetime's work.

It seems to me typical of obsessional creativity to posit alternatives, try to bridge them, and then transcend. The act of transcendence is what distinguishes obsessional creativity from an obsessional neurosis, in which a person stays at the level of trying to knit pieces back together, build bridges, make connections. Sometimes this activity is sadistic (the bridging involves demolition of the bridged parental figures, the expression of death wishes) and sometimes it involves much pain and suffering and self-punishment for the bridge builder. The obsessional neurotic works desperately to keep clean, to prevent breakups internal and external, and if this effort fails, if the defenses are not strong enough, the obsessional neurosis can intensify into paranoia. The obsessional creative character, by contrast, may have all of these habits to a degree, but he or she is also able to plunge right into the feared excremental realm, the *prima materia*, the lava in the center of the body, and find there the true self—which, miraculously, *is* a pure self. A dark night of the soul brings light—to use the religious terms that very commonly surround these experiences; or an orgy of undifferentiated, all-into-all sexuality leads to a prophetic utopian ecstasy—to use the sort of terms to be found in the writings of the Marquis de Sade (before he became quite paranoid in his later years).

The plunge can be construed as an active penetration or as a passive, meditative being-swept-away, but, in whatever the mode, the record of such a journey will reflect the habits of a mental lifetime. In 1930, after Jung had taken his plunge into the *prima materia* and begun to make an encyclopedia of archetypal forms as a consequence, he reverted to an abandoned form and made a typology of creative people. There are, of course, two types, a dualism. In "Psychology and Literature," Jung constructs the psychological creator, who draws on his own personal experience in creating, and the visionary creator. The visionary—the pure creator—brings us literary reports of trans-personal experiences like Jung's own, which have both sadistic and masochistic features, active and passive dimensions. The report is:

Sublime, pregnant with meaning, yet chilling the blood with its strangeness, it arises from timeless depths; glamorous, daemonic, and grotesque, it bursts asunder our human standards of value and aesthetic form, a terrifying tangle of eternal chaos, a *crimen laesae majestatis humanae*. On the other hand, it can be a revelation whose heights and depths are beyond our fathoming, or a vision of beauty which we can never put into words.

In the details of Melanie Klein's work, rather than in the dualistic theoretical frame, there are many clues to the features of the obsessional creativity Jung exemplifies. For example, she makes a very interesting and illuminating descriptive distinction between the condition stemming from a period of incorporating part-objects and the one stemming from an effort to incorporate the whole loved object (the mother); that is, she notes a period between the "paranoid-schizoid" and the "depressive" in which anality is the dominant chord:

> If we compare the feelings of the paranoiac with those of the depressive in regard to disintegration, one can see that characteristically the depressive is filled with sorrow and anxiety for the object, which he would strive to unite again into a whole, while to the paranoiac the disintegrated object is mainly a multitude of persecutors, since each piece is growing into a persecutor. This conception of the dangerous fragments to which the object is reduced seems to me to be in keeping with the introjections of part-objects which are equated with faeces (Abraham), and with the anxiety of a multitude of internal persecutors to which, in my view, the introjection of many part-objects and the multitude of dangerous faeces give rise.

If this typically obtuse and forbidding Kleinian lingo is translated into something a bit more intelligible, what it means is that the paranoiac tends to identify all the broken up pieces of its images of loved ones, all its part-objects, like breasts and penises, with feces. Paranoia is a condition in which internal persecutors are imagined and experiences as anal—and also felt as anal when they are projected and experienced as persecutors in the world.

Obsessional creators fight against both the fragmentation of their internal images and the simultaneous allure and horror of the dissolving, suffocating, exciting, rejuvenating *prima materia*. They develop great capacities for making lists, putting things together, enumerating, outlining. They intellectualize in the mode of connection-making—and make excellent investigators, mystery story writers, as well as researchers and encyclopedists. But underlying this activity there is a dialectic of journey and return in relation to the excremental realm. When the journey—felt as a succumbing to temptation—is itself intellectualized, what appears is an ideology of egalitarianism. All people, as in the Stoic cosmology, are made of the same cosmic stuff, and they will return to it—dust to dust, ashes to ashes. All differences are bridged and negated: between the sexes, between generations, between predecessors and parental family groups, even between the forces of light and the forces of darkness. All share what Jung called a "collective unconscious."

It is false to this creative character, however, to insist on very many general features. The four females (Weil, Yourcenar, Stein, and Anna Freud) and the two males (Johnson and Flaubert) I sketched were very different. The diversity comes from the fact that both an obsessional neurosis, and the obsessional creativity that can prevent such a neurosis, arise from so many pronouncedly distinct developmental courses—so many that one would need to be quite obsessional to enumerate them, as Anna Freud once jokingly noted on the basis of her excellent self-knowledge:

> The variations in the symptomatology of the obsessional neurosis seem to me accounted for by the many elements which enter into its causation such as the prominence of either the sadistic or the anal tendencies in the id; the excessive use of any one or of several of the relevant defense mechanisms; the different rate of growth in id and ego; the prominence of either mother or father as the main target of the child's death wishes; the interaction between intersystemic [id, ego, superego] conflicts and intersystemic conflicts [love-hate, passivity-activity, femininity-masculinity], etc. There are so many elements, and the possible combinations between them are so endless, that it needs not an analyst's but a mathematician's mind to calculate their number (5:247).

Chapter Nine

Gender Questions, Socio-Cultural Contexts

A SUMMARY, AND A NEW QUESTION

In the history of Western European characterology, as I have noted before, two types of characterologies appear again and again. First, there are the dualistic characterologies of which Carl Jung made such an encyclopedic study in his *Psychological Types* (1920). Some dualists have preferred to focus attention on a single key or determining line of demarcation, but Jung thought that a distinction between introverts and extraverts could summarize all of the various dualistic schemes, from the Greek physiological ones in which the four humors were presented in two pairs—hot and dry vs. cold and wet—to the gendered distinctions— masculine vs. feminine—to the cultural and intellectual ones—Apollonian vs. Dionysian. The second sort of characterologists are pluralists who posit more than two types, and, further, argue that each type is defined by a single trait which dominates in it. They do not, as the dualists do, define a type by the absence in it of its opposite; they define it by the presence in it of a dominating trait.

The characterology that I have been developing in this book is pluralist, but it does not rely on any one-to-one correlation between a dominating trait and a character-type. I assume that there are three character regions or complexes in which an array of elements intersect. Each person is a unique instance of her or his type; and each of the three types is a dynamic configuration of the different elements in different proportions. Proceeding cumulatively, adding layer after layer, angle after angle, I have been suggesting that each region or complex of character will reveal to an analytical approach these elements:

- a predominating libidinal phase (oral, anal, phallic)
- a predominating libidinal type (erotic, obsessional, narcissistic, usually to be found in mixed forms)
- a predominating psychic structure (id, superego, ego)
- characteristic patterns of behavior and mechanisms of defense
- characteristic pathological syndromes and affinities with or developed predispositions to neuroses (hysteria, obsessional neurosis, narcissism)
- characteristic affinities with or developed predispositions to psychoses (melancholia, paranoia, schizophrenia)
- characteristic theories or images of creativity (based on psychic splitting, based on psychic purging, and based on sublimation)
- characteristic images for psychic organization or character-ideals (artisanal/sexual, spiritual, political) and corresponding characteristic conceptual orientations in social visions (classist or hierarchical, universalist or cosmopolitan, and focused on charismatic leadership) and cosmologies/cosmogonies (demiurgic crafting, emanationist, evolutionist).

Reading back through these elements, the three creative characters I have been studying look like this:

Artisanal/sexual character-ideal	Spiritual character-ideal	Political character-ideal
Creative splitting	Creative purging	Creative sublimating
Tend toward:	Tend toward:	Tend toward:
melancholia	paranoia	schizophrenia
hysteria	obsessionality	narcissism
Id-dominated	Superego-dominated	Ego-dominated
Erotic-obsessional	Obsessional-narcissistic	Narcissistic-obsessional
Oral	Anal	Phallic

Within these three regions or complexes of character there are, as I have been noting all along, many variations or subtypes, and also many mixed cases. Because of the range of defenses they use and the degree of intellectualization in the defenses, the variations seem to be particularly numerous in people of the obsessional type with a spiritual character-ideal, as the four women studied in Chapter 4 (Weil, Stein, Yourcenar, Anna Freud) and the two men studied in Chapter 7 (Johnson, Flaubert) indicate. In creative people generally, the character-ideal types may be the clearest part of the configurations, both because character-ideals are the relatively late products of adolescence and because they usually involve a good deal of conscious secondary elaboration and referencing to existing intellectual and cultural traditions. This makes the character-ideal types very useful diagnostically and biographically as clues to the fuller regions of character that subtend them.

This tripartite characterology is tripartite (let me finally say explicitly) because it rests upon the conviction that people are ruled predominantly either (1) by their internal instinctual drives, or (2) by the ego they develop to control their instinctual drives and direct their being-in-the-world, or (3) by their conscience or superego as it represents intrapsychically the weight of their pasts in the form of their important external (usually parental) figures for identifications, and as it represents their societal and cultural traditions.

Put in less psychoanalytic and more philosophical terms, the characterology I have been developing rests upon the conviction that people are dominated either (1) by their libidinized caring for the future (for their own loves and works and immortality, or for the life of the species), or (2) by their present-mindedness and zeal (in Darwin's word) for understanding, or (3) by their sense of the past, their voluntary and involuntary memories (in Proust's terms). This philosophical schematization reflects the emphasis on temporal modalities so central to phenomenology and existentialism rather than utilizing only the spatial orientations central to distinctions like the one Jung drew between extraverts and introverts.

The importance of societal and cultural traditions for an individual and for the different types may be most obvious in the superego-dominated type, the obsessional with a spiritual character-ideal, the Proustian distiller of memories. But all individuals and each of the types live in societal and cultural conditions and all are aided or hindered by their conditions as they develop, as they love and work.

It is these relations between the creative characters and social-cultural contexts that I want to explore, in a general and schematic way, in this chapter. But I want to approach this huge topic from a particular angle, a particular part of the library of "Culture and Personality" studies produced by anthropologists and sociologists. I want to focus on a pair usually crucial to dualistic characterologies—masculine/feminine—and use the pair as an arena for examining the ways in which social arrangements and cultural traditions impinge on creative characters. This pair is particularly instructive because, throughout much of the Western European tradition, it has been interpreted as equivalent to creative/uncreative. That is, creativity has been assigned to males and (in more complicated ways) to masculinity, while women have been acknowledged as reproducers, not producers, and femininity as a character-designation has signaled, if not total absence of creativity, at least only limited sorts of creativity. I am going to make a survey map of the ways in which "creativity" and "genius" have been gendered by thinkers of the three different character and character-ideal types, and then track how such gendering has influenced understandings of female creativity. This map will, then, open a more general inquiry into the ways in which different types of societies encourage or discourage creativity of different sorts.

GENDER AND GENIUS

In recent years, a rich historical and biographical literature by European and American feminists has appeared that is devoted to exploring a network of questions about creative women in European and American contexts. How have their works, their voices, been suppressed or slighted in a tradition that predominantly values male creativity? And how can "herstory" be recovered? In what ways did their families and societies and larger cultural milieus discourage creative women, denigrate or flatly deny their abilities—or, much more rarely, in what ways did they receive encouragement, support, recognition? Are there elements in "female psychology" that have compelled women to cooperate in their cultural devaluation or at least not to recognize it as such? Is there such a thing as "feminine creativity" (as distinct from "masculine creativity") that would be crystal clear if only it could flourish outside of conventional cultural constraints? Or is "feminine creativity" necessarily a defensive weapon of subversion or deconstruction forged by women who have grown up in hostile cultural territory? Are there types of productivity and genres of work that are particularly "feminine," in and of themselves or as strategies for coping with oppression?

218

In pursuit of these questions, feminist scholars often display a tension between their desire to speak of something completely general—"the cultural position of women," "female psychology," "feminine creativity,"—and a clear acknowledgment that cultural positions, psychologies, and creativities are both and conjointly (in some as yet to be understood way) quite individual and quite culture-specific. The cultural positions of women in Periclean Athens and in the Renaissance city-states and in mid-nineteenth-century English towns are currently being seen to be as different as the lives of Aspasia (Pericles' highly cultivated mistress) and Christine de Pisan and the three Bronte sisters (very different characters and creative types who grew up under quite similar conditions). Differences are being appreciated, but the hope remains that common features might appear if the particular historical and biographical territories were thoroughly explored. A similar sense of specificity combined with hope for future generalizations is present in cross-cultural comparisons, as contrasted to the more numerous trans-historical comparisons within one culture or series of cultures. Prevailing winds in feminist studies are not good for the kind of universal statements that were sailing in structuralist anthropology and historiography two decades ago, when it could be flatly declared that the binary masculine/feminine is to be found in every culture in one form only—the patriarchal or sexist masculine over feminine construed as culture over nature.

On the topic of how "creativity" and "genius" have been gender-tagged within the Western European tradition, recent feminist scholars point to historical developments. For example, Christine Battersby, in a book called *Genius and Gender* (1989), argues that eighteenth-century estheticians and theorists of creativity envisioned a new type of "genius" by appropriating for male creators a number of attributes that had been, during the Middle Ages and Renaissance, attributed to women—passionateness or emotionality, sexual appetitiveness, wild imagination. Male creators with these feminine traits, who were different from ordinary males and could live only as outsiders, on the margins, in bohemias, were then idealized by Romantic genius-worshippers and by twentieth-century portraitists of the lonely, misfit virile artist with a streak of feminine intuition. A woman could not be such a genius, even if she approximated to bisexuality by having a "masculine mind."

This kind of historical delineation seems to me both right and wrong. It certainly is the case that the male genius with feminine traits came to be idealized among the Romantics, but, as I have noted, this type was as central to Plato's vision of the man who can metaphorically give birth to children of his soul as it was to the Romantic Nietzsche's male mother idea. I think visions of the male mother or the feminine male creator are common in all historical periods among thinkers of the artisanal/sexual character-ideal type. What varies historically, it seems to me, is the cultural recessiveness or dominance of this type, and thus the influence it has on both contemporaries and later historians writing about this type's visions of creativity and evaluations of femininity. There are pluralities of views of creativity and of femininity—as well as of anything else—to be found in each cultural location and period. But each view has a different weight, a different registration. Reconstructing historically these complex interplays of views, centuries or even just decades later, is as difficult as reconstructing an adult's childhood or adolescent fantasy life in an analysis. Similar methodological problems of selective evidence, manifest and latent layers of record, preconceptions in the mind of the reconstructor, and so forth, arise. "Romanticism" is now a label for an era, but during the Romantic era there were views abroad that were not Romantic. So the interesting question becomes: what social and cultural conditions promote Romanticism (which then, in turn, promotes certain social and cultural conditions for its supporting surround)?

In the present Euro-American place and period, gender issues are central to many types of inquiries thanks to the feminist intellectual revolution in course. The hope has been articulated that centuries of inquiry distorted by what is sometimes called "the male gender lens" will be superseded with the removal of this lens. Female creativity, historically and for the present and future, might then appear as quite different from male creativity. But this view, it seems to me, is reductionistic, or, in a current critical term, "essentialist," on the topic of "the feminine." That is, it assumes that "the feminine" is one thing, like an Aristotelian essence hidden behind all appearances or accidents of condition or context. In the characterology I have been developing, there are three broad types of creativity that both women and men exhibit. A historical approach, tuned to social and cultural contexts, can illuminate the ways and degrees to which any one kind of creativity tends to be more characteristic of a time and place, but a historical approach is not necessary for initially sketching the types.

In other words, while respecting and adapting the historical approach to "genius and gender," I think it is crucial to make a complementary typological approach—a synchronic approach. The pair masculine/feminine receives different readings and different emphases for different characterologists as well as in different periods and locations—including our immediate cultural context, in which the pair is at the center of so many discourses that it often seems to be considered the key to all other creativity mysteries.

In the last chapter, I suggested that dualistic characterologies—among them those focused on the pair masculine/feminine—are frequently produced by people of the spiritual or ascetic character-ideal type. Their fundamental characterological demarcation follows their own aspirations for character-organization, that is, they separate the pure and the impure, those liberated from the bondage of the flesh or the world and those, unredeemed or unredeemable, who are stuck in the mire of themselves or their surroundings. Masculinity has generally been associated with purity, and femininity with impurity, even among men and women who outwardly seem to worship female purity and saintliness, or who wish—for ideological-psychological purposes—to elevate femininity above masculinity (say, feminine relationship-cultivation over crass masculine judgmentalness). But in recent years, femininity has also been elevated and feminine creativity declared to be superior to legalistic hyper-rational masculine logicality.

Such gender-tagging also runs counter to another element in the worldview of people of this character-ideal type: their cosmopolitanism, their tendency to find all distinctions between people other than the basic pure/impure one to be superficial, inessential, anti-humanistic or inhumane. For the Stoics, both men and women were citizens of the world.

This contradiction can be seen in a specific focus in Carl Jung's work. Neither Jung's basic dualistic characterology nor the eight combinatory types with which he complicated it were explicitly organized along gender lines. Neither introversion nor extraversion were said to be specifically masculine or feminine, and Jung indicated that women can be either introverted or extraverted. The general position is quite in accord with the spiritual character-ideal projected as a cosmopolitan or universalist worldview. Nonetheless, when Jung turned his attention to creativity and considered men and women, he came to an asymmetrical stance that contradicted his equalitarianism. He elaborated Freud's emphasis on universal bisexuality by arguing that both men and women have masculine and feminine psyches (he called them *animus* and *anima*), and each is creative out of the psychic function opposite to their anatomical sex. In short, as he said in a 1945 essay called "The Relations Between the Ego and the Unconscious":

> Just as a man brings forth his work as a complete creation out of his feminine nature, so the inner masculine side of a woman brings forth creative seeds which have the power to fertilize the feminine side of the man.

Women produce seeds to fertilize the feminine in men, that is, they inspire men. But men do not inspire women by producing seeds to fertilize the feminine in women—for women's creativity is not feminine, it is masculine. Males are the true creators; women are apprentices, or muses.

Generally, people of the spiritual character-ideal tend to be equalitarian universalists in theory but male-celebrating in fact. Or, rather, their universalizing theory is really male-celebrating, but that is not obvious until the topic of creativity or leadership arises, at which point the unconscious fantasy emerges and the males move into first place. In Jung's scheme, a masculine woman (which psychoanalysts would associate with a phallic mother) is made subservient to male intellectual work—a result that certainly accords with typical obsessional mechanisms such as intellectualization that defend against forbidden desires. Many women with spiritual character-ideals speak of creativity with the same bias but for different reasons. Such a woman imagines her own creativity as masculine, an attribute of her liberated, purified self, which she identifies (often quite consciously and explicitly, but sometimes only unconsciously) as masculine, and she divests herself of her femininity in fantasy. This is the common pattern noted earlier in very different forms in Simone Weil, Marguerite Yourcenar, Gertrude Stein, and Anna Freud. Women of this sort may, further, like many Romantic estheticians, idealize a masculinity in themselves that is (conventionally speaking) feminine—that is, emotional, intuitive, sensitive, nurturing, and so forth. The masculinity is not unapproachably virile, not—specifically—unattainably phallic. Psychologically, spiritualizing or asceticism in the form of masculinizing is Oedipal safety for a woman: by becoming a pure, strong (if not particularly virile) male in her fantasy of herself, she moves away from incestuous desires for her father and also desexualizes her love of her mother while retaining it. In their late adolescences, creative women of this sort very commonly express their character-ideals in chivalric terms; thus Willa Cather in her twenties, as exemplified by her melodramatic credo text *The Kingdom of Art*:

> In the kingdom of art there is no God, but one God, and his service is so exacting that there are few men born of woman who are strong enough to take the vows. There is no paradise offered for a reward to the faithful, no celestial bowers, no houris, no scented wines; only death and the truth.

An alternative form of the fantasy is an image of a woman who has slipped the bonds of conventional frail domestic femininity and become spiritually Amazonian, strongly self-assertive and perfectly altruistic.

Spiritualizing fantasies are quite different from fantasies involving a masculine part of the mind and a feminine part of the mind in metaphorical intercourse, or what Virginia Woolf calls "consummation . . . of a marriage of opposites." This is the basic androgynous fantasy or *ars combinatoria* of people with artisanal/sexual character-ideals. And it is usually fitted into a pluralist characterology, not a dualistic one of the sort generated by people with spiritual character-ideals. A figure of androgynous mind is the ideal or highest type in pluralist characterologies generated by artisanal/sexual people, whether or not they make gender distinctions central to their full schemes.

People with artisanal/sexual character-ideals often follow the Platonic formula in sketching a pluralistic characterology. They imagine a lowly appetitive or materialistic character-type (in which femininity is associated with the appetitive part of an individual's psyche); a median type in which spirit dominates; and a highest, most creative type which is rational and masculine but in which femininity is transmogrified into an ability for mothering or propagation of (metaphoric) children of the soul. These character-types are sketched for males only, even if woman are not simply relegated to being characterless or to being in the lowest group. The fact that Plato wanted to educate women for guardianship and leadership in his ideal republic, following the actual Spartan example, did not pull his characterology toward compassing females. Intellectual or philosophical appreciation of women like Plato's may well rest on an unconscious conviction that females are really males.

Envy of female reproductivity and maternal-identification are usually obvious in the characterologies developed by males with artisanal/sexual character-ideals, who are, as I have noted, frequently of a quite androgynous sexual make-up in terms of attitudes, and sometimes in terms of homosexual object preferences. When Virginia Woolf set about praising androgyny in *A Room of One's Own*, she, by comparison, very carefully avoided all description of minds—male or female—giving birth or sowing seeds.

Woolf's ideal was a writer using both sides of his or her mind equally: "The androgynous mind is resonant and porous; . . . it transmits emotions without impediment; . . . it is naturally creative, incandescent and undivided." But this ideal implied for her that the "manly-womanly mind . . . does not think specially or separately of sex." The person of androgynous mind is not "sex-conscious" in the manner of men who are always defending themselves against women (particularly against the threat of women's suffrage or liberation) or in the manner of women who are always defending themselves against men or reciting a history of oppression. That is, the price Virginia Woolf had to pay for articulating for women a non-sexist equalitarian concept of androgyny was a drastic constriction of female creativity:

> It is fatal for a woman to lay the least stress on any grievance; to plead even with justice any cause; in any way to speak consciously as a woman. And fatal is no figure of speech; for anything written with that conscious bias is doomed to death. It ceases to be fertilized.

The image is of a woman who is deprived or deprives herself of her masculine fertilizing half. She is at odds with the masculinity in herself, excluding it. To be fully androgynous, she must not give special privileges or a voice for special pleading to her feminine self. Not being "sex-conscious" really comes down to not excluding masculinity—for a woman.

The three character-types implicit in Woolf's text are womanly, manly, and womanly-manly (or manly-womanly). The womanly character lacks masculine power and capacity to interest male readers, the manly one so lacks feminine "suggestive power" that female readers are left untouched by it, "however hard it hits the surface of the mind it cannot penetrate within." While the manly mind is impotent with female readers and the womanly mind is unseductive (frigid?) with male readers, the androgynous one has all kinds of potency. The desire and hope behind the artisanal/sexual character-ideal is very clear here: the person who can live up to this ideal can win all love.

Among males of the artisanal-sexual character-ideal type, women artists and writers are admitted to the republic of letters and perhaps even encouraged if they are of the type idealized by such men: that is, if they are as close as it is possible for a woman to be to the male with feminine creative capacities, to the male mother. Such a woman is both a familiar and always—by virtue of her anatomical sex—destined to be lesser. She never represents the threatening notion that women could be creative (rather than just reproductive) in their own ways. George Sand was the modern European writer who most nearly conformed to the type—judged from the perspective of those male Romantics who felt her to be a kindred spirit—as testimonial after testimonial to her life and work shows. Thus Balzac: "She is boyish, an artist, she is great-hearted, generous, devout, and chaste; she has the main characteristics of a man; ergo, she is not a woman." Portraits of George Sand as a creative man who is not really threatening to male artistic or sexual prerogatives (for example, because she is "chaste") then appear in scientific guise in the twentieth century, as for example in this assessment from Andrew Gemant's 1961 work *The Nature of Genius*, which assumes that Sand's masculinity was somehow demonstrated by her life:

> Nearly always highly gifted women, approaching in some degree the nature of a genius, are masculine. In certain instances we have proof of that masculinity, as in George Sand. Eminent women scientists are nearly always plain or have definitely masculine features. They are actually half men, physically and mentally, their primary sexual organs happening to be female.

The reigning impulse here is not the Jungian one for making creative females subservient to creative males with feminine attributes, cast in the role of inspirers. Rather there is a fantasy about two ranks of males— real ones, and female ones. The impulse is to make a hierarchy.

People with political character-ideals are generally, as I have often noted, evolutionists. As characterologists, they imagine their lowest character-type as early, primitive, archaic, while their highest type lives in the present or is imagined as a future paragon of civilization and refined greatness. In Aristotle's scheme, this kind of schematizing intersects very clearly and uncomplicatedly with the masculine/feminine pair: the lowest type is purely female, the highest purely male. But other evolutionary thinkers have found the matter of gender more complex. Freud's characterology, so multidimensional and so tied to a theory of

225

universal bisexuality, attributes the highest (artistic and scientific) abilities and creativity to males, but does not imagine that the paragon character is purely masculine.

Thinkers of the political character-ideal type also generally tend to imagine the psyche as tripartite. They speak with Aristotle of an irrational part and two sorts of rational parts of the psyche; or they speak with Aristotle's Christian heir Thomas Aquinas of the unified soul with manifold operations of sensation and locomotion, of *intellectus*, and of *voluntas*; or with Immanuel Kant of understanding (*Verstand*), reason (*Vernunft*), and judgment (*Urteilskraft*); or with Sigmund Freud of id, ego, and superego (or, in his earlier scheme, unconscious, conscious, and a censoring preconscious), or with Hannah Arendt (to indicate that this way of conceptualizing is not foreign to women) of willing, thinking, and judging. The three parts are not gendered, that is, they are not feminine or masculine or some mixture, though the ideal psyche may be imagined as belonging to a person who is characterologically a gender mixture.

The psychological experience that underlies these visions, it seems to me, is ego-centered. These people, strongly narcissistic, who put such stress in their lives and character-ideals on maintaining personal and psychic integrity, controlling unruly internal forces, on channeling and sublimating energy, developing intellectual discipline and capacity for systematization, experience themselves as having a fortress self. They guard against disruptions from below (appetitive, sexual, aggressive) and against threats from the outside in the form of either disruptive changes or rigid, inhuman rules and social conventions. They often conceive of the forces threatening from below and from outside as temporal forces, located in the past or located in the future, and they connect their evolutionary scheme to overcoming the representatives of the past and triumphing rebelliously by leading the elements of the future.

Men of this sort tend to identify their great creative moments or periods with achievement of psychic harmony or relaxation in the midst of great tension or effort, necessary pain and exertion. Like the austere, regulated Kant, they speak (as he did in the *Critique of Judgment*) of thinking that is "recreation of the mind," or of mental activity that consists of "playfulness among the faculties," or of creative production that is "purposive purposelessness," esthetic enjoyment that is "disinterested delight." Or they say something like what Freud said in *Jokes and Their Relation to the Unconscious* about the aimlessness of fantasy:

> When our psychic apparatus does not actually act in search of some urgently needed gratification, we let this apparatus itself work for pleasure gain. We attempt to gain pleasure from its very activity.

It is the systematic, balanced, harmonious quality of their minds and of their perceived tripartite constructions that appeals to these thinkers, and sets them apart from others who also use tripartite constructions, but for different purposes. G. W. F. Hegel, for example, used trinities repetitively for a philosophical activity that he, like Plotinus or Spinoza, imagined as a means to purify and free his mind, and The Mind (the universal *Geist*), of material restraints. But in his case the number three seems to have had the magical, numerological allure it often has for ascetic, obsessional types—like Freud's Wolf Man in his trinitarian religious phase—for whom dyads (father-son or mother-son) are too frightening.

Insofar as people with political character-ideals imagine creativity as a process of sublimation, they think of the ideally creative mind as sexless or desexualized (or, rarely, as genderless but undelimitedly sexual, as in the example of Hélène Cixous that I will turn to in a moment). Darwin, for example, imagined people evolving into angelic consciousnesses. Hannah Arendt worked for years on a complex, three-volume study called *The Life of the Mind* in which The Mind was never gendered or associated with genders. Simone de Beauvoir's *The Second Sex* contains an extensive and rich description of mental life from someone of this character-ideal type, but it also departs from the approach common to this type by considering the experiential repercussions in women— including herself—of sexist social conditions and the age-long sexist disparagement of women's creativity. A genius, Beauvoir says in her final chapter, must be free to "regard the universe," and such freedom and sweep has to this point in history required not a particularly gendered mind but male prerogatives, the masculine-human condition:

> Today it is already less difficult for women to assert themselves; but they have not yet completely overcome the age-long sex-limitation that has isolated them in their femininity. . . . The fact is that the traditional woman

is a bamboozled conscious being and a practitioner of bamboozlement: she attempts to disguise her dependence from herself, which is a way of consenting to it. To expose this dependence is in itself a liberation; a clear-sighted cynicism is a defense against humiliations and shame: it is the preliminary sketch of an assumption. By aspiring to clear-sightedness women writers are doing the cause of women a great service; but—usually without realizing it—they are still too concerned with serving this cause to assume the disinterested attitude toward the universe that opens the widest horizons. . . . For the individuals who seem to us most outstanding, who are honored with the name of genius, are those who have proposed to enact the fate of all humanity in their personal existences, and no woman has believed herself authorized to do this. . . . Once again: in order to explain her limitations it is a woman's situation that must be invoked and not a mysterious essence; thus the future remains largely open.

Women can, free of sex limitations, think like men. Masculine thinking in social conditions of masculine freedom is the standard, but this did not feel to Beauvoir like a particular standard. Masculine seemed to her the universal.

Currently, the French daughters of Beauvoir, while they pay her homage, see things differently. The one most of her characterological type, however, seems to me to be Hélène Cixous, judging not from biographical information but from her famous text "The Laugh of the Medusa." Cixous is a celebrant of the universe within, too, but she describes it without privileging masculinity. In the mode of evolutionary prophecy, she evokes the woman who will emerge at the end of "the Phallic period," in "the new history," the woman who will produce *l'écriture féminine* out of her bisexuality. But her singing, flying writing will flow from her "vatic" bisexuality, not from some "neuter" bisexuality that only reflects either denial of all sexual differences in herself or insistence that she is not a castrated being:

to this self-effacing, merger-type bisexuality, which would conjure away castration. . . . I oppose the *other bisexuality* in which every subject not enclosed in the false theater of phallocentric representationalism has founded his/her erotic universe. Bisexuality: that is, each one's location in self [*repérage en soi*] of the presence—variously manifest and insistent according to each person, male or female—of both sexes, non-exclusion, either of the difference or of one sex, and, from this "self-permission," multiplication of the effects of the inscription of desire, over all parts of my body and the other body.

Women's writing is explicitly supposed to rise up from and celebrate the female body, which has been derided in male characterologies and theories of creativity.

> To write. An act which will not only "realize" the decensored relation of woman to her sexuality, to her womanly being, giving her access to her native strength; it will give her back her goods, her pleasures, her organs, her immense bodily territories which have been kept under seal; it will tear her away from the superegoized structure in which she has always occupied the place reserved for the guilty (guilty of everything, guilty at every turn: for having desires, for not having any; for being frigid, for being "too hot"; for not being both at once; for being too motherly and not enough; for having children and for not having any; for nursing and not nursing . . .)— tear her away by means of this research, this job of analysis and illumination, this emancipation of the marvelous text of herself that she must urgently learn to speak.

Cixous is specifically anxious to challenge all forms of the male notion that motherhood and creativity are antithetical with the notion that women write from her their maternal bodies: "A woman is never far from 'mother' (I mean outside her role functions . . .). There is always within her at least a little of that good mother's milk. She writes in white ink." But Cixous also rejects ferociously any prescriptions about how and when and for what purposes a woman acts on her "gestation drive."

> Either you want a kid or you don't—that's your business. . . . We are not going to refuse, if it should happen to strike our fancy, the unsurpassed pleasures of pregnancy which have actually always been exaggerated or conjured away—or cursed—in classic texts. . . . And if you don't have that particular yearning, it doesn't mean that you are in any way lacking. Every body distributes in its own special way, without model or norm, the nonfinite and changing totality of its desires.

Cixous's universe within is a universe of desires, and her gloried-in narcissism ("beyond selfish narcissism") is simply and powerfully summarized: "I want all. I want all of me with all of him."

GENDERED INDIVIDUALS IN SOCIAL CONTEXTS

Freedom to encompass the universe and all human life and desire in it is psychological or philosophical freedom as the narcissist, the person of political character-ideal, imagines it. But this freedom is not the same as freedom from corrupting impurity or materiality; and it is not the same as freedom from internal splitting or intrapsychic disbalance (however defined) between masculinity and femininity or between shaping artisanal force and shaped material. These differences among conceptions of creative freedom, however, signal clearly the Euro-American ways in which women have been said to be uncreative or less creative than men. There are three ways:

—The obsessional, ascetic assessment: women are impure. This may mean too sexual (and too involved in reproduction) or too enmeshed in earthly sex or love relationships; too material or too materialistic; too unruly, undisciplined, unpredictable, inconsistent.

—The erotic, artisanal/sexual assessment; women are not masculine enough, not enough of a bisexual mixture, or they are too masculine but unable to be really masculine because of the limitations of their anatomies; they are uninspired (especially if inspiration is considered female, and women are not thought to have female Muses); they are unable to shape and mold their passions, their appetites. (When women are said to be unruly in the sense of unable to establish or submit to rules, the complaint usually comes from a person of spiritual character-ideal, while a charge of unruliness in the sense of being unable to shape and mold their mentally procreative powers more typically comes from a person with an artisanal/sexual character-ideal, who is afraid of too much passivity or submissiveness and imagines self-control as an activity.)

—The narcissistic, political character-ideal assessment: women are at a lower evolutionary stage, missing either a key developmental step (toward transcendent universalism in Beauvoir's social analysis) or a key ingredient of psychic function (reason, as Aristotle bluntly said) or of psychic structure (superego, as Freud argued in his portrait of the female's unresolved Oedipus complex, her perennial parental love).

These assessments of women as lesser creators or noncreators are often lumped together in feminist critiques and viewed as, simply, specific instances of male misogyny or sexism. This approach is, it seems to me, reductionistic. It ignores the influence of character-types on assessments of creativity in general, and thus it closes off what looks to me like the clearest route to understanding in psychological (if not social) terms how and why female creativity is disparaged. But the approach also

230

ignores how women—who share character-structures with men—share the assessments.

I have indicated summarily, in sketch, how women of different character-ideal types attribute creativity to masculinity, but I would like to pursue this discussion in more detail along one line before turning to a consideration of how social contexts enforce or reinforce the various equations of creativity and masculinity. Many efforts have been made to isolate something—a single thing—called "female creativity" or "feminine creativity," and each effort supposes that the single thing is largely independent of social context, common to all women. This idea needs consideration before the "Culture and Personality" topic can be pursued.

Phyllis Greenacre was one of the few psychoanalysts—male or female—of her generation to give her attention to differences between creative men and women. She did this in an essay called "Woman as Artist" (1960), while all of her earlier papers on childhood and adult creativity and on the related topics of transitional objects and fetishism, split selves and imposters, used only male examples.

"Woman as Artist" begins by noting the fact that fewer women than men have gained reputations as creators and moves immediately to a caveat unusual for the time of its publication: Greenacre acknowledges that having abilities and gaining recognition are not the same thing, that is, she acknowledges social constraints on women's achievement of success and renown, if not upon the development of their abilities. But her focus is not on these constraints; it is on constitutional and psychological differences between men and women and on neurotic barriers to creativity that are specific to women and greater than those specific to men.

Turning to physiological issues first, as she did in all of her papers on creativity, Greenacre ruled out of consideration the obvious involvement of adult women with procreativity, with both child-bearing and child-rearing, and turned her attention to factors in childhood and adolescence. She stated, as most psychoanalytic and non-psychoanalytic researchers do, that girls are typically verbally precocious in relation to boys, that they are more concerned with emotional and personal relationships, and less concerned with muscular activities, manual activity, logical precision, need for externalization, experimentation, adventure, "and what might be called executive expansion." On the basis of these observations, Greenacre concludes: "Woman's creative work seems stamped with attributes resembling her biologically creative functions, as it is most often involved in problems of human relationship and interpretation, and rarely shows a high degree of originality in other respects."

Greenacre, like most other researchers who hold this view, offers no support for it and no argument for why these observed differences are not largely—or at least much more largely than Greenacre concedes—consequences of social training and expectation rather than of any biological or physiological givens. Greenacre's view seems to me to reflect widely shared prejudices, but also to be quite specifically typical of people of the artisanal/sexual character-ideal—whether male or female—who model creative production on biological reproduction and then assess differences between males and females on the basis of their relationship to biological reproduction.

Focusing on anatomical sexual differences, Greenacre remarks:

> While the exposure of the male genitals promotes their stimulatability, it also heightens the direct threat and fear of injury to the organs; but the whole problem is a focused one. The castration problem of the little girl, with its devious explanations and its excess of hypothetical guilt, is linked with her envy and confusion due to her awareness of the difference from the boy and her inability to see her own organs clearly. It gives rise to a type of competitiveness which cannot be met directly with reality testing and so must depend on displacement, rationalization and fantasy. The girl's resolution of her envy of the boy's phallus, with the realization that she will later be able to have a child, contains so great a deferment that its acceptance cannot be achieved until she has reached the degree of maturity to tolerate this postponement. . . . Child-bearing remains in feminine psychology heavily stamped with a tacit attitude of considering it essentially a substitute, although possibly a superior recompense, for the original inferiority in her presumed genital deficiency.

Greenacre goes on to stress the importance for creative women of their fantasies that they do have a phallus, of their "heightened bisexuality." When they must fulfill female functions—when they menstruate, when they give birth—their fantasized creative selves, often quite split off from their ordinary-life selves, are threatened with a kind of castration. They may come to fear their creative selves, abandon their creative imaginations, in order to mend such a split; and they may give up their creative enterprises, unless actively urged along in them by parental figures, particularly their fathers. They may also, by identifying with an encouraging or alluring father figure, produce another split, between a father-identified self and one still dependent on and enmeshed in the maternal care that comes from a mother who is also becoming a rival. The girl, in this complex Oedipal tangle, tends toward "caution growing out of ambivalence—the forerunner of tact—the need for careful balance and infantile diplomacy. This in turn restricts the full expansiveness of creative originality." What the pre-Oedipal developmental story of such a girl might be, Greenacre does not say, although she might have been open to the suggestion that a girl who felt her "presumed genital deficiency" so keenly would also have known earlier losses—for examples: of her mother's love (or her security in her mother's love); or her oral or anal erotic pleasures through a traumatic weaning or a too rigid step into cleanliness.

Greenacre's Oedipally focused developmental descriptions presume splitting, presume strong penis envy and conflict over phallic fantasies; they identify psychic splitting as the source of creativity, and also as the demarcation of it, the signal for its vulnerability to pathological splitting. They show how a woman with these characteristics comes to identify creativity and masculinity as phallic power. The descriptions seem to me excellent for one period in the life of one type of creative woman: they focus on the Oedipal—to the almost complete neglect of the pre-Oedipal—period of the woman whom I identify by her artisanal sexual character-ideal and her erotic-obsessional libidinal type, who is hysterical in the sense of prone to play out her conflicts (including penis envy) in the medium of her body and especially her oral arena (she, for example, finds expressing her opinions orally very anxiety-producing, or she cannot stop talking or eating or drinking long enough to paint or write). Greenacre's descriptions also distinguish females of this type from their male counterparts, the imposters or poseurs whose hidden creative self is very likely (but not necessarily) a phallic feminine one, a male mother. But these descriptions do not seem to me generalizable to all women, or even to all women of this type: they put all of the developmental emphasis on penis envy and the Oedipal configuration, and these features are said to be uninfluenced by familial or social conditions.

Even more focused on developmental factors independent of social conditions—and even earlier developmental factors, as well—is Melanie Klein's theory that all women (not just one type) work creatively from one basic impulse: to make reparations for the harm they imagine they

233

have done their mothers in fantasized sadistic attacks upon their mothers' bodies. They work out of the "depressive position" that succeeds their "schizoid" sadistic phase in the second year of life. As Klein argued in "Infantile Anxiety-Situations Reflected in a Work of Art and in the Creative Impulse" (1929):

> The little girl has a sadistic desire, originating in the early stages of the Oedipus conflict, to rob the mother's body of its contents, namely, the father's penis, faeces, children, and to destroy the mother herself. This desire gives rise to anxiety lest the mother should in her turn rob the little girl herself of the contents of her body (especially of children) and lest her body should be destroyed and mutilated. In my view, this anxiety, which I have found in the analyses of girls and women to be the deepest anxiety of all, represents the little girl's earliest danger-situation. I have come to see that the dread of being alone, of the loss of love and loss of object-love, which Freud holds to be the basic infantile danger-situation in girls, is a modification of the anxiety-situation I have just described.

The woman purges herself of her basic anxiety by restoring her mother—and herself—in the medium of art. She fills up all empty or deranged spaces with paintings, writings, musical compositions. The man, too, works restoratively, but in him there is a specific focus to his sadism and thus to his reparation: his sadistic desire is a "struggle with the father's penis in the mother." But both men and women heal themselves and purge themselves of their aggressivity and sadism in art.

Klein's descriptions, and also her own need to find one determinative experience that all people share, her cosmopolitan psychoanalysis, lend themselves well to guiding an exploration of the obsessive, the person who tends toward depression and even paranoia, the person with a spiritual or ascetic character-ideal, who is in her creative activity trying to clean up, to order, to purify. But the descriptions are not particularly illuminating for the Greenacre creative woman or for the more narcissistic universalizer, the woman of political character-ideal, for whom I do not think there yet exists a coherent psychoanalytic guiding formulation. (I will return to this problem in a moment.)

If the early developmental factors to which psychoanalysts like Greenacre and Klein have pointed are examined out of social or cultural context, it seems to me that they cannot either mark or explain the life-course of a woman who is able, first, to continue her development past childhood in a creativity-supporting way and, second, to act upon her creative impulse, to find a medium or genre, workable working conditions, an arena. How does she differ from her sister who falters developmentally and expressively? In short, there is no distinction between possessing a childhood creative impulse or a psychological reason for creativity, and developing a creative character. The two psychoanalysts note a psychologically inhibiting condition toward which their types tend—chronic dissatisfaction with her anatomy or her recompenses and splitting for Greenacre's woman, and depression for the Kleinian woman who cannot purge her aggressivity. But only Greenacre gives an indication of how the inhibiting condition might be avoided. She suggests, but does not consider in any detail, that a paternal identification can play a crucial influence in the girl's creativity. Klein does not consider environment at all.

As long as a theorist of creativity operates with the idea that creativity is one thing—one impulse, one mental mechanism, one developmental configuration, one character-trait—the variety of living conditions in which creative people flourish will seem to the theorist just baffling, as will the variety of creative expressions, modes, and products. Differences among creative characters, and reflections of those differences in peoples' conceptions of creativity, are crucial, I think, to understanding how social conditions generally, or what Beauvoir calls "sex limitations" specifically, impinge on people and become part of their characters. One person's freedom may be another's bondage; and one person's bondage, another's freedom. In the most basic public sense, all women are trapped alike by being always "the other" (as Beauvoir says of every member of the second sex), as all who live in physical or political chains are enslaved. But this public sense does not speak to how conditions become part of character or how different characters react in the same conditions.

Let me make a preliminary sketch, based not on clinical evidence but on the evidence of many biographies of women, of conditions that seem to me to sustain womens' creativities at the point of late adolescence or post-adolescence, and in the various characterological types. I am going to turn to an exploration of "social character" just below, but this sketch will mark the kind of survey and inquiry that, it seems to me, can be yielded by an activity that might be called "comparative biography."

—The Greenacre woman, who (as Greenacre says) can "play out bisexual roles dramatically," who tends toward imposture and use of her internal splitting in her art, which often is quite dramatic (regardless of its genre), is a woman who gravitates toward social and cultural contexts in which roles, and particularly gender roles, are not rigidly assigned. She needs a bohemia—a Greenwich Village, a Bloomsbury, a 1930s Paris or Berlin—where there is a collective relishing of the carnivalesque or gender-experimental. For the more overtly or determinedly homosexual woman, this may be a lesbian world, a city of ladies or a Lesbos in the archetypical sense of the word. An explicitly counter-cultural society is not as necessary for a woman of this character type who is a performer and has been able to find in her acting, her dancing, her music playing, in the specific milieus of a theater, a troupe, an ensemble, a way to enjoy her psychosexual motility, her role liability. As an adolescent in a family or a social setting in which her nightmare is the daily fare—gender roles are strictly assigned, and only men are considered creative—a creative woman of this type who does not give up may turn away from her creative medium to lavish her creative energy on an illness (sometimes raising hypochondria to a kind of art form) or to experiments in being a product, being passively shaped and molded by someone else.

—The more obsessional type with a spiritual or ascetic character-ideal gravitates toward or organizes an environment which is convent-like or monastic, where her self-strictures accord with the prevailing strictures. It is much less likely that she will be making a rebellious break with her family to come into such an environment—usually the prevailing family style tends toward the obsessional. Her character-structure has been sanctioned and promoted in the religious life (particularly Christian) of Europe (and then America) since the Middle Ages, and she has not generally been viewed as any threat to patriarchal prerogatives. This reason alone might be sufficient to explain why women of this type are, I think, the most frequently recognized and celebrated (perhaps also the most frequently existing) creative characters. She can be a mystic, a saint of the militant or the pacifist sort, a healer or one who cleanses societies of their diseases, their unsightly people, their bad memories. Whether a Joan of Arc or a Florence Nightingale, she is not a usurper; she may even be welcomed as the perfect soul-sister among the rule-worshippers in such all-male institutions as churches and armies. Even so, she may choose to live on the margins of her society: she may flourish in an actual convent or an institution like one, a women's college (in the early twentieth century rather more than now), a clinic like Anna Freud's in London. The chief rule-enforcers in such milieus may be female, but they will often be experienced by their followers as asexual or masculine, as a Mother Superior who is both mother and father; and the chief rule-enforcers often are predominantly masculine in their own fantasies (as Gertrude Stein was in both her little household group of two and in her salon). If her obsessionality is characterological but not overly inhibiting, not neurotic, and if she is not very sadistic, she can be a superb team-player, conscientious and exacting in her formulation and execution of orders, completion of tasks. She will rejoice in lucidity, even if the lucidity is eccentric, as Gertrude Stein's was—for the lucidity in her works, like lucidity as a central category of her poetics, is consonant with freedom from impurity and opaqueness in her life. The obsessional creative type's nightmare is exactly the kind of counter-cultural unstructured, experimental, role-reversal atmosphere toward which the bisexual play-actor turns like a plant to the sun. This is not because the obsessional is not bisexual in mental attitude—she often is—but because she is ascetic and loves not lability but predictability. If she is overtly homosexual, her partner will have to be very like herself in terms of purity (or, if she is not, the partner will have to live elsewhere in a basement of impurity and dirty sexuality that the creative woman can visit and then leave, with much guilt).

—The narcissistic universalizing or all-embracing woman with an energy-channeling political character-ideal (such as "vatic bisexuality," for example) is the most likely of the various characterological types to have grown up in a "team" of some sort with males. Because, as I noted just above, her psychology has been so little studied, I will gesture toward it in both psychoanalytic and social-psychological terms. Biographical portraits yield a number of possibilities: she is raised with a brother or other close male contemporary in something like equality, or she feels enough an equal to consider herself in a unit with him, as Emily Dickinson did with her brother Austin; she is paired in her imagination (particularly if she is an only child) with a male who is on her same track (although this figure is not necessarily a split-off secret creative masculine self, as the artisanal/sexual type often has); one or both parents has an image of her that is quite masculine (a father's image will be easier for her and for anyone who studies her to see than a mother's, which implies a very forbidden desire for the daughter to be a lover, perhaps a better lover than the father) and she partakes of this parental narcissistic investment in her, conforming to the expectation, making it her own, as she elaborates it in fantasy. As she grows up, she enjoys male company and considers herself an equal; she often pairs herself (as Beauvoir did with Sartre, as Hannah Arendt did with her second husband, Heinrich

Blücher, and also with a succession of female best friends). The partner (man or woman) is her mirror while she is his or hers; their relationship may or may not be sexual in the narrow sense, but it will be full of erotic charge. Familial and societal contexts that permit or even promote such mirroring relationships are nurturing to her creativity: her sex and her gender are not stressed, they can be in the background as they are in her fantasy, in which she is pan-sexual or supra-sexual. (She does not move between roles, needing the changes; she plays everyone at once.) A family peer unit like Emily Dickinson's with her brother and sister-in-law, or a largely male intellectual cafe circle like Beauvoir's, or a friend-ship circle of the sort Hannah Arendt referred to as her "tribe," is crucial for her (and she may, as well, excel as a literary or artistic extoller of friendship and crafter of paeans to her friends). Her intelligence is usually rebellious or culturally innovative, and, as she usually comes up against constraints for this, she needs a mentor who sanctions her, whose narcissistic investment in her can echo earlier ones from her parent(s), but in the key of achievement and intellectuality, not (except disguisedly) of sexuality. A social situation in which there is some tradition of respect for extraordinary women (even if they are thought of as somehow monstrous or unnatural) is what she needs and looks for and, if she cannot find it, she invents it in a utopia or an elaborately idealized version of whatever milieu she has been able to find. She is at once a fiercely independent person and enmeshed in the lives of her mirrors, her supporters, her mentor—her extended narcissistic family, as it were. Rarely does she allow anyone to know her vulnerabilities, her dependencies, and she stays away from the exhibitionistic bohemian contexts of role-players as well as from the strict—over-strict, to her—societies of more obsessional types, both of which make her feel her fortress self too keenly, as they represent unchained id and enchaining superego to her. Much of the power of her work comes from her capacity to, in Beauvoir's words, "enact the fate of all humanity in her existence," so she avoids alliances or allegiances that seem to her too particularizing, too paro-chial. Thus Hannah Arendt was a Zionist, but a "cosmopolitan Zionist," and Simone de Beauvoir a socialist, but a "socialist internationalist." (The author of *The Second Sex* was for many years reluctant to call herself a feminist because her humanism found feminism too narrow an allegiance. Others of this type as well like to set feminism in a larger political context, and await women's liberation in a more general—

often socialist—liberation.) This type's zeal for understanding finds any partiality of view or narrowness of ideology an entrapment; she makes an excellent student of totalitarianism, or of the history of sexism, or of any form of life and thought that denies freedom or spells evolution away from freedom.

Among modern European-American men, the sweep and all-embracingness of a narcissistic universalizing mind has often enjoyed epic literary forms as well as scientific-theoretical ones; among women, political philosophizing stands out as a mode of choice—one that would not have occurred to Emily Dickinson in her late nineteenth-century Amherst. Rosa Luxemburg's is a paradigmatic voice. She, who grew up with three brothers in a polylingual house where the expectations of culture were high for the boys and the two girls, was criticized in her Gymnasium as a rebel and needed for her wider world the company of her Social Democratic peer groups in Poland, Switzerland, and Germany, as well as the partnership of her companion Leo Jogiches, her mirror-other. The attitude she inspired in the men around her is very sharply summarized in an epitaph she jokingly suggested to August Bebel—who repeated it approvingly—as appropriate for her and her peer-group friend Clara Zetkin: "Here lie the last two men of German Social Democracy." Her political sympathies were always republican and democratic; where others saw leaders and elites as the key forces in political affairs, she always countered with praise of the people. Considering from her war-time prison cell the "mighty sweep of the Russian Revolution," she argued in the hard-hitting, tough, and vivid prose typical of her kind of character against many of the Bolshevik practices current in 1918:

> The freeing of Russia was not an achievement of the war and the military defeat of czarism, not some service of "German bayonets in German fists," as *Neue Zeit* under Kautsky's editorship once promised in an editorial. [Events] show, on the contrary, that the freeing of Russia had its roots deep in the soil of its own land and was matured internally.

Her thinking—and not just because she was trained as a zoologist—was characteristically evolutionary, organic, systematic, an enactment or reenactment of the people and events she thought about.

239

SOCIAL CHARACTER: PROLEGOMENA TO
FUTURE THEORIZING

It seems to me that the easiest kind of "Culture and Personality" reflection is the sort I have just offered: descriptions of milieus that suit characters that have been, more or less, formed before they found the milieus. It is far more difficult to discuss how social conditions are formed into characters, woven into developmental processes. People are as likely to revolt against their characterological milieus as to reflect them, adapt to them; most frequently, they do both in mixtures that are difficult to determine for any given individual, and quite impossible to generalize about. Further, characterological milieus—in families, in kin-groups, in local societies, in national societies, and so forth—are describable, perhaps even typeable, with very broad strokes, but such strokes may be too broad, too vague, to allow for much correlation between the milieus they present and individuals.

Similarly, it is easy to observe that each society, small or large, will promote or inhibit not just certain kinds of characters but certain kinds of intelligence (in the widest sense of the term) and certain kinds of creativity. Oral cultures do not value literary production; some complexly literate cultures do not promote oral talents, while some do, at least in forms that link to literary ones. Some cultures give music instruction for children great emphasis, either in classrooms or in apprenticeships; some do not. In some milieus, the physical abilities for creativity in, say, dance, are cherished; in others spatial abilities are cultivated in more cerebral and less total-body forms. These kinds of socio-culture specificities certainly play a role in the unfolding of creative lives and the formation of creative characters. But it is not possible, it seems to me, to elaborate in any but the vaguest ways how cultural preferences are woven into individuals' stories or into a story of outstanding abilities or achievements.

The methodological complexities of what might be called social characterology and its subdiscipline, social theory of creativity, are further compounded by the way the history of such efforts has unfolded. In the European tradition, this history is, of course, interwoven with the history of individual characterology, and it has been so since Plato delineated the Athenians as an ideal philosophical leadership group in comparison with, on the one hand, the appetitive Phoenicians and Egyptians, and, on the other hand, the spirited, north-dwelling Thracians and

Scythians. His assumption about groups and individuals was the simplest one, the one eugenicists and utopians generally embrace: as the group is, so the individual will be; the group's nature is imprinted on the individual; individual nature is group nature writ small. Social determinists of all sorts lean on such an assumption, even those who are hopeful about some form of creative liberation from social determinism or some form of social determination toward liberation or enhanced creativity. The hopeful recurrently find themselves in the kind of quandary faced currently by those feminists who, believing that there has never been a non-patriarchal society or a woman raised non-patriarchally, look forward to a new world in which a social reform like shared parenting will change the history of boys becoming public men like their fathers and girls reproducing their mothers' role in the domestic realm. In the new world, girls will be free for public lives and accomplishments—as boys will be free to be richly parental. Faced with this unlikely proposition, which calls for a totally novel future to be produced by people immersed in the old ways, other feminists counter with a history in which matriarchies once existed, were suppressed—and will inevitably rise again, restoring women to their lost creativities.

In general, social determinism must banish from its thoughts all domains such as "the unconscious" that are, by their definition, out of reach of social forces in one of two senses: either "the unconscious" is timeless and impervious to social forces, even familial ones; or the effect of social forces on "the unconscious" is too complex and too invisible to be comprehended. There is, however, a modification of this second and looser interpretation that can permit social determinism to proceed fairly simply with its assumption that a social milieu can be seen writ small in an individual. That is to make the unconscious consist only of identifications with or internalizations of figures in the social surround. Thus, the idea that modern middle-class patriarchal families are templates for their childrens' psyches requires the idea that girls identify overwhelmingly and continuously with their mothers and boys at first with their mothers and then, after a struggle to disidentify with them, with their fathers, for the preservation of their masculinities. Social determinism constructed in terms of "object relations" (not instinctual drive theory or even a theory of character more rich than the pair "feminine/masculine") can present, however, only a very limited range of female or male types and only a single sort of social milieu.

Short of some form of social determinism, social characterologists are hard pressed to link group characters and individual characters. Usually they simplify their problem by selecting out some facet of social character to call essential and proceeding from there. In other words, like characterologists, theorists of social character tend to emphasize a particular feature or structure of social character and reduce all others to it. For example, David Riesman, author of *The Lonely Crowd: A Study of Changing American Character* (1950), offered this very honest and self-conscious general orientation and selection rationale:

> "Social character" is that part of "character" which is shared among significant social groups and which, as most contemporary social scientists define it, is the product of the experience of these groups. The notion of social character permits us to speak . . . of the character of classes, groups, religions, and nations. . . .
>
> [The] link between character and society—certainly not the only one, but one of the most significant, and the one I choose to emphasize in this discussion—is to be found in the way in which society ensures some degree of conformity from the individuals who make it up. In each society, such a mode of ensuring conformity is built into the child, and then either encouraged or frustrated in later adult experience.

Riesman's stress, that is, rests on the weight in each individual of the group's collective past. In external terms, he refers to social mores and morals, rituals, traditions, and prevailing opinions; in intrapsychic terms, to what Freud called "the superego" and to what in the "object relations"–oriented social psychoanalysis we just met above would be called, collectively, identifications or internalizations. Riesman might have focused (in Freud's terms) on ego-effecting features of societies or on id-effecting ones, but he realized that "modes of ensuring conformity" lent themselves well to existing sociological methods for defining conformity and deviance, norms and deviations. Neither a sociology of desires nor a sociology of intelligence forms (either a cognitive sociology or what is known as sociology of knowledge) was part of his repertoire.

I want to look in more detail at Riesman's study in order to clarify what seem to me its strengths and weaknesses and to survey the enormous range of historical development he thought should be reflected in a social characterology. Riesman argued that there have been two major Western European and American revolutions in modes of ensuring conformity. In the first revolution, which developed between the seventeenth and late nineteenth centuries, "tradition-directed" social character gave way to "inner-directed"; in the second, unfolding at the mid-twentieth century, "other-directed" people began to flourish. The first revolution came about as a long period of nearly zero population growth ended in Europe and the sway over individuals of rigidly organized clans and implacable traditions abated. A balance between high birth rate and high death rate, shaping societies in which the majority is young and the generations turn over very rapidly, gave way to a high growth rate as new knowledge for improved food production, communications, hygiene, and disease control reduced the death rate. Along with the population explosion went explosions in personal mobility, capital holdings, technological innovations, and colonization. Such conditions, Riesman concluded, both produce and require the "inner-directed" social character Max Weber had identified in *The Protestant Ethic and the Spirit of Capitalism*:

> As the control of the primary group is loosened—the group that both socializes the young and controls the adult in the earlier era—a new psychological mechanism appropriate to the more open society is "invented": it is what I like to describe as a social gyroscope. This instrument, once it is set by parents and other authorities, keeps the inner-directed person, as we shall see, "on course" even when tradition, as responded to by his character, no longer dictates his moves.

It was Freud, the early twentieth-century theorist of the superego as an individual's amalgamated internalized parental voices, the precipitate of the Oedipus complex, who recognized Kant's Categorical Imperative, dating from the late seventeenth century, as the most powerful form of psychological gyroscope. As Freud wrote: "The superego—the conscience at work in the ego—may . . . become harsh, cruel and inexorable against the ego which is in its charge. Kant's Categorical Imperative is thus the direct heir of the Oedipus complex."

Living on the last cusp of the "inner-directed" society that Kant epitomized, Freud could also see emerging the next type Riesman notes—the "other-directed" person. Societies characterized by "incipient population decline" and by the replacement of entrepreneurial producers with consumer-service producers, are conducive to other-direction. Like Freud, Riesman saw the avant-garde of this type in the new middle class of post-World War I America:

> The other-directed person learns to respond to signals from a far wider circle than is constituted by his parents. The family is no longer part of a

closely knit unity to which he belongs but merely part of a wider social environment to which he early becomes attentive. . . . As against guilt-and-shame controls, though of course these survive, one prime psychological lever of the other-directed person is a diffuse anxiety. This control equipment, instead of being like a gyroscope, is like radar.

The other-directed person values social acceptance, strives to be able always to manage his or her relationships, and has an exceptional sensitivity to the needs and wishes of other people. "While all people want and need to be liked by some people some of the time, it is only the modern other-directed types who make this their chief source of direction and chief area of sensitivity." Riesman's other-directed types are, one might also note, very like the feminine characters posited by Greenacre and also by recent American feminist theorists of gender difference like Nancy Chodorow and Carol Gilligan: both are relationship-oriented, non-domineering, and alert to the nuances of social interaction and meaning; girls of this sort are maternal in this other-directed mode long before they are mothers.

Riesman also added to his historical and social characterology an important plurality of qualifying marks. He noted that people can belong to the three main historical character-types in three universal modalities: (1) they are well adjusted, socio-psychologically fitting their cultures as though made for them; (2) they are anomic and socio-psychologically unfitted ("ranging from outlaws to "catatonic" types who lack even the spark for living, let alone rebellion"); or (3) they are autonomous, meaning that they are capable of fitting but may choose or not choose to conform. Different societies can be characterized by the frequency with which these well-adjusted, anomic, or autonomous types appear in them and by the importance these types assume in them. But it is important to note that "autonomous, adjusted, and anomic types can be brothers and sisters within the same family, associates on the same job, residents in the same housing project or suburb." That is, these types are ultimately comprehensible only in the categories of individual developmental psychology or with the techniques of fiction and biography; sociology or social characterology stops outside their doors; a return to individual characterology is announced.

Another very important qualifying train of thought runs through Riesman's theory. Currently, there are in the world small societies in which a historical stasis in tradition-boundness or a historical progression through one or both of the other types is clear, or in which one of the three types clearly dominates. But all large societies and most small ones are scenes of "characterological struggle" among people of all three types. This is particularly so in American society considered as a whole, Riesman argues, for it contains each of the character-forming milieus in chaotic abundance: rural and immigrant tradition-bound clans; educated, middle-class entrepreneurs and traders (sometimes typified by their "Protestant ethic"); and the new relationship managers and culture manipulators and image consumers.

The concept of "characterological struggle" and the three qualifiers— adjusted, anomic, and autonomous—strike me as the most important contributions of Riesman's approach. The typology of tradition-directed, inner-directed, and other-directed, while suggestive, seems too broad, too vague, and too dependent on the single social factor, modes of ensuring conformity, that Riesman deemed crucial. In effect, what Riesman offered was a typology of superego controls: there is a relatively uninternalized superego-as-tradition, the classic Freudian superego made up of internalizations and identifications, and a "modern" unrigid superego characteristic of people embedded in their social milieus (as Freud said women were embedded in their Oedipal families, falling short of the "dissolution of the Oedipus complex" that spells a firm superego). At the very least, emphasis on modes of ensuring conformity will make it hard to appreciate either societies in which social conformity is not a value or not valued, or societies in which individualism is valued but does not presume "inner-directed" characters; societies centrifugal with expressed desires or selfhoods cultivated without shame, to speak summarily and in the terms the structural theory suggests.

A less single-dimensional social theory—one acknowledging at least a richness of factors equal to the richness of factors that are obviously necessary in individual characterology—would have to begin, it seems to me, from the idea that societies or cultures are each delimitations or canalizations of the vast array of societal developmental possibilities, as individual characters are precipitants of a vast array of individual developmental possibilities. This is the idea that frames the anthropologist Ruth Benedict's *Patterns of Culture* (1934):

> The course of life and the pressure of environment, not to speak of the fertility of human imagination, provide an incredible number of possible leads, all of which, it appears, may serve a society to live by. There are the

schemes of ownership, with the social hierarchy that may be associated with possessions; there are material things and their elaborate technology; there are all the facets of sex life, parenthood and post-parenthood; there are the guilds and cults which may give structure to society; there is economic exchange; there are the gods and supernatural sanctions. Each one of these and many more may be followed out with a cultural and ceremonial elaboration which monopolizes the cultural energy and leaves small surplus for the building of other traits. Aspects of life that seem to us most important have been passed over with small regard by peoples whose culture, oriented in another direction, has been far from poor. Or the same trait may be so greatly elaborated that we reckon it as fantastic.

Benedict shapes an analogy between cultural life and speech: as any spoken language uses a small selection out of all the possible sounds that human beings can make, any culture uses a selection of the possibilities available.

Every human society everywhere has made such a selection in its cultural institutions. Each from the point of view of another ignores fundamentals and exploits irrelevancies. One culture hardly recognizes monetary values; another has made them fundamental in every field of behavior. In one society technology is unbelievably slighted even in those aspects of life which seem necessary to ensure survival; in another, equally simple, technological achievements are complex and fitted with admirable nicety to the situation. One builds an enormous cultural superstructure upon adolescence, one upon death, one upon after-life.

In an approach like Benedict's, Riesman's "modes of ensuring conformity" would be only one ingredient of a society or culture, and its weight in any given location would have to be reckoned rather than presumed. Similarly, modes of organizing gender roles and relations would be specific, and it would make little sense to use a word like *patriarchal* without qualification. Cultures have—to borrow Anna Freud's term—"developmental lines." Each one will go along the multitude of possible developmental lines in a different way, at a different pace, with different accumulations of fixations and repressions, typical behaviors, traits, symptoms, proclivities toward pathology, ideologies or societal myths and religions, and so forth. Neither at the level of humankind nor in smaller units are there norms for cultural development in the normative-prescriptive sense; there are simply courses of development that appear more frequently than others in particular regions or locales but are not superior by virtue of their commonness. There may be broad cultural types—the equivalent, to use Benedict's linguistic analogy, of language families—but these ought to arise before the eyes of a relativist as, in the narrower project of individual characterology, types appear tentatively through the multiplicity of individual developmental lines.

I do not, in other words, think that social characterology can operate at the macro-historical, across-the-centuries level where Riesman wanted to situate it. His types seem to me as little useful as the more commonly employed socio-characterological designations "Western" (or more recently "Euro-centric") and "Eastern." At the most, socio-characterological study makes sense in smaller socio-cultural units, where the "pattern of culture" can be determined with some clarity, and where "social character" as that part of an individual's character that she or he shares with a group can be specified. Whether that sharing takes place peacefully, in a state of antagonism or rejection, or in an autonomous mode can also be specified, both from the direction of sociology and from the direction of biography—as, for example, when a member of a rebellious subculture or "lost generation" is considered from the angle of the generation and as an individual.

When the socio-characterological enterprise is pared down a bit from Riesman's model, another dimension emerges to the very definition "social character." Riesman did not consider that "social character" means different things at different stages in an individual's life, as different groups assume different importances in an individual's life. In childhood "social character" may mean, most importantly, family character; in latency and adolescence will be added perhaps peer-group character, perhaps initiation-group (e.g., church, army) character, depending on how the culture weights and tries to shape the training years; in young adulthood, "my society" and "my culture" as constructions or interpretations become more important. As a person becomes an adult, "social character" becomes more reflective; as an object of explicit self-identification, concern, caring, rebellion, it changes its meaning.

In the transition from adolescence to adulthood, when creative people form what I call their character-ideals, they also take a position in relation to their socio-cultural surround. They are much more likely than the relatively uncreative to be not just—to use Riesman's terms—well adjusted, anomic, autonomous, but self-consciously so, self-constructingly so. Riesman's definition of "social character" is unidirectional—societies shape characters—as all social determinists, strict or loose, believe. What is missed in this approach is any way to understand the diversity of human beings, and particularly of creative ones, who manifest their particularity in more ways than the less creative. For the creative, it seems to me, the key ingredient of "social character" is the fit between the person's conscious or unconscious character-ideal, projected as a social ideal, and the person's experience of his or her society and his or her place in it. In the mode of biography, much can be said about how a subject is an Italian or a Nigerian, a peasant or an aristocrat, the product of rural gentry or the child of indentured servants, elementary-schooled or university-educated, a Caucasian or a person of color, masculine or feminine, and so forth, a composite of social factors of national identity, class and caste identity, racial identity, gender identity, with the appropriate weight given to each in the particular case. But the subject's "social character" will also include how the subject's social ideals, the social dimension of the character-ideal, register against the realities of the experiences reflected in the composite, the social realities.

It is a cliché of the European tradition that creative people live in a condition that the anthropologist O. Manoni described as "disharmony almost amounting to conflict between the social being and the inner personality." (Manoni, in his *Prospero and Caliban* [1966], was noting that this disharmony, which he in the imperial European manner attributed to "the civilized," did not seem to exist among the Merina of Malagasy, whom he was studying.) To my mind, such a disharmony comes about when a person's characterologically rooted social vision is experienced as a standard and the person's "social being"—the actual, felt social experience—is experienced as painfully off the standard. This can be a condition for creativity. But so, also, can a harmonious relationship between social vision and social being.

Riesman's qualifying categories "well-adjusted," "anomic," and "autonomous" gesture in the direction of this individual dimension of "social character." But he gives no indication of what would make a person feel at home in, or alienated from, or independent of the social group with which he or she grows up, shares characteristics. There is nothing psychodynamic about his approach: it is all "social" and no "character." Drawing on the kind of quick sketches I made before of late-adolescent creative women and their longed for or despised social milieus, let me set out a few biographical rules of thumb. When people of the artisanal/sexual character-ideal, whose social visions tend to be hierarchical or classist (perhaps timocratic—favoring rule by the special honorable few) but who also relish having their own needs for gender-role indeterminacy reflected in the hierarchy, perceive themselves to be constrained in role-rigid societies and ill-fabricated cultures, they become anomic, actively (like Oscar Wilde) or depressively (like Virginia Woolf). When people of the spiritual or ascetic character-ideal, social cosmopolitans or banishers of superficial differences among humans, find that their personal rules and regulations are supported by their society's, they adjust well, while those who do not tend to become to some degree paranoid (and in some cases, like Samuel Johnson's, they vacillate between periods of adjustment and periods of paranoia). When people of the political character-ideal, whose social vision is evolutionary, progressive, experience their society as de-evolutionary, regressive, they pose their dilemma to themselves dramatically: they can retreat, disengage, set up independent camp, or they can set out to change things, be active; they can idealize a contemplative life, or an active reforming one (or they can do both, as Aristotle did in his *Nicomachean Ethics*, to the confusion of later readers). People of this sort often relish their autonomy even while they acknowledge their socio-characterological rootedness (as Freud did, for example, in pointing out his Jewish traits and joking about his "Jewish science" while he stayed aloof from Jewish religious practice).

Creative people are inventors of imaginary societies for living in and being creative in, and these fantasies both reflect and measure the societies and cultures in which they have lived. They need conditions and people in the surroundings who support them in at least one sense: the conditions promote and the people discover and patronize or matronize the creative person's talent, and, more deeply, the creative person's secrets—whether these secrets be secrets of sexuality and sexual role, of forbidden desires and crucial ceremonial regulations of desires, or of grand erotic and achievement ambitions. Real people may be sources of identification, but they are internally wrapped with layers of fantasy. Ernst Kris once described the creative adolescents he studied as "museums of identifications," a constantly rearranged storehouse of many, many acts of modeling and imitation. Apprenticeship systems tacitly recognize this psychodynamic process.

The creative person's fantasy conditions and people license his or her creativity—or, in more guilty types, tolerate it or forgive it; they deem

249

the person a chosen one, an elect one, an inheritor, an exception; their voices, heard inwardly, are the voices of vocation. If there is a good deal of accord between the fantasy social-ideal and "social being," actual experience, the creative person feels little need to keep elaborating the fantasy into adulthood. At the opposite end of the spectrum, there is the perennial social rebel, the perennially disappointed critic, whose work will have a dimension of social critique, whether of theory or praxis. A person's social character tells not only the story of how character assimilates context, but the story of how what might be called a "social romance"—an extended version of Freud's "family romance"—is lived with, lived through, acted out, woven into work.

These are gestures at the many combinations and permutations of individual characters and societies in their interactions and impingements. These gestures leave both unasked and unanswered a question I can ask but cannot answer: Are the character-types that seem to my eye to stand out in the life-stories, descriptions of creative process and images of creativity, works and deeds, poetics, of people in the specific European and American cultural traditions and "patterns of culture" with which I am familiar—are they to be found projected in other cultural traditions, other patterns, with which I am not familiar? I would expect that basic characterological and libidinal orientations—to the id, the ego, the superego in the terms Freud's structural theory provides—and the developmental phases in their broadest, least culturally influenced forms, would be similar across cultures, while specific formations and developmental emphases would not. That is, heightened interest in genitalia and increased erotic involvement with caretaking figures may be generally characteristic of children who are developmentally able to run around, to explore on their own, and who are in the period of intense eroticized activity familiar everywhere to weary adults who are caring for toddlers. Whether the specific forms of the "negative" and "positive" Oedipus complex proposed by Freud are similarly ubiquitous is unlikely. But that does not mean that some form of unconscious love for caretakers is not universal. And the further along the developmental lines from childhood to adulthood you look, the more variety there is, and the more influence particular cultural forms have. In every culture, the developmental line from adolescence to adulthood unfolds, but the transition to adult roles, adult forms of work and creative achievement, takes place under very diverse conditions of ritual celebration or disregard, difficulty or ease, upheaval or regularity. "Social character" in the interactional sense that I have tried to sketch, something that cannot be richly described until adulthood, seems multiform, as multiform as the notion "patterns of culture" implies. All cultures have images of the mind, social visions, and cosmogonies, which, to me, means that everywhere there are people who project their experiences of psychic order outward, who develop character-ideals. But I doubt that the typology of character-ideals I have sketched, with its corollary typology of cosmic visions and social romances, is, in the broader arena of "patterns of culture," rich enough to encompass all projectors of character-ideals, all creative characters. The typology may, however, be rich enough in its survey of basic projective elements to serve as a map for further inquiry— as long as the map does not come to seem more real than the land by virtue of its simplicity.

Bibliographic Notes

I have chosen not to encumber the text of *Creative Characters* with footnotes, but I would like to provide the bibliographic notes below, both in order to indicate for interested readers what literature exists on the topics I have considered, and in order to sketch the sources on which I have drawn in constructing my argument and my biographical vignettes. (Quotations from Freud and Anna Freud will be indicated in my text with volume and page numbers indicating their collected writings.)

My INTRODUCTION surveys the existing literature on creativity, which is, I think, most efficiently to be found in anthologies of essays. I recommend three collections from the 1950s: H. A. Anderson, ed., *Creativity and Its Cultivation* (Harper & Row, 1959); *The Nature of Creative Thinking* (New York University Press, 1958); V. Tomas, ed., *Creativity in the Arts* (Prentice-Hall, 1964); two collections of pieces from the 1960s: S. Rosner and L. E. Abt, eds., *The Creative Experience* (Grossman, 1970); P. E. Vernon, ed., *Creativity: Selected Readings* (Penguin, 1970); and from the 1970s: R. J. Sternberg, ed., *The Nature of Creativity: Contemporary Psychological Perspectives* (Cambridge, 1988); F. D. Horowitz and M. O'Brien, eds., *The Gifted and the Talented: Developmental Perspectives* (American Psychological Association, 1985). A fairly recent popular survey is Daniel Cohen, *Creativity—What Is It?* (Evans, 1977).

A great deal of work on "the creative process" refers to a popular anthology edited by Brewster Ghiselin, *The Creative Process* (University of California Press, 1952). An example of how "the creative process" can be analyzed into segments or stages is Rosamond Harding, *An Anatomy of Inspiration* (Heffer, 1948). Arthur Koestler's book is *The Act of Creation* (Dell, 1964). The "self-actualizing" theorists I glance at are Abraham Maslow, particularly *Motivation and Personality* (Harper, 1970), and the much more original and interesting Otto Rank, particularly *Art and Artist: Creative Urge and Personality Development* (Knopf, 1932) and *The Double* (University of North Carolina Press, 1971). There is also an anthology of some of Rank's relevant writings in English: P. Freund, ed., *The Myth of the Birth of the Hero and Other Writings* (Knopf, 1959). Anthony Storr's *The Dynamics of Creation* was issued in paperback in 1985 by Athenaeum; also of interest are his essays on creativity in *Churchill's Black Dog, Kafka's Mice and Other Phenomena of the Human Mind* (Grove, 1988). Others have noted shortcomings in the existing literature on creativity, most recently Robert W. Weisberg, *Creativity, Genius and Other Myths* (Freeman, 1986).

The history of theories of character in the European tradition was very interestingly tracked by A. A. Roback in *The Psychology of Character* (Kegan Paul, 1927), and Roback also published an extensive bibliography on the topic. But there is unfortunately no contemporary general history of the topic (although Christie Kiefer's *The Mantle of Maturity* (SUNY Press, 1988) deals with development of character historically). Jung's approach is presented in *Psychological Types*, vol. 6 of *The Collected Works of C. G. Jung* (Princeton University Press, 1971). The quotations from Picasso come from the fascinating collection of his writings and sayings edited by Dore Ashton, *Picasso on Art* (Viking, 1972). The Benjamin quotations are from pp. 305 and 321 of *One Way Street* (New Left Books, 1979). Characterological typologies are certainly not a mode much in intellectual fashion in our current deconstructionist times, as I noted above in my Preface, but they were crucial to the Continental modes of post-World War II political and social thought, descended from Max Weber, to which I am much indebted, and which I will sketch bibliographically when I come to Chapter 9 below. Let me just note here a good post–World War II analysis of the importance of characterological typologies that is combined with a good catalogue of its methodological problems: T. W. Adorno et al., *The Authoritarian Personality* (currently in paperback from Norton), Chapter 19, especially "Types and Syndromes."

In the opening section of CHAPTER 1, I quote L. M. Terman from Vernon's anthology *Creativity* (see above) and Nietzsche from *The Gay Science*. The material on Plato and Aristotle is all quoted from easily available translations; I have added the Greek in transliteration where there is any linguistic issue at stake or where the Greek text is questionable. As there is no translation of the four-volume *Stoicorum Veterum Fragmenta* that Johannes von Arnim edited (Teubner, 1903–24), I have presented Zeno's thought without much resort to quotation. The modern scholarship on the Stoics is very uneven in quality and fixated on particular lexical problems, it seems to me, so I cannot recommend any improvement over Arnold's *Roman Stoicism* (Cambridge, 1911) for a historical overview and introduction to the whole of ancient Stoicism. My own brief presentation is close to that offered by J. Christensen, *An Essay on the Unity of Stoic Philosophy* (Copenhagen, 1962), which is one of the few philosophically interesting works on Stoicism. A good sampling of more recent British work is A. A. Long's *Problems of Stoicism* (Athlone, 1971).

The opening of CHAPTER 2 focuses on Kant, and specifically on his *Anthropology from a Pragmatic Point of View*, for which I used the V. L. Dowdell translation (Southern Illinois University Press, 1979), particularly pp. 203–06. On the history of the notion of "the unconscious," see Henri Ellenberger, *The Discovery of the Unconscious* (Basic Books, 1970). I have used Walter Kaufmann's translations of Nietzsche throughout, for consistency's sake, and have indicated the particular works in my text. For more on Phyllis Greenacre's work, see the notes for Chapters 8 and 9 below; Kubie's book is *Neurotic Distortion of The Creative Process* (University Press of Kansas, 1958), and see also the essays on creativity in his *Symbol and Neurosis: Selected Papers* (International Universities Press, 1978). Generally, see Harry Slochower, "Contemporary Psychoanalytic Theories on Creativity and the Arts," in J. E. Strelka, ed., *Literary Criticism and Psychology* (University of Pennsylvania Press, 1976). The biographical literature on Freud is enormous—see the survey in Peter Gay's *Freud* (Norton, 1988). In this chapter I have cited letters from the Freud/Jung collection, the single volume edition of Freud's *Letters*, the Jones biography, and Max Schur, *Freud: Living and Dying* (International Universities Press, 1972). For the section on Proust, I drew upon the great *A la recherche du temps perdu*, but also the collections *Marcel Proust on Art and Literature, 1896–1919* (Meridian, 1958) and *Against Sainte-Beuve and Other Essays* (Penguin, 1988), which contains the text I cited at length, and an interesting compendium of Proust's philosophical aperçus that Justin O'Brien edited, *Maxims of Marcel Proust* (Columbia University Press, 1948). I have found George Painter's two-volume *Marcel Proust* (Chatto and Windus, 1959) to be still the best biography, but learned from André Maurois's *The Quest for Proust* (Cape, 1950) and M. L. Miller, *Nostalgia: A Psychoanalytic Study of Proust* (Houghton Mifflin, 1956).

CHAPTER 3, on character-ideals, connects three types of character-ideals with three types of projected cosmogonic visions, and for considering such visions two anthologies have been very helpful to me: C. Doria and H. Lenowitz, eds., *Origins: Creation Texts from the Ancient Mediterranean* (AMS Press, 1976) and Charles H. Long, *Alpha: The Myths of Creation* (Collier, 1963), which ranges over many ancient and modern cultures. There is a large psychoanalytic literature on the ego-ideals, in which I found Anna Freud's *The Ego and the Mechanisms of Defense* (1936) and Erik Erikson's *Identity and the Life Cycle* (1959) to be the most provocative. These texts were interesting to review in light of a recent work by J. Chasseguet-Smirgel, "Essai sur l'idéal du moi," *Revue française de psychanalyse* 37 (1973), and the same author's *Creativity and Perversion* (Norton, 1984); and also of Joseph Sandler et al., "Ego Ideal and Ideal Self" in Sandler's *From Safety to Superego* (Guilford Press, 1987). See also Stanley Kaplan and Roy Whitman, "The Negative Ego-Ideal," in *International Journal of Psychoanalysis* 46 (1965). Anna Freud and Erikson are also the key theorists of adolescence, but I also learned a great deal from Peter Blos's 1962 volume *On Adolescence* (Free Press), and particularly from his "Character Formation in Adolescence," *Psychoanalytic Study of the Child* 23 (1968).

My portrait of Freud in his adolescence in CHAPTER 4 takes off from K. Eissler's "Creativity and Adolescence: The Effect of Trauma in Freud's Adolescence," *Psychoanalytic Study of the Child* 33 (1978), which, like most of Eissler's biographical work on Freud, is very suggestive and very tendentious. Eissler offers the excerpts I have requoted from Freud's letters to Silberstein (which have recently been published by Harvard University Press). There is a discussion of Freud's negative attitudes toward Americans in Peter Gay's *Freud*. The Richard Ellmann biographies that I have drawn upon in the second section of this chapter are *Yeats: The Man and the Masks* (Macmillan, 1948) and the recent *Oscar Wilde* (Vintage, 1988). Goethe has been studied psychoanalytically in enormous detail by Eissler, who noted the poet's fascination with pregnancy. The Hopkins poem is titled "To. R. B." and can be found as number 53 in W. H. Gardner, ed., *Gerard Manley Hopkins: Poems and Prose* (Penguin, 1953). Simone Weil's "Spiritual Autobiography" has been republished recently in *The Simone Weil Reader* (McKay, 1977).

256

Marguerite Yourcenar has not yet been the subject of a good biography, so the interview collection called *With Open Eyes* (Beacon Press, 1984) is particularly useful. The literature on Gertrude Stein, on the other hand, is huge, but I have used her own works for my sketch, as I have not found a biography I feel confident in. The quotation from *A Novel of Thank You* comes from an article on Stein by Ulla Dydo in *Raritan* 7 (1987). Anna Freud's "altruistic surrender" is discussed in detail in my own *Anna Freud* (Summit Books, 1988).

My discussion of Freudian characterology in CHAPTER 5 owes a good deal to Otto Fenichel's discussion of character in his *The Psychoanalytic Theory of Neurosis* (Norton, 1945), but I have not found a good discussion of the many dimensions of Freud's characterology in the psychoanalytic historical, theoretical, or clinical literatures. For brief gestures, see A. Valenstein, reporter for a session on "The Psychoanalytic Concept of Character," *Journal of the American Psychoanalytic Association* 6 (1958). The literary quotations in this chapter are identified in the text, with the exception of the paragraphs by Father Yelchaininov, which are taken from G. P. Fedotov, ed., *A Treasury of Russian Spirituality* (Harper, 1965).

All citations in CHAPTER 6 from Anna Freud's eight-volume *Writings* are noted with volume number and page number in the text. The quotation from Georgia O'Keeffe is from Lauri Lisle's biography *Portrait of an Artist* (Washington Square, 1986). There is a large psychoanalytic literature on character and character pathologies beyond what I have cited in the text by Abraham, Glover, Reich, Jones, Hartmann, and Kohut (all easily available in essay collections or books by these authors). A succinct series of articles appeared in the 1930 *Medical Review of Reviews*: K. Lewin, "The Compulsive Character"; S. Lorand, "The Reactive Character"; F. Wittels, "The Hysterical Character." Also interesting for my purposes: Richard Sterba, "Character and Resistance," *Psychoanalytic Quarterly* 20 (1950); J. J. Michaels, *Disorders of Character* (Thomas, 1955); Hermann Nunberg, "Character and Neurosis," *International Journal of Psychoanalysis* 37 (1956); Steven Hammerman, "Masturbation and Character," *Journal of the American Psychoanalytic Association* 9 (1961); Jeanne Lampl-de Groot, "Symptom Formation and Character Formation" (1963), reprinted in her *The Development of Mind* (International Universities Press, 1971); Jacob Arlow, "Character Perversion," in *Currents in Psychoanalysis* (International Universities Press, 1971).

CHAPTER 7, focused on biographical writing, uses for close study W. Jackson Bate's *Samuel Johnson* (quoting from the 1979 Harcourt edition), Philip Spencer's *Flaubert* (quoting the 1952 Grove edition), along with William Berg et al.'s *Saint/Oedipus: Psychocritical Approaches to Flaubert's Art* (Cornell University Press, 1982), Leon Edel's *Henry James* (for which I consulted both the four-volume complete edition and the 1985 single-volume abridgement, quoting the latter), and Phyllis Rose's *Woman of Letters: A Life of Virginia Woolf* (quoting from the 1979 Oxford edition). The last section of this chapter shifts approach: I wanted to show what kind of biographical sketch can be offered on the basis of the characterological theory I am developing, and then to compare it to other sorts of biographies. My Darwin sketch relies mostly on Darwin's own early writings and his *Autobiography*. In Howard Gruber's *Darwin on Man* (Dutton, 1974), Paul H. Barrett has provided transcriptions and annotations for several of the early notebooks, and I have quoted these in my text (indicating them by Barrett's titles). For Emily Dickinson, I drew upon Thomas Johnson, ed., *The Poems of Emily Dickinson* (Harvard University Press, 1955), although I found very suggestive the two works I criticize, Cynthia Griffin Wolff's *Emily Dickinson* (Knopf, 1986) and John Cody's *After Great Pain: The Inner Life of Emily Dickinson* (Harvard University Press, 1971).

Behind CHAPTER 8 stands a shelf of psychoanalytic studies of creative people and of creativity. Some of these focus critically on Freud, like Sarah Kofman's *Childhood of Art: An Interpretation of Freud's Aesthetics* (Columbia University Press, 1988). Some are general (and to my mind quite unsatisfactory) studies like Silvano Arieti's *Creativity: The Magic Synthesis* (Basic Books, 1976); some are works with a particular thesis to argue, like Edmund Bergler's *The Writer and Psychoanalysis* (Doubleday, 1950), which focuses on orality as "the psychic mechanism" of writers, or Andre Haynal's *Depression and Creativity* (International Universities Press, 1985), or William Niederland's "Clinical Aspects of Creativity," *American Imago* 24 (1967), which concentrates on creativity as restitution or overcoming of defects, or Marion Milner's fascinating *On Not Being Able to Paint* (Heinemann, 1957). Some contain essays on many topics, like Ernst Kris's *Psychoanalytic Explorations in Art* (International Universities Press, 1952) or John Gedo's *Portraits of the Artist: Psychoanalysis of Creativity and Its Vicissitudes* (Guilford Press, 1983) or Gilbert Rose's *Trauma and Mastery in Life and Art* (Yale University Press,

1987). The journal *Psychoanalytic Perspectives on Art* (Analytic Press, starting in 1985) also ranges over many topics and includes many psychobiographical studies. There is an empirical literature, too, like the recent *The Creative Process: A Functional Model Based on Empirical Studies from Early Childhood to Middle Age*, ed. Smith and Carlsson (International Universities Press, 1990) and much interesting clinical work, like that presented over the years by the Gifted Adolescents Project (New York), which Ernst Kris organized. Along with Kris's volume, I find most interesting the work of Freud's associates, especially Hanns Sachs, *The Creative Unconscious* (Sci-Art, 1942) and *Masks of Love and Life* (Sci-Art, 1948), and Robert Waelder, *Psychoanalytic Avenues to Art* (International Universities Press, 1965).

Robert Waelder's essay "On Psychoses" is from his collected essays, *Psychoanalysis: Observation, Theory, Application* (International Universities Press, 1976). Also helpful to me in thinking about schizophrenia was Thomas Freeman et al., *Chronic Schizophrenia* (International Universities Press, 1958), which I cite in my text; Freeman's brief "The Psychopathology of the Psychoses" in *International Journal of Psychoanalysis* 51 (1970); M. Katan, "Structural Aspects of a Case of Schizophrenia," *Psychoanalytic Study of the Child* 5 (1950); H. Searles, *Collected Papers on Schizophrenia* (Hogarth, 1965); and Bellak and Loeb, *The Schizophrenic Syndrome* (Grune and Stratton, 1969). The literature on the psychoses is immense, even if one does not—as I do not—take into account the range of it which concentrates on biological and/or hereditary causation. For melancholia or depression, which I consider with reference to the artisanal/sexual character-ideal, I learned a great deal from Phyllis Greenacre's *Emotional Growth* (International Universities Press, 1971), which I cite in the text, as well as from her *Trauma, Growth and Personality* (International Universities Press, 1952), and from Edith Jacobson's *Depression* (International Universities Press, 1972). For an overview, see James Coyne, ed., *Essential Papers on Depression* (New York University Press, 1986). For paranoia, which I discuss in relation to obsessionality and the spiritual character-ideal, I found these summaries helpful: H. Bonner, "The Problem of Diagnosis in Paranoiac Disorder," *American Journal of Psychoanalysis* 107 (1951); N. Cameron, "Paranoid Conditions and Paranoia," *American Handbook of Psychiatry* (Basic Books, 1959); W. Niederland, "Paranoia: Theory and Therapy," *Psychiatry and Social Science Review* 4 (1970). But Freud's case studies, particularly of the Rat

Man, the Wolf Man, and Schreber (about which Niederland has also written a book, *The Schreber Case*), still seem to me among the richest places to read about obsessionality and paranoia.

In CHAPTER 9, I have not made an attempt to survey views on female psychology, but I have offered a bibliography and a quick survey of the terrain elsewhere in my anthology *Freud on Women* (Norton, 1990). Christine Battersby's *Gender and Genius* (Indiana University Press, 1989), which I cite in my text, contains a bibliography on women and creativity. Hélène Cixous's "The Laugh of the Medusa" can be found in Marks and Courtivron, *New French Feminisms* (Schocken, 1980). Phyllis Greenacre's essays are in her *Emotional Growth*, Melanie Klein's are in her *Contributions to Psychoanalysis, 1921–45* (McGraw-Hill, 1964). In Sondra Fraganis's *Social Reconstruction of the Feminine Character* (Rowman and Littlefield, 1986) there is a survey of approaches to "feminine character" in the sociology of knowledge (starting with Viola Klein, *The Feminine Character*).

The post-war literature on "culture and personality" that has been particularly suggestive to me follows (in chronological order): Abraham Kardiner, *The Psychological Frontiers of Society* (Columbia University Press, 1945); C. Kluckhohn and H. Murray, eds., *Personality in Nature, Culture and Society* (Knopf, 1948), and David Rappaport's review of this in *Psychoanalytic Quarterly* 18 (1949); S. S. Sargent and M. W. Smith, eds., *Culture and Personality* (Wenner-Gren, 1949), which includes Eric Fromm's "Psychoanalytic Characterology and Its Application to the Understanding of Culture"; Erik Erikson, *Childhood and Society* (Norton, 1950); T. W. Adorno et al., *The Authoritarian Personality* (Harper, 1950) and the other volumes in the American Jewish Committee's late 1940s and early 1950s series "Studies in Prejudice"; G. B. Wilbur and W. Munstenberger, eds., *Psychoanalysis and Culture* (International Universities Press, 1951), which includes Hartmann, Kris, and Loewenstein; "Some Psychoanalytic Comments on 'Culture and Personality,' " a paper that is indebted to the work of Geza Roheim, for example, *Psychoanalysis and Anthropology: Culture, Personality and the Unconscious* (International Universities Press, 1950).

Index

Index